CAPITALIST
PUNISHMENT

ALSO BY **VIVEK RAMASWAMY**

Woke, Inc.

Nation of Victims

CAPITALIST PUNISHMENT

How Wall Street Is Using Your Money to
Create a Country You Didn't Vote For

VIVEK
RAMASWAMY

BROADSIDE BOOKS

HarperCollins books may be purchased for educational, business, or sales promotional use. For information, please email the Special Markets Department at SPsales@harpercollins.com.

Broadside Books™ and the Broadside logo are trademarks of HarperCollins Publishers.

FIRST EDITION

Library of Congress Cataloging-in-Publication Data has been applied for.

ISBN 978-0-06-333775-6

23 24 25 26 27 LBC 5 4 3 2 1

To my two sons, Karthik and Arjun, and to their generation.
May they live with purpose and liberty.

Courage is contagious.

CONTENTS

INTRODUCTION

D o you want your retirement funds to be used to force US tech companies to adopt racial hiring quotas? Or to force US energy companies to produce less oil to fight climate change? And are you okay with sacrificing investment returns to pursue these objectives? If your answer is "Yes," save your money and don't buy this book.

But if your answer is "Hell no!," don't read this book at bedtime. What you are about to discover is the largest financial scam in modern history. You're probably among its victims, though you probably don't know it yet.

You might recall the spectacular rise and fall of Sam Bankman-Fried, popularly known as SBF. The thirty-year-old rapidly built FTX, his Bahamas-based cryptocurrency exchange, into one of the largest financial empires in the world. His net worth in early 2022 exceeded $20 billion. The young man was described as the John Pierpont Morgan of our time, America's next Warren Buffett. His was also the leading voice in Washington, DC, for the so-called responsible regulation of the cryptocurrency sector. He donated tens of millions of dollars to Democratic candidates in 2022 while pledging over a billion in years to come. Perhaps owing to these acts, a prominent ESG (environmental, social, and governance) ratings firm assigned a higher leadership and governance score to FTX than it did to ExxonMobil. Months later, FTX declared bankruptcy after more than $8 billion in customer funds went missing—after it came to light that SBF had siphoned those funds away to another hedge fund that he separately owned.

He's not one of us, Wall Street insiders would have you believe. SBF was the weird kid who wore shorts and slept on bean bags. His headquarters were in the Bahamas, not on Park Avenue. His high ESG score was just an unfortunate coincidence, they'll say. But here's the dirty little secret: SBF wasn't an exception to the rule but an embodiment of it.

SBF is probably going to prison. But the most elite practitioners of the game won't. Take my 2006 summer internship employer, Goldman Sachs. It was one of many Wall Street firms that sold complex mortgage-backed securities to investors that turned out to be worthless. One trader who worked there back when I did was a twenty-eight-year-old by the name of Fabrice Tourre, who liked to refer to himself as "Fabulous Fab." His emails revealed what many suspected at the time: that Goldman's bankers knew they were selling worthless securities but continued to do it anyway. He boasted in June 2007 about selling "abacus bonds to widow [*sic*] and orphans."[1] He quipped, "More and more leverage in the system, The whole building is about to collapse anytime now. . . . Only potential survivor, the fabulous Fab . . . standing in the middle of all these complex, highly leveraged, exotic trades he created without necessarily understanding all of the implications of those monstruosities!!!"[2]

Well, the house *did* collapse, and it triggered the largest recession since the Great Depression. The stock market lost trillions of dollars in value, wiping out the savings of millions of Americans. The ensuing financial crisis cost the less genteel Wall Street firms, such as Bear Stearns and Lehman Brothers, their very existence.

That would have almost certainly been Goldman's fate, too, except for a notable noncoincidence: Goldman's most recent CEO, Henry "Hank" Paulson, was the US treasury secretary at the time. Paulson had recently pocketed nearly half a billion dollars from selling his Goldman Sachs shares prior to the crash—and avoided payment of capital gains taxes because he was US treasury secretary (yes, that's legal if you're a senior government official).[3] His position was what enabled him to use taxpayer money to bail out Goldman Sachs, too.

Fool me once, shame on you. Fool me twice, shame on me. A decade later, Goldman was playing a new version of its old game—not exactly its pre-2008 subprime mortgage "greed is good" game but a new post-2018 game instead. It was the same game at its core but under the cover of a virtuous-sounding three-letter acronym: ESG.

One of Goldman's flagship mutual funds, its so-called Blue Chip Fund, was struggling to gain assets. But Wall Street's savviest firm soon found its fix: in June 2020, Goldman Sachs rebranded its Blue Chip Fund as its U.S. ESG Equity Fund.

If you were one of the many investors who had decided to pass on investing in Goldman's flailing Blue Chip Fund and Goldman later marketed a fund called U.S. Equity ESG Fund, you would understandably assume that it was a *different* investment opportunity. But you'd be wrong.[4] As it turned out, the three largest holdings of the two funds—Microsoft, Apple, and Alphabet—were identical. That's because Goldman Sachs cleverly defined "ESG" in its legal filings so that it didn't have to do much differently from what it had already been doing with its existing S&P 500–tracking, non-ESG Blue Chip Fund. It promised to screen out gambling, alcohol, tobacco, coal, and weapons stocks—but very few companies in the S&P 500 make those products anyway. It also promised to "conduct a supplemental analysis of . . . a range of environmental and social factors" but never said what that meant.[5] The only real difference was its fee, which it raised by a mere basis point—not enough to make much more money on it but enough to signal that it was now marketing an even more premium product.

When the disgraced pharmaceutical entrepreneur Martin Shkreli bought the rights to a floundering HIV drug and jacked up its price while changing absolutely nothing about the drug, he was ostracized from society and eventually imprisoned. But the market had done its job: medical insurance companies had refused to pay for the drug because they had seen through the trick.

By contrast, when Goldman jacked up the price on a floundering fund and slapped an ESG label on it, clients didn't flee. They flocked to it. Why? Because market actors are human beings, not automatons, a fact that efficient market theorists often forget. We humans tend to be very good at sniffing out crooks when they act like greedy villains, but we're hopelessly bad at it when they act like saints.

Goldman's particular ESG-related sin eventually became so commonplace on Wall Street that it earned its own idiom: greenwashing. The investors in Goldman's ESG fund thought they were getting something other than just the S&P 500. But they were not. Left-wing critics of ESG get upset about this practice, and rightly so. Greenwashing is fraudulent: it tells investors that they are getting one thing (exciting investments that combat climate change and societal injustices) when in fact they are getting another (standard investments that are just supposed to make money). It's the sort of ESG-directed criticism that the *New York Times* views as fit to print.[6]

But greenwashing isn't the biggest ESG scam. Dedicated ESG funds represent a relatively small minority of total funds in the asset management industry. The real problem is the inverse: greensmuggling. That occurs when *non-ESG* funds smuggle *ESG* policies into their investment practices. Again, investors believe that they are getting one thing (standard investments that are just supposed to make money), when in fact they are getting another (objectives that include combating climate change and societal injustices). Unlike greenwashing, the greensmuggling problem is over $100 trillion in scale. But you won't read about it in the *New York Times*.

The perpetrators of *that* scam make Goldman Sachs look quaint. They're not Wall Street banks. They're the institutions that own them. They own the *New York Times*, too.

Meet BlackRock, State Street, and Vanguard, the three largest and most influential financial institutions in US history. They're known as the "Big Three" on Wall Street, but you may never have heard of them. You probably don't know what they do. As this book goes to print, these three companies manage more than $20 trillion, almost as much as the entire US gross domestic product. That's more than the inflation-adjusted net worth of John D. Rockefeller, Andrew Carnegie, Henry Ford, and Cornelius Vanderbilt combined.

Unlike the great industrialists, the Big Three don't simply invest their own money; they invest yours. If that were all they were doing—investing your dollars in the market to deliver returns—it wouldn't be a problem. Big isn't *inherently* bad. Scale even provides benefits. BlackRock, State Street, and Vanguard can offer historically low fees to their clients precisely because they're big enough to make such a business profitable.

But there's a catch, a recurring theme you'll see throughout this book: if you get something for free, you're not the customer; you're the *product*. In Silicon Valley, that means you get to use Google, Facebook, and Twitter "for free," but in return, you give up your privacy, your personal data, and your freedom to decide what you see on the internet. Modern internet users awoke to that reality only after the tech titans got so big that no one could do anything to solve the problem.

Something similar happened on Wall Street: everyday investors can access ultracheap index funds offered by BlackRock, State Street, and Vanguard. But the real price isn't the nominal fee that the Big Three charge them; it's their voices and votes as shareholders in the global economy.

This scheme isn't just financial, it's *ideological*, one that uses the money of US citizens to secretly advance agendas that they may find revolting. It's happening on such a large scale that it may be what Arizona's attorney general in 2022 called "the biggest antitrust violation in history."[7] If that sounds grandiose, consider the following: if the CEOs of the largest US oil companies were to get together in a closed-door conference room and decide to slash oil production, thereby causing prices to rise at the pump, they'd go to jail for price-fixing. Yet the largest *shareholders* of those companies—ExxonMobil, Chevron, ConocoPhillips, Marathon, and so on—are none other than the Big Three. And those asset managers are working together to pressure *all* of those companies to cut oil production.

Take what happened to Chevron in 2021. A Dutch nonprofit submitted a shareholder resolution demanding that the US oil giant reduce its Scope 3 emissions. That requires Chevron to take responsibility for not just its own emissions but those of its suppliers and customers as well.[8] This makes as much business sense as McDonald's assuming responsibility for reducing the body weight of anyone who eats a Big Mac. The Dutch nonprofit was clear that its objective was to fight climate change, not to help Chevron's business—which helps explain why it proposed a commercially nonsensical mandate. Predictably, Chevron's board resoundingly opposed the proposal. Then something curious happened: BlackRock, State Street, and Vanguard all voted for it anyway. They used trillions of dollars belonging to hardworking Americans—the money in many of your 401(k) accounts and pension funds—to do it.

The vote had its intended effect. Chevron sheepishly changed course by agreeing to a litany of climate-related policies. The oil behemoth adopted Scope 3 carbon intensity targets. It tripled its prior multibillion-dollar investment in a nebulously named division called Chevron New Energies whose leader described the move as the company's earning its "social license." Chevron publicly advocated for a new tax on its main product: oil. And the company's management groveled to its new masters by vocally endorsing the Paris Climate Accords; if the United States wasn't going to ratify the Paris Accords, Chevron would do it instead. BlackRock and State Street even gave Chevron a nice pat on the back in 2022, praising the company's progress toward its Scope 3 goals—like a good daddy and mommy rebuilding the confidence of their once-disobedient child.

You might wonder what happened to the oil and gas projects that US companies dropped in recent years. Chevron, for example, abandoned a gas extraction project in China's Sichuan Basin. Daddy BlackRock would be proud. It's another small step in the long trek to stave off global climate change, you might assume.

Again, you'd be wrong. Gas production continued[9] anyway—under new ownership. PetroChina, the listed arm of China National Petroleum Corporation, acquired the project from Chevron for what was undoubtedly a fire-sale price. And in another noncoincidence, one of PetroChina's largest foreign shareholders is none other than BlackRock.

There are many losers in this game. Chevron loses: the company allocates its capital according to social mandates instead of investment returns. Clients in BlackRock's US funds lose: they are invested in companies such as Chevron that are encumbered by social and environmental mandates. Climate activists lose: the more firms such as Chevron shift oil production to places such as China and Russia, due to poor extraction practices in those countries, the more methane leaks into the atmosphere (and every unit of methane is eightyfold worse for global warming than carbon dioxide). Ukraine and other countries lose: the less oil and gas the United States produces, the more dependent the West becomes on Russian and Chinese energy sources and the more emboldened the dictators of such countries become. Citizens lose: their investment accounts are used to advance agendas they never voted for.

The winner is, of course, BlackRock. In a predictable twist, during the short period between the moment Chevron dropped its project in the Sichuan basin and PetroChina started drilling at the same site, BlackRock revealed that it had become the first foreign asset manager to launch a wholly owned mutual fund business in China. The first gas started flowing from the new PetroChina facility in November 2022, but Chinese money had begun flowing to BlackRock long before that.

This isn't just a tale about the US energy industry. In 2022, BlackRock did something similar to the United States' largest technology company: Apple. An ESG proponent called on Apple to conduct a racial equity audit in its workforce. Apple's board opposed the proposal, just as Chevron's board had opposed the Scope 3 emissions proposal. But once again, BlackRock and State Street voted for it nonetheless, and the proposal passed. As this book goes to print, Apple is conducting that racial equity audit. Meanwhile, BlackRock is among the top shareholders of Xiaomi, the largest smartphone producer in China. Apple's workforce looks like a multicultural kaleidoscope compared to that of Xiaomi, but there is no public record of BlackRock calling for the latter to conduct a racial equity audit—or for that matter to assess how equitably the firm treats its Uighur compatriots.

It's not even a tale about just the United States. On the contrary, developing nations may prove most vulnerable to ESG-inflicted woes. Take the implosion of Sri Lanka. Three years before the country's economic crisis beginning in 2019, the World Economic Forum (WEF) urged it to adopt "affirmative-action programs," "good environmental policies," and, most specifically, "high-productivity organic farming."[10] Sri Lanka resisted. But it was ultimately too poor to say no. In 2021, it banned nonorganic fertilizers. It was showered with praise from environmental groups.[11] It was awarded a $28 million grant by the European Union and World Bank for its "move towards a more sustainable, resilient and productive agriculture."[12] Then the country's economy collapsed. Crops were devastated, food prices soared, and people began to starve. Cars became children's playgrounds[13] as fuel became scarce. Rolling blackouts left citizens without power. The president fled. Protesters breached his residence and swam in his pool. Three years later, Sri Lanka's desperate financial situation has not improved, but its ESG score has: it now boasts a near-perfect ESG rating of 98.1.[14]

At the heart of this game is not a trick but a worldview—what Klaus Schwab, the executive chairman of the WEF, has called "the Great Reset." "Whether it's pandemics, climate change, terrorism or international trade, all are global issues that we can only address, and whose risks can only be mitigated, in a collective fashion," he has said. This vision calls for the dissolution of boundaries in our lives—between capitalism and politics, between nonprofits and for-profits, even between nations. It calls on leaders in the private sector to step in and address the failures of government leaders, and vice versa.

A response to the Great Reset is now well under way. I call it the Great Uprising—a movement of citizens in the United States and other democratic nations who reject the dissolution of those boundaries. They are the ones who say "Hell no!" They are the ones who stood up to an empire two and a half centuries ago to say that we settle our differences through free speech and open debate in the public square, through the electoral process and the ballot box, where every citizen's voice and vote count equally—not by self-appointed elites in cloistered rooms in the backs of palaces.

Those two forces collided in 1776 and gave birth to a great nation. Now, in 2023, they're about to collide again. We'll soon find out whether they will break the great nation they once birthed.

CAPITALIST PUNISHMENT

Chapter 1

WHAT IS ESG?

I t's a bit difficult being a public critic of the World Economic Forum (WEF) when it advertises you as one of its representatives. The WEF and its chairman, Klaus Schwab, are the organizing force behind the Great Reset, stakeholder capitalism, and ESG—all the economic agendas I'll explain and oppose in this book. The WEF is the head of the snake. Every year, it summons business leaders, celebrities, and politicians to the resort town of Davos in the Swiss Alps to determine the future shape of the world. Given my opposition to the WEF's imperious ideology, I still don't know how I became listed as one of its Young Global Leaders.

My supposed career as a Young Global Leader began in October 2020, when a WEF representative sent me an email congratulating me on my nomination to the program. On a call with him, I politely but firmly said that I wanted nothing to do with it; I reiterated that refusal on another call. I thought that was the end of it. But a few months later, I received another email from the same guy congratulating me on being named a Young Global Leader and inviting me to make connections at its annual conference in Davos, where my training in global leadership would presumably begin.

"I'm flattered by your nomination, but I don't think it's the right fit for me," I responded. "I believe I mentioned that when we spoke, but I'm sorry if that was unclear for any reason."

"In any case, they made an announcement this morning Geneva time, and you were named a 2021 honoree," he replied. He told me that 120 billionaires had attended Davos the prior year and that my company Roivant Sciences would get some good PR from my being a Young Global Leader, though I'd have to clear press releases with the WEF first. He also mentioned that the honor might help with promoting my upcoming book; I'm not sure he knew it was titled *Woke, Inc.*

I could not get those guys to take me off their list. After I started complaining about it on Twitter a few months later, I finally got an email from the World Economic Forum apologizing for the confusion, saying it had never heard me decline and promising to remove me from its site in a day or two. That didn't happen. Instead, I got more calls and emails from the original WEF rep telling me it would be a mistake to try to take my name off the program. Looking back on all those exchanges, it reminds me of the Dr. Seuss story *Green Eggs and Ham*. *I do not want to be a Young Global Leader*, I kept insisting to no avail. *I would not like it with billionaires. I would not like it with Davos airs. I would not like it anywhere.*

Many months later, as the next crop of Young Global Leaders was announced, the WEF naturally replaced the press release mentioning my membership. I was finally quietly scrubbed from its site. But the damage was done. People on social media still cite it and warn everyone that I'm some kind of secret double agent whenever I criticize the World Economic Forum's plans. The author of one article inferred from the Young Global Leader program description that I had attended a five-year Davos training course with people such as Elon Musk and PayPal cofounder Peter Thiel. The writer noted our public opposition to the WEF's agenda and stated, "their connection to the WEF shouldn't be ignored—we should be able to recognize and appreciate some of the good work they are doing while reserving some skepticism given their history."[1] I'm sure those two had as little choice as I did; Klaus Schwab should probably name all his critics WEF leaders.

My experience of being drafted into the WEF's Young Global Leader program is a microcosm of the way it conscripts everyone into its plans: it turns out you've been drafted, too. You didn't even receive the courtesy of a notification. The program you're enrolled in is called "stakeholder capitalism," and its main seminar is "ESG." This chapter outlines the syllabus of the course the WEF signed you up for.

Investing based on ESG considerations has taken the financial world by storm over the last several years, but before you can understand all that's bound up in the intentionally bland phrase "environmental, social, and governance," you have to understand where it came from. That starts with stakeholder capitalism. I've already written at book length about stakeholder capitalism, so I'll present only a brief overview here; my target in this book is the ESG movement, its main method of implementation. Today's ideological battles are the renewed hostilities of a war that began more than fifty years ago. The opposing generals were the economists Milton Friedman and Klaus Schwab.

The German-born, Geneva-trained Schwab represented the post–World War II European view that all parts of a society had to work in concert for the community to prosper and that wise leaders representing every institution needed to coordinate their efforts to produce that harmony. As Western Europe took on the daunting task of rebuilding itself in the decades following the war, it made some sense for every sector of society to view itself as embarking on a common project with every other part; churches, states, schools, nonprofits, and corporations all had to pull in the same direction and keep one another's interests in mind. Thus was stakeholder capitalism born. The American law professor Merrick Dodd had anticipated it decades earlier,[2] but the idea took root and flourished in the soil of postwar Europe. Stakeholder capitalism held that businesses had to make decisions for the benefit of all members of society, not just their employees and owners.

That European view clashed with American individualism. It's no surprise that as global markets brought stakeholder capitalism across the Atlantic, it met its strongest opposition here. To us, wary of aristocracy and unravaged by war, pursuing the common good was a task best left to democratic government. The main question for financial markets was not about what use of capital was best for society but who had the right to decide. In the American mind, investors' freedom to use their money as they saw fit was an important end in itself. Stakeholder capitalism's insistence that unelected leaders have a duty to shepherd society toward greatness struck us as little more than modern noblesse oblige.

In 1970, the Chicago School economist Milton Friedman argued in the pages of the *New York Times* that "there is one and only one social responsibility of business—to use its resources and engage in activities designed to increase its profits so long as it stays within the rules of the game, which is to say, engages in open and free competition without deception or fraud."[3] He insisted that when corporate executives take responsibility for solving social problems, they essentially steal shareholders' money to do so, because shareholders haven't expressly invested their money for social purposes. Market participants found his argument compelling; his stance ruled the Western financial world until the last fifteen years or so.

Now stakeholder capitalism is in the ascendant again. How did it make a comeback? In short, the 2008 financial crisis provided ample ammunition for critics of greed-is-good profit-above-all capitalism, and the ESG-focused version of stakeholder capitalism is the ideology that emerged from the dogpile.[4] But ESG's eventual victory is only the end of this story. There was a lot of quiet work that paved the way.

Back in the 1970s, Klaus Schwab had lost the battle with Milton Friedman but continued to wage the war. A year after Friedman's broadside against stakeholder capitalism, Schwab founded the European Management Forum, which eventually gained more global management aspirations and renamed itself the World Economic Forum. (I agree, "World Management Forum" would have sounded a little too sinister.) In 1973, it published the first Davos Manifesto, beginning with the assertion that "The purpose of professional management is to serve clients, shareholders, workers and employees, as well as societies, and to harmonize the different interests of the stakeholders." It concluded by arguing that achieving a level of profitability is a necessary means to the end of serving society and all its other stakeholders.[5]

The WEF's influence gradually grew over the decades as it gathered elites from all institutions to realize the Davos vision of stakeholder capitalism: self-appointed global leaders, young and old. Since Friedman's doctrine of shareholder primacy was dominant in capital markets, the WEF chipped away at it through advancing narrower philosophies that could smuggle aspects of Schwab's vision into Friedman's view. The WEF usually sanitizes its agenda with anodyne three-letter acronyms.

That's what ESG ultimately amounts to: the latest and greatest way to disguise stakeholder capitalism as shareholder centric. Go back further in the evolution of ESG, and you'll find two ancestors: CSR and SRI.

CSR stands for "corporate social responsibility"; it brought tenets of stakeholder capitalism into corporate boardrooms, shaping *executive* behavior. SRI stands for "socially responsible investing"; it brought stakeholder capitalism into capital markets, shaping *investor* behavior. But stakeholder capitalism is the mother ship that used these three-letter doctrines as vehicles to carry its ideology piecemeal into various spheres of shareholder capitalism.

Like the larger philosophy it now belongs to, CSR was first proposed in the United States but only caught fire decades later in post–World War II Europe. The idea that businesses had social responsibilities beyond shareholder profit began to take shape as a reaction to the wealth of nineteenth-century robber barons; back then, those duties were generally discharged through the owners' personal philanthropy.[6] Charity was a way of guaranteeing that they would leave their communities at least as well off as they had found them, or at least try to. After World War II, theorists shifted the burden of helping society to businesses themselves. The economist Howard R. Bowen coined the term *corporate social responsibility* in his 1953 book *Social Responsibilities of the Businessman*.

The idea didn't really catch on until the 1970s, when institutions such as the WEF started to tie it together with European-style stakeholder capitalism. As the law professor Ramon Mullerat put it, "The European Union (EU) has been the continent that first became a convert to the CSR movement," because "in Europe there have been traditionally more CSR consistent values, norms and perceptions than in other areas of the world; European corporations have tended to hold stronger and broader approaches to stakeholder relations."[7] Basically, Americans started thinking that business owners should treat their employees well, not hurt people, and give back to their communities. Then, decades later, Europeans got their hands on CSR and combined it with their idea that corporate executives should direct and coordinate the interests of all society's members.

European stakeholder capitalism has gradually colonized American corporate social responsibility. The idea that corporations have some social responsibility slowly morphed into the broader theory that their responsibility is to shape society. CSR initially tended to focus more on making sure businesses didn't harm the communities they belong to, minimizing what economists call negative externalities. Stakeholder capitalism requires corporations to lead civilization into the future. As the two blend together, CSR now increasingly demands the same.

This ongoing shift demonstrates an important point: unless strictly confined, a corporation's notion of the scope of its social responsibility will always grow more expansive. With greater responsibility comes greater power. Milton Friedman's vision of shareholder capitalism required corporations to profit within society's rules, but stakeholder capitalism requires them to profit by creating the rules. Like light, the corporation's social duty will travel across the universe until some barrier stops it.

Unlike light, however, it travels in a particular direction: left. Not only does the meaning of "social responsibility" expand to give corporations more responsibility over time, it has become a mere vehicle to carry progressive policies past democratic checks. Liberals have tended to be the ones pushing the notion of CSR, so their very notion of what corporate social responsibility entails is also progressive. They phrase the goals of CSR broadly in terms that all can agree on, such as "equality" and "fighting pollution," but the specific policies always end up being liberal favorites, such as DEI training and Scope 3 emissions caps. When liberals can't pass their favored policies through democratic means, they use the power of definition to say it's a matter of social responsibility for corporations to force progressive agendas on everyone. It becomes the *corporation's* social responsibility to pass unpopular liberal policies precisely because the *government* can't pass them.

The World Economic Forum is now openly driving the shift from CSR's do-no-harm to stakeholder capitalism's do-all-good, and ESG is its main mechanism. You don't have to take it from me; the WEF sums it up perfectly well: "The most recent evolution in the journey of corporate sustainability is ESG: a set of Environmental, Social, and Governance criteria to measure and evaluate a company. What separates ESG from precursor programmes [such as CSR] isn't just a change in acronyms, but the paradigm shift from a shareholder-centric philosophy to one that is undeniably focused on all stakeholders."[8]

It adds that "Storytelling remains paramount with ESG, but it's validated with specific metrics that gauge a company's holistic performance," such as rigorous "DEI metrics," including diversity scorecards and annual equality reports. Though "CSR programmes from company to company look quite different—each housing a variety of loosely connected activities ranging from philanthropic causes to employee volunteerism . . . ESG issues, on the other hand, are fundamentally intersectional. 'E,' 'S,' and 'G' are not separate categories, but rather interconnected. Let's consider climate issues for example—ESG looks not only at an organization's environmental impact, but also the social justice issues around the disproportionate impact climate change has on low-income populations."[9]

This is no conspiracy theory; after decades of careful line blurring during Milton Friedman's era, the WEF is now blatantly saying that we should just replace shareholder capitalism's notion of corporate social responsibility with stakeholder capitalism's ESG. What is ESG? The traffic cop that writes tickets to enforce stakeholder capitalism. The finishing blow that completes the transformation of "corporations shouldn't hurt people" into "corporations should rule them."

That's the story of CSR; it's not so much evolving into ESG as being selectively bred into becoming it. SRI, on the other hand, is ESG's direct ancestor.

The True Purpose of ESG

As the prominent ESG rating provider MSCI puts it, "The practice of ESG investing began in the 1960s as socially responsible investing, with investors excluding stocks or entire industries from their portfolios based on business activities such as tobacco production or involvement in the South African apartheid regime."[10] MSCI's history of its movement is a bit off. Socially responsible investing (SRI) probably actually began in the 1700s, when Quakers refused to participate in the slave trade.[11] Today, ESG proponents would twist themselves into knots presenting intersectional economic arguments about why using forced labor doesn't maximize long-run profit; the Quakers just thought it was wrong.

They later expanded that ban to guns, alcohol, and tobacco—"sin stocks."[12] What changed in the 1960s was that the secular community finally picked up on long-standing religious investment practices. That was amped up in 1971 when antiwar Methodist ministers created the Pax

World Fund, the first sustainable investment fund, which allowed all investors to join their congregation in opposing companies that played a role in the Vietnam War.[13] Then, in the 1980s, divestment as a tool for social change was used to pressure the South African government to end apartheid. Back then, SRI held that divesting from harmful industries was *responsible*, not necessarily *profitable*. The same method is employed today by the "Boycott, Divest, Sanction" movement to protest the Israeli government's treatment of Palestinians.

When I was a student at Harvard in the mid-2000s, its endowment led a movement to divest from Sudan. Back then, its endowment was the largest of any university's by far. But its next target was divestment from the fossil fuel industry, which backfired, at least as a strategy for increasing risk-adjusted returns. The University of Texas's oil holdings are bringing in record amounts of cash during a bear market, and UT's endowment is now poised to overtake Harvard's. As Yale University finance professor William Goetzmann put it, "The University of Texas has a cash windfall when everyone is looking at a potential cash crunch. Adjusting your portfolio for social concerns is not costless."[14]

I covered the basic logic of divestment, and the reasons it necessarily sacrifices returns, in my first book.[15] In short, the hope is that if enough powerful market actors divest from a socially undesirable enterprise or set of activities (or nations), it will eventually increase the cost of capital for such enterprises enough to nudge them to change their behavior. But this strategy is unlikely to be effective in creating behavioral change, because in a liquid global market, when one party divests from an activity for a noneconomic reason, it simply creates an opportunity for another party to collect a higher rate of return by investing in that activity for purely economic reasons. If an investor screens investments for something other than financial performance, some financial performance is necessarily sacrificed and some other investor is given a discount. This is what the capital manager Cliff Asness calls "the cost of virtue."

State Street Global Chief Investment Officer Lori Heinel admitted as much when BlackRock and State Street were questioned by Texas state officials: "Over the years we've debated whether ESG is a performance enhancement and, as CIO, I've been steadfast in saying by definition, imposing a constraint on a portfolio, if you just do basic investment principles, that's a constraint. And so I've steadfastly encouraged our teams to not think of ESG as a performance enhancement, for example."[16] Yet at the same time, State Street proudly declares "We are encouraging our portfolio companies to adopt more sustainable practices, and embedding ESG across our own business to build a more resilient and inclusive future."[17]

ESG was born as the more precise successor to SRI. The term was first used in 2004 by the United Nations Global Compact, a sustainability initiative announced five years earlier at Davos in an address to the World Economic Forum. In a report titled *Who Cares Wins: Connecting Financial Markets to a Changing World*, the UN rejected the idea that virtue has a cost, suggesting that when practiced in a particular way, socially responsible investing could actually increase returns.[18] SRI was imprecise about what counted as "socially responsible," so ESG tried to fill that gap by referencing "environmental, social, and governance" factors, which has the benefit of sounding slightly more precise and better thought out. That was what gave it much more expansive influence and staying power than SRI had.

The new name elided a number of important distinctions. Though the goal of SRI was explicitly to achieve a particular noneconomic end, ESG was born to blur the line between social and economic ends. That was why "governance" was tacked on at the end. Governance is usually associated with better investor oversight of companies to improve long-run economic performance.

ESG is built on a dirty semantic trick: historically, no one really expected socially responsible investment to increase returns. But everyone expected good corporate governance to be important for a company's financial performance. So ESG just takes the regular old unprofitable social investing considerations, throws regular profit-focused governance concerns into the same acronym, then claims that the whole acronym is obviously concerned with shareholder profit. Then it says some stuff about intersectionality to take the profit-focused governance stuff and claim that the environmental and social stuff are profit focused, too. It governance-washes the rest of the acronym. The boundary between what's good for society and what's good for shareholders becomes blurred.

That's the main distinction that ESG was created to elide: whether the enterprise of virtue-acronymized capitalism was to improve *society* or to create greater value for *shareholders*. The SRI answer was clearly the former. But ESG was born to enable the movement to have its cake and eat it, too; its answer was "both." Old-fashioned SRI wasn't that popular, because it promised only virtue, not wealth. Because of that limitation, asset managers bound by fiduciary duty couldn't force SRI on their clients. But once it was dressed up as ESG and started promising virtue *and* wealth, suddenly asset managers were free to use their clients' money to pursue social agendas. With SRI, *individuals* had to choose to divest from sinful industries; ESG forces *everyone* to divest.

CSR was originally about corporate owners and executives making sure they didn't make the world worse through their business activities. SRI started out the exact same way, just from the investor side of the equation. People didn't want to spend their money in ways that harmed the world. Both of those precursors to ESG didn't pretend that they were about maximizing returns.

In contrast, the ESG movement contends that all it needs to do is refocus capitalists on their own long-run interests and that doing so will also solve all the world's injustices. This assertion is founded on stakeholder capitalism's nebulous promise that since we're all in this thing called life together, what's best for the group in the long run will also necessarily be best for the individual.

But what's best for a family isn't automatically what's best for each member of it. What's best for a company isn't automatically what's best for each of its employees. What's best for $X + Y$ isn't automatically best for X. Individuals can have long-run interests that conflict with those of the groups they belong to. It feels odd to have to explain this point through argument and analogy, but it seems necessary. We're all connected and all that—he who saves one life saves the world entire—but using an investor's money to help other people does not automatically make them richer if they just wait long enough.

The debate between stakeholder and shareholder capitalism cannot be resolved by saying that what's best for all stakeholders in the long run is necessarily also best for shareholders. That's wishful thinking. It's a catechism born from the effort to cram European stakeholder capitalism into US shareholder primacy. ESG advocates reflexively invoke the long run as though it were a mystic shield against evil. But the cost of virtue cannot be overcome simply by waiting. There is no escape from choosing how to balance competing moral and financial interests. These are deeply personal decisions everyone must make for themselves. There is no one-size-fits-all answer, and creating new acronyms will never provide one.

How ESG Spread Everywhere

SRI's divestment strategy lives on in its successor, ESG, but only as a small part of it. There are two kinds of ESG investing now. In the introduction, I called the problems associated with them greenwashing and greensmuggling. The latter is the one that brought ESG into your portfolio.

The first, less common kind of ESG investing is simply the old-fashioned sustainability fund, now sometimes called an ESG fund, where an asset manager takes an index and cuts out a few companies that are viewed as sin stocks. It's the classic divestment approach, but this time with the extra promise that avoiding sinful companies will somehow make the investor more money in the long run. "Unsustainable" is the

ESG term of art for "sinful"; ESG divestments sometimes seem motivated by the biblical belief that evil cannot prosper forever. Typical targets for divestment these days are fossil fuels, guns, tobacco, alcohol, gambling, private prisons, and defense. The original sustainability fund that divested from companies enabling the Vietnam War still avoids investing in defense companies, but it's abandoned its Methodist roots. Now it dresses everything up in modern language about ESG and long-term profit.[19]

Why should we believe that divesting from Lockheed will make money in the long run? Is the United States not going to have an army in the future? It's hard to see why it's moral, sustainable, or profitable to defund the arms production necessary to stop Russia from conquering Ukraine or China from taking Taiwan. But it has become accepted ESG dogma that war is bad, therefore defense companies are bad, therefore the arc of the moral universe will somehow bend to make them unprofitable in the long run. As Japan[20] and Europe[21] belatedly realize the need to arm themselves and the United States wakes to China's military modernization,[22] ESG's allergy to the defense industry naturally opens up opportunities for other investors.

The truth is that most ESG fund providers know that they're probably sacrificing risk-adjusted returns for their clients when they divest from a company over moral disapproval. But they offer ESG funds because they can charge much higher fees for them. To avoid sacrificing too much return, the name of the game is for the ESG fund provider to make as few actual divestments as possible; that's greenwashing.

In this spirit, Pax World Management, the original sustainability fund provider, was fined by the United States Securities and Exchange Commission for violating its own rules and quietly investing in companies involved in alcohol, gambling, and military contracting.[23] It turned out that they were profitable enterprises, and Pax couldn't bring itself to part with those returns. But it didn't want to give up its high ESG fees, either. It currently charges an annual fee of around 1 percent on its flagship ESG-themed fund,[24] compared to the average mutual fund fee of around .4 percent.[25] It enjoyed the best of both worlds—until the SEC caught it.

It's pretty extreme greenwashing for an ESG fund to benefit from its name and violate its own divestment rules in pursuit of returns. Garden-variety greenwashing involves charging high ESG fees while never actually promising to divest from much to begin with. Sometimes, as Goldman Sachs did, a firm will take an underperforming fund and rebrand it as an ESG fund, carefully constructing its divestment rules so that they sound impressive but don't actually require it to change its holdings much. It's a double win because suddenly, the firm gets more inflows to the fund and can charge higher fees. The dog becomes the darling—a real Cinderella story for the asset manager. Not too great for the new investors, though, since it's still just a rebranded underperforming fund.

I won't spend too much time on greenwashing because it's well known; everyone in finance is talking about the proliferation of greenwashing today, and regulators worldwide are trying to crack down on it. As they do, ESG funds will have to make more divestments to keep the name ESG, they will underperform as it becomes clear virtue has a cost, and sustainability funds will gradually dwindle until only true believers who are willing to sacrifice returns invest in them. That, of course, is their right. Even when our values differ, I respect anyone who sacrifices something to pursue theirs.

My main concern in this book is the second kind of ESG investing, which I call *greensmuggling*. This is a much bigger problem. There's actually not much money invested in the old-school divestment approach, relative to the rest of the market. The real problem is that ESG strategies are infiltrating the rest of the market. Giant asset managers such as BlackRock, Vanguard, and State Street are using the power of the shares they own to force all the companies in their non-ESG funds to adopt ESG policies.

BlackRock provides a prime example of greensmuggling. One month after its CEO, Larry Fink, wrote a letter to America's CEOs saying "every company must not only deliver financial performance, but also show how it makes a positive contribution to society,"[26] the Parkland shooting happened. BlackRock's executives realized that the company was the largest shareholder of every gun manufacturer and retailer in the United States. They started doing damage control, issuing a statement decrying "the terrible toll from gun violence in America" and saying that the shooting "requires response."[27] They met with gun retailers and manufacturers and pressured them to sell fewer guns by either getting out of the gun business altogether (as Kroger chose to) or voluntarily raising the age limit for gun purchases from eighteen to twenty-one. How does this help shareholders? It doesn't. It was all done in the name of social responsibility.

Here's the thing: BlackRock couldn't use its dedicated social responsibility funds to lobby gun sellers and makers, because those funds had to divest from gun manufacturers and therefore didn't have a shareholder's voice or vote anymore.[28] So BlackRock leveraged the massive weight of all the billions in its *non-ESG* funds to convince gun sellers not to sell guns. It used its supposedly profit-focused funds to advance social goals that had nothing to do with profit. The millions of investors in those funds, many of them gun owners, had never signed up for that; they just wanted diversification and profit. BlackRock's companywide commitment to ESG made it smuggle social activism into *all* its funds.

A few short years later, greensmuggling of ESG policies into all regular funds is becoming commonplace. ESG proponents have even come up with a name for the practice, a more flattering one than mine: IFSI, which stands for "investing for sustainability impact."[29] Essentially, it's the opposite of divestment. Instead of avoiding supposedly sinful companies, the new strategy is to invest in them as usual and use the voice and vote of each shareholder to make them less sinful by imposing ESG policies on them. There's "instrumental IFSI," in which imposing a sustainability goal on a portfolio company is supposed to be a means to the end of increasing its profit, and "ultimate ends IFSI," in which the sustainability goal is an end in itself and doesn't have much to do with shareholder profit. It's just a new name for stakeholder capitalism. That was what BlackRock was doing.

This approach avoids the obvious problem that divestment leads to underperformance. Sure, if you're BlackRock, your index fund clients arguably might make less money if you force gun sellers not to sell guns. But that profit will disappear from the entire market, so your index fund won't underperform any other asset manager's; everyone will make less money together.

The new term, IFSI, describes and legitimizes a strategy all the major asset managers have been pursuing for years. When BlackRock and others respond to critics by saying that they're *not* divesting from oil and gas, they're right. The real problem isn't that the likes of BlackRock are divesting from ExxonMobil and Chevron; it's that they're *invested* in ExxonMobil and Chevron and slowly changing the essence of what those companies do. Just as gun sellers make less money when they sell fewer guns, oil companies make less money when they're pressured to produce less oil.

ESG continues its inexorable advance. After the 2008 financial crisis, Wall Street leapt to embrace it to distract the mob at its door. Occupy Wall Street demanded a reordering of modern capitalism itself. By contrast, the growing DEI movement, the "social" part of ESG, merely demanded the capitalists make a few tweaks. Applaud diversity. Add women and minorities to your boards. Muse about the racially disparate impact of climate change. Occupy Wall Street began with a complaint about inequality but was divided and appeased by promises of diversity. Worrying about class is out; race, sexual orientation, and gender identity are in.

The DEI branch of ESG is still going strong, but the environmentalism part became supercharged in 2017, when President Trump announced his intent to pull the United States out of the Paris Climate Accords. As the experts at Davos worried that global governments wouldn't take adequate action against climate change, ESG suddenly demanded that corporations behave like governments. Shortly after Trump's announcement, the Climate Action 100+ group sprung up to commit businesses to meet the Paris Accords' goal of limiting global warming to below 2°C.[30] If the citizens of countries wouldn't voluntarily make the politically correct sacrifices, billionaire business leaders would sign them up for it instead. Quasi-governmental environmental corporate alliances keep popping up. The Net Zero Asset Managers initiative asks its members to pressure all their portfolio companies to cut their greenhouse gas emissions so the world can reach net zero emissions by 2050.[31] The new Glasgow Financial Alliance for Net Zero, GFANZ, coordinates those asset managers with similar coalitions in banking, insurance, and consulting.[32]

Whatever the merits of these climate efforts, which I'll discuss in more detail in chapter 3, it's hard to believe this is all about shareholder profit. Special Presidential Envoy for Climate John Kerry agrees. As he recently put the problem, "that money is not giveaway money. It's not concessionary funding. It belongs to people, you know. An entity like BlackRock doesn't own the money. They're working for clients. The clients own the money, and some of the clients want the best return they can get on that investment, and you don't get that necessarily from climate. Or you have pension funds—big pension funds—with, you know, millions of American workers who anticipated retirement based on that fund. They are subject to fiduciary responsibility, and they have to live up to that."[33]

Couldn't have said it better myself.

Your Money

It's quite simple: a solid CSR framework expresses a corporation's commitment to social responsibility, so a business should probably still hire people to staff that department.[34] It definitely needs a top-notch ESG department to measure its success on those commitments and coordinate with the WEF and the rest of the stakeholder capitalist community to make sure it's achieving the Sustainable Development Goals (SDGs) of the United Nations' Principles for Responsible Investment (PRI).[35]

Diversity, equity, and inclusion (DEI) efforts are an important part of the *S* in ESG and have many intersectional links to the *E* and *G*, so the corporation needs to hire people to run those, too, both internal directors and external auditors and consultants.[36] An asset manager's ESG department must make sure the firm practices IFSI to ensure that all of its portfolio companies do a good job at all of the above.[37] All of this will obviously increase shareholder profit in the long run.

ESG. DEI. CSR. SRI. PRI. SDG. And now there's something called IFSI, and it's supposed to be good. This is what it looks like when an institution is captured by an ideology.

Allow me to suggest the obvious: there's no reason to think that any of this stuff is really about maximizing your investment returns; it's just an extensive apparatus to eliminate political dissent from the global marketplace. The self-appointed global leaders at Davos do it because they don't trust governments or the people who elect them to do things right. A bunch of leeches in the growing ESG-industrial complex have latched on to all this both to advance their political agenda and to extract directing, consulting, and auditing fees from corporations at every step of the chain. It all comes from your bank account in the end. And your vote means less every day.

This is what the modern battle to rule the world looks like. It's fought not with bullets but with acronyms. One way to steal from people is to distract them from what you're doing. A safer way is to bore them. Then they'll distract themselves. Leave financial stuff to the experts. Leave it to your financial advisor, your asset manager. Leave it to BlackRock, Davos, the credentialed DEI and ESG experts; they've given one another certificates that they're experts.

But the acronyms you ignore eventually find their way into your life. You wake up one day and find yourself at the beck and call of strange ideas, and you don't know where they came from or what they mean, only that you're required to pretend you believe them with all your heart. Why do you have to go to so many mandatory HR trainings? Why are you supposed to accept that your race inevitably dictates your career outcomes? Why does your employer want to know your sexual orientation? Why is everyone talking about sustainability, regardless of their job?

The alphabet soup of neologisms the WEF serves up is all stakeholder capitalism in the end. It all comes back to one simple question: Who has the right to decide what to do with your money? The WEF always thinks it's the one that ought to be calling the shots.

As I finished writing this chapter, I saw yet another tweet warning everyone that I'm a WEF Young Global Leader, that my public anti-ESG persona is fake, and that I'm "controlled opposition."[38] Once a Young Global Leader, always a Young Global Leader. Maybe if this book does too well, the WEF will name me Klaus Schwab's successor; it seems I can't decline these things. After I corrected him about my being a Young Global Leader, the tweeter suggested that I sue the WEF, saying that it was deliberately trying to undermine my criticism of it. I probably won't. I don't think there was any malice in what the WEF did; everyone I talked to there was sincere and professional.

The WEF means well. That's actually the problem. It's absolutely sure it knows what's best for you. When you disagree, it doesn't matter, because it assumes that you can't possibly be fully informed. You must not know how many billionaires go to Davos; you must not know how good stakeholder capitalism will be for your career. That's the story it tells itself about how it can force programs on you while respecting your autonomy: it's fulfilling the will you would have if you were fully up to speed on all the good the WEF is doing. The WEF cannot fathom that a rational person could disagree with it. That's what makes it so dangerous. It cannot fathom that you don't want to be a follower of stakeholder capitalism in exactly the same way it couldn't fathom that I don't want to be one of its Young Global Leaders.

That's the crux of the problem with ideologies such as ESG: you are the best judge of your own will, your own rationality. The WEF will not give you the option of leaving its program. Believe me, I know. But the power ultimately lies with you, because the fundamental fact remains that all of this stuff is made possible by your money.

That's what this book is about. I will tell you exactly what is being done with your money and how it's affecting you and tell you exactly what legal, political, and financial tools are available for you to take back control of your money and your life. You live in a cage made of your own money. But you can also fashion your money into the key.

Chapter 2

THE BIGGEST FIDUCIARY
BREACH IN US HISTORY

E SG is in the law's crosshairs. In August 2022, nineteen state attorneys general sent a letter to BlackRock CEO Larry Fink warning of "rampant" illegality at his company due to BlackRock's ESG activities.[1] Three months later, Goldman Sachs paid millions of dollars to the SEC to settle a federal investigation into several of its ESG investment funds.[2]

Many find ESG's legal woes inexplicable. What could possibly be unlawful about BlackRock or Goldman offering ESG options to interested investors? In this chapter I'll explain ESG's "rampant" illegality, but unraveling that legal mystery requires a quick stop back in medieval Britain.

The Sacred Law of Trusts

Some eight hundred years ago, England's myriad courts of equity—Church courts, the Court of Chancery, even the Exchequer of the Jews—began to fashion a new legal concept, which would one day be called the most important innovation in the history of the common law. This innovation was not the jury. It was not the privilege against self-incrimination. It was *the trust*.

The great common-law historians Frederick Pollock and Frederic William Maitland made valiant Crusaders the heroes of this story.[3] Noblemen riding off to fight the Infidel would sometimes convey title to their lands to a trusted friend so that he could collect rents, pay taxes, cut timber, provide for the lord's wife and children, and so on. Occasionally, the faithful friend proved to be faithless: he would take the estate for himself and refuse to return it when the nobleman returned. Because the faithless friend was now the owner, the nobleman had no legal recourse. If the poor, betrayed, now-homeless lord sued in a court of law, he would lose.

England, however, had courts not only of law but of equity, where fairness could trump legality, and their judges saved the day. They came up with the idea that there were two different kinds of ownership and two different kinds of owners of the land in question. The faithless friend was the *legal* owner, but the lord remained the *beneficial* owner, the *"equitable* owner," a term still used today. Yes, the friend owned the land, but he held it *in trust*. He had all the powers of ownership, but a duty as well—the duty to manage the property for the benefit of the nobleman and return it to him upon request.

The valiant Crusader part of this story is probably apocryphal. The real origins of the trust appear to have had more to do with tax evasion.[4] In those days, a chief source of Crown revenue was death taxes on feudal lands after the owner's demise. However, if a clever nobleman transferred his land to a trusted friend (or relative or attorney), who upon the nobleman's death reconveyed it to the lord's wife and children, no death tax would have to be paid because the "owner" had never died. Once again, however, the trusted friend occasionally proved to be untrustworthy, keeping the land for himself after the lord's death. And once again, courts of equity stepped in to return the land to its true owner.

Either way, medieval equity courts invented the trust to enable people to transfer property to a new legal owner while ensuring that the property would be used for specific purposes. The trustee would have an owner's legal rights but a fiduciary duty to exercise those rights in the beneficiary's interests. Today, trusteeships are universally recognized, and a trustee's fiduciary duties are still described as "sacred"—the highest known to the law.[5] Over the centuries, trusts became common, used not only for estate planning but also to pool capital into publicly held investments.[6] A lot of people could put a little money into a for-profit trust created, for example, to build a cotton mill or a streetcar line. Each of those investors was a fractional beneficial owner of the trust's assets. As legal owners, trustees would manage the assets and provide a return to the investors. In other words, trusts were the progenitors of the modern limited liability corporation; indeed, as late as the mid–nineteenth century, far more business enterprises in England were organized as trusts than as corporations. A century ago, most of the United States' oil companies were held in giant trusts, with John D. Rockefeller at the helm. Even today, exchange-traded funds (ETFs) are often held as trusts, and pension plans are typically trusts as well.

Nowadays, there are other legal devices for achieving similar results in the investment industry. A $100 billion investment fund owned by Black-Rock might be technically registered as a company. However, this technicality doesn't affect the company's core rights and duties. In essence, every large investment fund is a megatrust. BlackRock may "own" the $8 trillion it manages, but it holds those funds in trust for the assets' true owners—the investors—and everything it does with its investors' money, it must do "solely and exclusively" (as lawyers say) to advance their interests. BlackRock owes those investors the same sacred fiduciary duties recognized by the courts of equity centuries ago. Until fairly recently, the United States' largest asset managers fully understood and generally honored these fiduciary duties. Then came ESG, and the rails came off.

Greensmuggling: How ESG Really Works

On the left, the chief argument against ESG investing is that some ESG investment funds don't actually promote ESG at all. One example often pointed to is Vanguard's ESG U.S. Stock ETF. This is an index-style fund, like an S&P 500 fund. In fact, the problem is that it is a little too much like an S&P 500 fund. Day over day, year over year, it has had a 99.7 percent correlation—that's right, *99.7 percent*—with the S&P 500.[7] Basically, an investment in the fund *is* an investment in the S&P 500, but Vanguard calls it an ESG fund.

Why would Vanguard do this? Maybe because it's more profitable. If you invest in Vanguard's S&P 500 ETF, you pay a fee of three basis points. But for its ESG U.S. Stock ETF, Vanguard's fee is *nine* basis points.[8] Don't forget—worldwide, there was $46 trillion in professionally managed assets with ESG mandates, and that figure was projected to rise to $80 trillion by 2024.[9] At that asset level, with a few extra basis points, pretty soon you're talking about real money.

This problem is called *greenwashing*—the use of the ESG moniker to make investors think their money is promoting ESG causes when in reality it isn't. That was the basis of the federal investigation into Goldman Sachs.

Sometimes asset managers greenwash not for higher fees but simply to trick the market and capture pro-ESG investment dollars, like Goldman Sachs did in rebranding its Blue Chip Fund. Goldman Sachs was far from alone. In 2020, twenty-five funds similarly renamed themselves as "sustainable" or "ESG."[10] The ploy seems to work. In decline before their rebranding, many of the funds bounced back and added billions of dollars in new capital once the magic acronym "ESG" appeared in their name.[11]

That's the Left's legal critique of ESG, and the Left is right: not all ESG is greenwashing, but at least some of it surely is. According to this view, however, as long as ESG is real—as long as it's doing what it claims—it's perfectly lawful. That's the view of the Biden administration, which is pro-ESG and has recently enacted new rules to make ESG investing easier. Not so fast, say the nineteen state attorneys general who wrote to BlackRock. They argue that ESG, even when it's not a scam—in fact, *especially* when it's not a scam—can still violate fiduciary duties, particularly when public pension money is put to ESG use.

"How can it be illegal," you may be asking, "for me to use my investment dollars to promote ESG causes if that's what I want to do?" The answer is—it's not. You can invest your own money to promote any causes you like. But many investors, especially institutional investors, don't have that freedom. Pension funds are a clear example, which is why pensions have played a central role in driving the ESG debate.

Americans have a lot of money in pension funds—maybe $40 trillion, all told[12]—and some of the funds have jumped headfirst into the ESG game. In California, the board of California Public Employees' Retirement System (CalPERS), the largest state pension fund in the country with almost $500 billion in assets, signed on to the United Nations Principles of Responsible Investment (UNPRI). This means that the CalPERS board committed the state pension fund to "a set of core values in the areas of human rights, labour standards, and environmental practices"[13] to "better align investors with broader objectives of society."[14] CalPERS has publicly stated that it will seek to promote ESG objectives, such as biodiversity, human rights, and indigenous rights, in its investment decisions.[15]

Why do the board members running a $500 billion US pension fund believe they can use the retirement savings of hardworking public employees to further the world's "broader objectives" as determined by the United Nations? Because they have forgotten one thing: they're *trustees*.

The fundamental principle of trust law is the *sole interest rule*, which states that trustees must "administer the trust solely in the interest of the beneficiaries."[16] Thus, as the Supreme Court held in 1985 (the heyday of the socially responsible investment movement), a pension plan fiduciary must "discharge his duties with respect to a plan *solely in the interest of the participants and beneficiaries and . . . for the exclusive purpose of providing benefits to participants and their beneficiaries"* (emphasis added).[17]

You might think that this holding alone would have been sufficient, but sophisticated pension plan managers came up with a clever argument: they argued that retirees have all kinds of interests; some of them are financial, but others are "nonpecuniary," and pension fund trustees can lawfully advance both. If this view were accepted, pension fund trustees would be permitted to pursue social or political causes freely, so long as doing so could be said to provide their retirees with "nonpecuniary benefits."

But the Supreme Court rejected this argument in a 2014 case called *Fifth Third Bancorp v. Dudenhoeffer*. In that case, the Court squarely held that pension fund trustees are not permitted to make investments to advance *nonpecuniary* interests. Rather, they must act solely and exclusively to maximize retirees' *"financial* benefits" (emphasis added).[18]

Fifth Third Bancorp v. Dudenhoeffer was decided under a federal statute called the Employee Retirement Income Security Act, or ERISA, which governs many corporate pension plans. State law, which governs state pension plans, is even clearer on this point: "All fifty states authorize the assets of public retirement systems to be held in trust" and require that pension plan assets be devoted solely to the paying of benefits to plan participants.[19] Some states even include this principle in their constitution, expressly providing that "[a]ssets and funds established, created and accruing for the purpose of paying obligations to members of the several retirement systems of the State and political subdivisions *shall not be diverted or used for any other purpose*" (emphasis added).[20]

Under the sole interest rule, even "mixed-motive" investing is unlawful.[21] As Professors Max Schanzenbach and Robert Sitkoff put it, "Acting with mixed motives triggers 'an irrebuttable presumption of wrongdoing,' full stop."[22]

This rule is prophylactic. The point is to ensure that fiduciaries aren't tempted to use trust money to further their interests or preferred causes.

"The policy of the trust law is to prefer (as a matter of default law) to remove altogether the occasions of temptation rather than to monitor fiduciary behavior and attempt to uncover and punish abuses when a trustee has actually succumbed to temptation."[23]

For much the same reason, "social investing"—i.e., the investing of plan assets motivated by social or political considerations rather than solely by financial return—is prohibited in state pension systems. As stated in the comments to the Uniform Prudent Investor Act, "No form of so-called 'social investing' is consistent with the duty of loyalty if the investment activity entails sacrificing the interests of trust beneficiaries . . . in favor of the interests of persons supposedly benefitted by pursuing the particular social cause."[24]

Now you understand why several state attorneys general have warned their state pension trustees not to engage in ESG investing. ESG is a form of "social investing" or, at an absolute minimum, an example of "mixed-motive investing." However ardently some people may believe in the ESG agenda, state pension trustees aren't allowed to use other people's retirement savings to advance it. Whenever the board members of CalPERS or other pension funds do ESG investing, they take hardworking Americans' money—your money—and use it to promote their values.

Most pension funds, however, don't explicitly embrace ESG investing— at least not to the extent that CalPERS does. When they allocate billions of dollars to BlackRock, they don't put it into a BlackRock ESG fund, they put it into BlackRock's S&P 500 Index Fund or some other supposedly "passive" index fund, because all they're trying to do is maximize their risk-adjusted return. Most pension fiduciaries previously assumed that this meant they'd safely distanced themselves from ESG and its legal problems. Surely, they imagined, putting money into a BlackRock index fund can't raise any ESG legal issues? Yes, it can. Because BlackRock promotes the ESG agenda even with its index funds.

ESG doesn't simply consist of socially conscious investors choosing to put their money into ESG-friendly companies or ESG-themed investment vehicles. Far from it. All the big asset managers engage in greensmuggling, which is greenwashing's opposite number. Here's how it works.

The Big Three have made "firmwide commitments" to promote ESG. BlackRock, for example, boasts of its "firmwide commitment to integrate ESG information into investment processes across . . . all of the firm's investment divisions and investment teams."[25] This means that asset managers take concerted action to advance the ESG agenda not only through their explicit ESG investment funds, but throughout *all* their investment portfolios, including even their supposedly passive index funds. Take it directly from BlackRock: "we actually integrate ESG. . . . regardless of whether that portfolio has an ESG objective or not"; "A sustainable fund uses ESG integration, yes, but a non-sustainable fund also uses ESG"; "BlackRock now makes environmental considerations part of all our investment decisions."[26] Understanding how they do that is the key to understanding how ESG works.

Proxy Voting and "Shareholder Engagement"

The big asset managers push the ESG agenda through two primary mechanisms: (1) shareholder proxy voting and (2) "shareholder engagement," defined by Vanguard as "[d]irect contact with companies to discourage undesirable corporate behavior."[27] These "direct contacts"—for example, high-level in-person conversations or phone calls with corporate officers—often take place behind closed doors, and the specifics of the communications are rarely disclosed to outsiders. Shareholder engagement is less visible than proxy voting is. Still, it is even more powerful and effective, because of the tens of trillions of dollars in potential investment capital wielded by firms such as BlackRock, Vanguard, and State Street.

Through both mechanisms, ESG-promoting asset managers use their power as "shareholders in an attempt to . . . promote what they consider to be the right public policy. This takes place through dialogue with officers and proxy voting."[28] Again, asset managers that engage in these ESG-promoting practices—including BlackRock, Vanguard, and State Street—admit that they do so throughout all their investment portfolios, *including their nominally "passive" index funds.*[29] SEC commissioner Mark T. Uyeda described how the major US asset management firms use both shareholder voting and corporate engagement to push the ESG agenda on corporate America:

> In reviewing any large asset manager's stewardship website, mentions of ESG seem ubiquitous, from voting guidelines to engagements statistics. The information on these websites often document how an asset manager (1) establishes its expectations for ESG matters, (2) engages with companies that aren't meeting its expectations, and (3) may vote against one or more incumbent directors if those companies do not continue to meet expectations. For example, an asset manager publicly disclosed a case study where, following multi-year engagements, it voted against a director of a public company, who also chaired the board committee overseeing ESG matters, because the company had failed to disclose its forward-looking GHG reduction targets. This is one of many instances in which an asset manager did not support the election of a director on the basis of climate-related issues.[30]

With their $20 trillion in assets under management, the Big Three control the "equivalent of more than half of the combined value of all shares for companies in the S&P 500."[31] Due to this extraordinary economic and shareholding power, ESG promotion by firms such as BlackRock, Vanguard, and State Street has a profound impact on company policy all across the United States—often at odds with the best financial interests of the company and its shareholders.

For example, in 2021, an environmental activist group holding a minuscule number of shares of ExxonMobil nominated at that company's annual shareholder meeting a slate of new directors committed to reducing oil production. Whether one agrees or disagrees with this initiative as a matter of social policy, it is hard to see how reducing oil production is in the best financial interest of an oil company. Nevertheless, the Big Three asset management firms voted their proxies in favor of the activist slate of directors. As a result, the activist directors won, causing ExxonMobil to cut oil production, thereby reducing the company's revenues and contributing to a nationwide increase in gas prices.

This is a prime example of ESG promotion by BlackRock and other major asset managers serving to further social or political goals at the expense of investors. It is also concerning because oil projects abandoned by ExxonMobil can be picked up by rival companies such as PetroChina, the Chinese national energy company—one of whose largest private shareholders happens to be BlackRock, which owns over a *billion* shares of PetroChina.[32] There is no evidence that BlackRock notified any investor clients of this serious potential conflict of interest—i.e., that Exxon-Mobil's loss could be BlackRock's gain.

In other examples of ESG initiatives seemingly at odds with the best interests of shareholders and other investors, the Big Three voted their proxies in 2021 to cause Chevron to adopt Scope 3 emissions cuts and in 2022 to cause Apple to engage in a companywide racial equity audit. Whether you agree or disagree with such measures, they are motivated primarily not by the interests of shareholders but rather, as their proponents freely acknowledge, by a desire to advance the interests of certain social groups, society at large, or a company's other "stakeholders." For example, the proponents of Apple's racial equity audit claimed that it was required to determine "how [Apple] contributes to social and economic inequality" and to force Apple to "identify, remedy, and avoid adverse impacts on its stakeholders." Color of Change, one of the activist groups pushing for the audit, explains that its mission is "to hold companies accountable for the ways they perpetuate white supremacy."[33] Some may consider holding companies accountable for white supremacy to be a noble goal, but it's very different from maximizing return to those companies' shareholders.

With your retirement money—your pension, your 401(k), and so on—the Big Three use your shareholder voice and vote to promote ESG even when that money isn't in an ESG fund but only in an index fund. That's not legal. Like CalPERS' board members, BlackRock's Larry Fink has forgotten one thing: that the firm he oversees is a trustee. BlackRock has no right to use its investors' assets to promote its preferred social or political agenda, regardless of how noble some people may feel that agenda to be.

Several state attorneys general have issued opinions or guidance documents concluding that asset managers breach their fiduciary duties as trustees by using pension fund assets to promote ESG objectives. On September 1, 2022, the attorney general of Indiana issued a formal legal opinion concluding that public pension managers act unlawfully if they allocate capital to asset management firms such as BlackRock, Vanguard, and State Street that "engage with portfolio companies, or exercise voting rights appurtenant to investments based on ESG considerations."[34]

When your retirement assets are allocated to an index fund, the money is doubly entrusted. The pension plan is itself a trust, required by law to devote all assets solely to maximizing financial benefits. And the index fund is another trust, subject to the same fiduciary duty. Neither the pension's trustees nor the index fund's trustees can use their beneficiaries' money to promote the public policy outcomes they prefer. Yet that's exactly what BlackRock does when it pushes the ESG agenda through the shareholder voice and vote of people who never signed up for that agenda.

The Big Three's greensmuggling tactics have legal implications for other big players in the investment world, particularly investment advisors. They, too, may be in breach of their fiduciary duties if they put client capital into Big Three index funds without disclosing what the Big Three are doing with that money.

Often there's an intermediary between the owners of capital and the big asset managers. These intermediaries are called investment advisors. They make recommendations about where investors should put their money, and often they carry out investment transactions, placing clients' money in investment funds. JPMorgan Chase has investment advisors; so does Merrill; so do hundreds of other companies, large and small.

Investment advisors are usually not trustees (because they are not the legal owners of the assets in question), but they are still fiduciaries under both state and federal law.[35] As the SEC has stated, investment advisors must make a reasonable inquiry into their clients' objectives and must "adopt the [client's] goals, objectives, or ends."[36] In this way, investment advisors differ from pension fund trustees. Investment advisors may lawfully invest client capital in ESG vehicles, because individual investors are free to use their investment capital however they wish.

The corollary, however, is that investment advisors may not place a client's capital into investments promoting social, political, or other non-pecuniary objectives unless the client is aware that this is being done and has consented to it. Under well-established law, investment advisors have a fiduciary duty of disclosure: "As a general matter, an investment adviser, as a fiduciary, has a duty to disclose to clients all material facts. . . . Information is 'material if there is a substantial likelihood that a reasonable [client] would consider it important.'"[37] And as the Supreme Court has held, an investment advisor's "failure to disclose material facts must be deemed fraud" regardless of the presence or absence of any intent to deceive.[38]

How a client's shares will be voted is undoubtedly material information that investors have a right to know. Specifically, the fact that a client's shares will be voted to advance the ESG agenda is information that many investors will reasonably view as important—especially investors who don't support that agenda. Similarly, the fact that an asset manager will use a client's money for shareholder engagement to promote the ESG agenda is significant, material information that investors have a right to know.

At present, investment advisors frequently place client capital with ESG-promoting asset management firms—and even in explicitly ESG-themed investment funds—without informing their clients that they have done so. A 2021 report by Bloomberg tells the story.

Almost two years have passed since Larry Fink, the chief executive officer of BlackRock Inc., declared that a fundamental reshaping of global capitalism was underway and that his firm would help lead it by making it easier to invest in companies with favorable environmental and social practices. Lately, he's been taking a victory lap.

"Our flows continue to grow and dominate," Fink said Oct. 13 of so-called ESG, or environmental, social and governance funds, and similar investments. On the same conference call with analysts, he added: "BlackRock is a leader in this, and we are seeing the flows, and I continue to see this big shift in investor portfolios."

What Fink did not say is that BlackRock drove a significant part of that shift by inserting its primary ESG fund into popular and influential model portfolios offered to investment advisors, who use them with clients across North America. The huge flows from such models mean many investors got into an ESG vehicle without necessarily choosing one as a specific investment strategy, or even knowing that their money has gone into one.[39]

This practice is unlawful and has to stop. Placing client capital into an ESG vehicle or into a passive index fund whose shares are used to promote ESG objectives through proxy voting and shareholder engagement is an act of fraud if the investment advisor has not informed the client.

It's not categorically unlawful for investment advisors to place client capital into a BlackRock (or Vanguard or State Street) index fund. That's up to the investor. But as a fiduciary, the investment advisor first has to inform its clients about how BlackRock (or Vanguard or State Street) will use their money—their shareholder voice and vote—to promote the ESG agenda. Maybe the client will be fine with that. But every investor is entitled to know these facts before his or her money is used to promote someone else's values.

The "Long-Term Value Creation" Con

ESG advocates sometimes claim that ESG has nothing to do with achieving positive social or global impact; no, it's all about "long-term value creation." This claim is meant to save ESG from the sole interest rule, which states that investment fiduciaries must act exclusively with the motive of increasing returns. The idea is that in the long run, companies that adopt good ESG practices will succeed more often than the ones that don't.

Such claims have become more common recently as legal scrutiny of ESG has intensified. For example, after years of championing ESG for the sake of the world and to advance the interests of all "stakeholders," BlackRock CEO Larry Fink declared in late 2022 that BlackRock engages in ESG solely to increase "returns for shareholders."[40]

Courts are not likely to accept such post hoc rationalizations. Candid descriptions of ESG invariably acknowledge that its goal is and has always been to advance "socially responsible," "socially conscious," or "social impact" outcomes, even at the expense of "profit margin." The following are just a few examples.

- "The goal of the [ESG] movement is to ensure that companies take into account *not only their profit margin but also the impact they have on the world and society as whole*." (Emphasis added.)[41]

- "Environmental, social, and governance (ESG) investing criteria refers to a set of standards for a company's behavior used by *so-*

cially conscious investors to screen potential investments . . . to encourage companies to act *responsibly*," and to allow investors to "*[put] their money where their values are.*" (Emphasis added.)[42]

▪ "The corporate social responsibility (CSR) movement wants companies to consider the societal impact of their operations. A recent outgrowth of CSR has been to speak in terms of environmental, social, and governance (ESG) impact of a company's operations. . . . ESG reflects a way to measure the societal impact by providing metrics [to] investors and investment analysts."[43]

▪ "The PRI [the United Nations' Principles of Responsible Investment, signed on to by thousands of asset managers, including the Big Three] defines *responsible investment* as a strategy and practice to incorporate environmental, social and governance (ESG) factors in investment decisions and active ownership."[44] (Emphasis added.) Its signatories "embrace, support and enact a set of core values in the areas of human rights, labour standards, and environmental practices"[45] in order to "*better align investors with broader objectives of society.*" (Emphasis added.)[46]

Indeed, BlackRock itself used to candidly acknowledge that ESG investing was a form of "social impact" investing, notwithstanding recent name and wording changes in its public statements apparently adopted to obfuscate this fact. As late as 2021, BlackRock described its ESG US Equity Index Fund as "invest[ing] in a portfolio of equity securities of companies with *positive aggregate societal impact* outcomes."[47] In 2022, however, BlackRock quietly changed this fund's name to BlackRock Sustainable Advantage Large Cap Core Fund and now tells investors that the fund picks companies positioned to capture "climate opportunities."[48] Such rebranding shouldn't fool anyone. ESG is still exactly what its proponents have always claimed: an effort to achieve a "societal impact." Belated attempts to redescribe ESG in terms of capitalizing on market "opportunities" should not be trusted.

Even though the true motive behind ESG investing is and has always been "socially responsible investing" to achieve "positive aggregate soci-etal impact outcomes," ESG proponents nevertheless sometimes claim that ESG increases profitability, producing higher returns. And surely, ESG advocates argue, ESG investing can't be a breach of fiduciary duty if it produces superior financial outcomes?

This contention misses the point of the sole interest rule and its pro-phylactic prohibition of mixed-motive investing, the purpose of which is to avoid giving fiduciaries the temptation to use other people's money for their own preferred causes. The legal system doesn't want years-long tri-als in which judges have to resolve difficult empirical questions that even economists or financial experts may disagree on. That's why "[a]cting with mixed motives triggers 'an irrebuttable presumption of wrongdoing,' full stop."[49]

But if courts were to take up the question of whether ESG investing actually increases investment returns, they certainly wouldn't defer to the say-so of ESG-promoting asset management firms or pension funds. Rather, the burden of proof would fall on investment fiduciaries that seek to engage in ESG investment practices. "[U]nder the common law, a fidu-ciary who allegedly breached his or her fiduciary duty must justify his or her conduct."[50] Where "it is possible to question the fiduciaries' loyalty," "intensive and scrupulous" inquiry is appropriate, and substantial, objec-tive, and independent evidence must support the fiduciaries' claims.[51]

As the next chapter will show, proof that ESG investing increases in-vestor returns is at present wholly lacking. On the contrary, significant evidence suggests that ESG investing in fact produces *inferior* financial returns.

Chapter 3

DOES ESG MAKE MONEY?

C limate risk is investment risk."

That's what many people think is the elephant in the room. It's the mantra BlackRock created to try to meet its burden of proving that ESG investing will make money in the long run. In my first book, I mentioned that colleges that are sued over affirmative action have a mantra they intone in court as though they're prisoners of war, reciting their name, rank, and serial number: "We have a compelling interest in admitting a diverse class and race is but one factor of many we consider in our practice of holistic review."[1] "Climate risk is investment risk" serves the same function for asset managers worried about being sued over ESG investing.

The Big Three and the WEF would have you believe that to oppose ESG is to oppose science itself, that climate science and the dictates of ESG are one and the same. When those nineteen state attorneys general accused BlackRock of violating its fiduciary duty, the company trotted out its trusty ace in the hole: appeals to "climate risk" appear seven times in its response. But that's just an assertion, no matter how often it's repeated.

BlackRock directs the reader elsewhere for the proof: "BlackRock's belief that climate risk poses investment risk is backed by our publicly-available research."[2] It cites a BlackRock document titled "Seeking Outperformance Through Sustainable Insights."

Fair enough. So let's take a close look at that research. Let's talk about BlackRock's defense claiming that ESG investing doesn't violate fiduciary duty because climate risk is investment risk. That's difficult because, at least as of this writing, the link BlackRock provides to that article is broken.[3] Its grand defense of ESG investing leads to nothing; I like to view that as deeply symbolic. Fortunately, nothing on the internet is ever lost.[4] After examining an archived version, I see why the company took it down. BlackRock would have you believe that its ESG practices are the hand-picked emissary of science itself and that to disagree with them is to stand in opposition to thousands of scientific studies on climate change. Yet its arguments that climate risk is investment risk mention hardly a single scientific study.

BlackRock begins by saying "We believe that a key component of the outperformance we predict will be driven by a vast reallocation of capital toward sustainable assets and strategies in the coming years."[5] This is where the paper's one citation to climate research comes in, and it's not even about climate itself; it cites an Intergovernmental Panel on Climate Change report saying that $50 trillion to $100 trillion of investment will be necessary to reach net zero emissions by 2050, although Black-Rock clarifies in a footnote that this is "For illustrative purposes only."[6] Perhaps its hesitance is because it knows the world is nowhere near on track to reach net zero emissions by 2050. As Aniket Shah, Jefferies Group global head of ESG, put it, "I am not of the view we can get to net zero before 2050. I know that because I do research for a living. We would have to see more decarbonisation happen than happened in Covid in every year for the next 28 years. That's very clearly not happening."[7]

If BlackRock's main thesis is that $50 trillion to $100 trillion needs to be invested in ESG assets to reach net zero by 2050 and the world continues to fall woefully short of that target each year, does that mean Black-Rock's confidence in ESG's outperformance will get lower each year? No, because its real argument is simply that ESG will outperform in the long run because it will continue to become more popular. Put another way, a key component of BlackRock's argument for investing in ESG is that everyone else will invest in it.

In technical terms, this method of valuation creates what experts call a bubble. I described it in detail in my first book in a chapter titled "The ESG Bubble."[8] And guess what? Shortly after I published that and just a few months after BlackRock published the paper arguing for ESG outperformance due primarily to growing momentum, the bubble popped.

The proximate cause of the pop was the Federal Reserve raising interest rates to deal with inflation, some of which was due to the energy crisis caused by a shortage of fossil fuels. ESG funds tend to be heavy on tech stocks, mostly because producing software requires fewer emissions than producing material goods does. Rising interest rates hit growth stocks such as tech stocks hardest both because they make it harder for companies to borrow money to grow and because the value of their putative future earnings is less appealing relative to bond returns in the present. So ESG funds were hit hardest by the current bear market because they were hurt by the tech crash and missed out on the fossil fuel gains.[9]

That's why you have to be so careful about any backward-looking studies evaluating ESG fund performance. I'll let you in on the secret: you can come to whatever conclusion you want by choosing your preferred time frame. Before the late 2021 crash, there were any number of studies saying that ESG funds outperformed.[10] Today, there are any number of studies saying that ESG funds have underperformed.[11] There were studies supporting ESG underperformance even before the current bear market.[12] One analysis during the ESG boom found that 75 percent of ESG stock outperformance since 2013 was driven by ordinary balance sheet quality factors that had nothing to do with ESG and the rest of the outperformance was due to simple momentum as ESG stocks got good press.[13]

I'm going to take the high road here and not rest my case against ESG on the current state of the market. The real question is not what has happened in the past; it's what can be expected to happen in the future.

Here's a sign that BlackRock's argument about riding the momentum of future ESG inflows is insincere: Can you imagine that there will ever be a time when the Big Three say that ESG has become a crowded trade? After declaring its loyalty to sustainability and stewardship of the planet and joining every net zero alliance out there, do you think that after five more years of ESG inflows BlackRock will come out and say, "The green transition's priced in, time to take profit on all your ESG stocks and switch that money over to coal"? It would be crucified.

There is no amount of ESG buying that would convince the Big Three that the music's about to stop; ESG inflows like those of the last decade can only be used to predict more ESG inflows. ESG outflows like those happening today[14] can only be used to predict opportunities to buy ESG stocks low. The underlying ideology of stakeholder capitalism will never allow ESG advocates to declare that it's now time to sell ESG assets.

Likewise, there is no amount of divestment that will ever lead the Big Three to declare that fossil fuels are now undervalued. Even the current energy crisis caused by Russia's invasion of Ukraine was insufficient to alter BlackRock's ESG momentum thesis. In its response to the attorneys general, as further proof that climate risk is investment risk, it cited another BlackRock research piece titled "Taking Stock of the Energy Shock," summing up its finding as "the longer-term shift towards a less carbon-intensive economy is likely to continue."[15]

BlackRock must really be hoping that nobody follows these links. From beginning to end, the piece acknowledges the obvious: thanks to the West's efforts to wean itself off Russian energy, "Greater supply of U.S. and other non-Russian fossil fuels will be needed."[16] But it wriggles desperately to avoid the conclusion that this makes investments in US fossil fuel production more attractive. Witness this contortion:

We could also see carbon emissions edge up as the EU burns more coal and oil to make up for less Russian gas. But this isn't a sign that the transition to clean energy is being derailed, in our view. . . . We are set to see a shift in where fossil fuels are produced, not a surge in the total amount of fossil fuels consumed.

The drive in Europe for greater energy security should spur the development of clean energy. Tight fossil fuel markets, with sustained high prices, act like a carbon tax on consumers.[17]

So the argument is that a limited supply of fossil fuels will make them more costly, encouraging the production of more renewable energy. Might a limited supply of fossil fuels also raise the production of . . . more fossil fuels? Couldn't the "carbon tax" be lifted by pumping more oil?

Even if there will only be a shift from Russian fossil fuel production to US production, doesn't that make investing in US fossil fuel production more appealing? And why will global fossil fuel production shift, not increase? A couple of paragraphs later, BlackRock reluctantly acknowledges, "Pipeline capacity is already being built to more than double flows of gas from Russia to China . . . potentially delaying the shift to cleaner energy sources, such as renewables."[18]

Unable to come up with a valid argument that the current energy crisis is good news for the transition from fossil fuels to renewables, BlackRock ends the piece by throwing up its hands and saying "while traditional energy stocks are doing well in the short term due to greater demand for non-Russian output, clean energy stocks are also outperforming global benchmarks." The article closes with a chart showing that clean energy stocks are slightly outperforming the market and fossil fuel producers are massively outperforming it.[19]

So to recap, BlackRock produced an entire document littered with acknowledgments that US fossil fuel production must increase yet twisted that into its desired conclusion that clean energy investment is more justified than ever. It presented all this to the attorneys general as a piercing analysis that climate risk is investment risk, whereas its piece actually proves that fossil fuel divestment is investment risk. This demonstrates that BlackRock's thesis about riding the momentum of the clean energy transition is unfalsifiable: faced with clear evidence against it, it managed to interpret that as further proof of its ESG thesis. Anyone committed to the scientific method or fiduciary duty should invest based on falsifiable theories.

Here's how you know that ESG's a crowded trade: all the biggest players in the market are already in it and telling you to get in, too. The Big Three are in; the smaller asset managers that follow their lead are in. All the blue-state pension funds are already in. The European Union's in. Who's left to jump in besides you?

The momentum thesis has played out. ESG funds are underperforming the market and experiencing their first net outflows in a decade.[20] ESG funds are dropping like flies; they made up 4 percent of all US ETFs at the beginning of 2022 but 15 percent of all US fund closures by July.[21] The bubble can always reinflate, but "ESG will outperform because people will buy it" will never be a good argument. Yet that is, by BlackRock's own admission, a key component of its thesis. Its 2022 closures, by the way, included an ESG fund shuttered due to lack of demand.[22]

BlackRock's other arguments are just as bad, if not worse. For instance, it has harnessed AI-powered natural language processing to uncover the deep insight that "Companies with more green patents have tended to spend more on environmental research and development."[23] It includes a chart illustrating the correlation between companies having green patents and conducting green research. Why does this mean that ESG will outperform financially? Because "markets have tended to reward 'green' innovation." So it still comes back to the argument that ESG will outperform because people will invest in it.

Even BlackRock cautions readers not to take the sustainable insights too far: "For example, our research has found that business ethics controversies and regulatory issues are more likely, not less likely, for firms that disclose a richer set of ESG-friendly policies."[24] Perhaps sensing that its thesis is on shaky ground, it returns to the idea that "Assets under management in global sustainability funds have tripled over the past decade and crossed over $USD 1 trillion in 2020," throwing up a chart showing increasing ESG inflows.[25] That's the real argument: that the ESG tree will grow to the sky. As the cherry on top of its grand proof that climate risk is investment risk, the article closes with this:

> The material is for information purposes only. It is not intended for and should not be distributed to, or relied upon by, members of the public.
>
> It is not intended to be a forecast, research or investment advice, and is not a recommendation, or an offer or solicitation to buy or sell any securities or to adopt any investment strategy. . . . References to specific securities, asset classes and financial markets are for illustrative purposes only and are not intended to be and should not be interpreted as recommendations. Reliance upon information in this material is at the sole risk and discretion of the reader.[26]

Out of one side of its mouth, BlackRock says that you can't rely on its research at all; out of the other, it cites it to meet its legal burden of providing substantial, independent, objective evidence that ESG investing makes money.

You may think that critics of ESG are opposing thousands of scientific studies on climate change. But the most prominent ESG asset manager's famous thesis that "climate risk is investment risk" is not based on those studies; it does not cite or discuss them. It is based mostly on one claim: ESG will outperform in the long run because people like you will buy it, and you will buy it because it will outperform. Doesn't that sound like a Ponzi scheme?

Are you in?

The Limits of Climate Change

The planet has warmed since the late 1800s, though there's some disagreement over how much of that has been caused by human activity; Obama administration undersecretary for science Steven Koonin argued that the attribution of warming to humans is often overstated.[27] In its most recent report, the Intergovernmental Panel on Climate Change (IPCC) claimed that "The likely range of total human-caused global surface temperature increase from 1850–1900 to 2010–2019 is 0.8°C to 1.3°C, with a best estimate of 1.07°C."[28] The IPCC is probably the best representative of scientific consensus. I'll accept its premise for the sake of exploring the underlying economic issues about the cost of mitigating climate change. It turns out that there's a lot of distance between the premise that human activity causes climate change and the conclusion that ESG investments will be profitable.

One key question is the cost of "abatement," the strategy of slowing climate change by reducing carbon emissions. Removing carbon from the atmosphere is another potential long-term strategy, but, like efficient battery technology or nuclear fusion, current technology isn't effective enough, and it's unclear when it will be. We need to estimate the cost of abatement and compare that to the expected cost of warming to predict what level of investment in ESG assets might even be warranted.

This is the fundamental problem with international agreements such as the Paris Accords, which aim to cut greenhouse gas emissions to constrain warming to within a target such as 2°C or even 1.5°C; that looks at only one side of the equation. It considers only the cost of emissions; it doesn't weigh that against the cost of cutting them. As the Yale University climate economist William D. Nordhaus said in his speech on the topic when accepting the Nobel Prize, "However attractive a temperature target may be as an aspirational goal, the target approach is questionable because it ignores the costs of attaining the goals. If, for example, attaining the 1.5°C goal would require deep reductions in living standards in poor nations, then the policy would be the equivalent of burning down the village to save it."[29]

Because this focus on only one side of the cost equation afflicts the Paris Accords, the problem also extends to the burgeoning number of net zero financial alliances meant to enforce them in the private sector. BlackRock's own citation to the IPCC was based on the level of ESG investment necessary to reach the Paris Accords' goal of limiting warming to 2°C by cutting emissions to net zero by 2050. Not only is that approach unrealistic, it's too simplistic.

So what are the expected cost of climate change and the expected cost of cutting emissions to limit it?

First, let's look at the cost of climate change. In Nordhaus's own pioneering model, DICE, "damages are estimated to be 2% of [global economic] output at a 3°C global warming and 8% of output with 6°C warming."[30] The good news is that we can deemphasize the worst-case scenarios about extreme rises in temperature and the exponentially more serious damages associated with them. Even climate activists are increasingly acknowledging that the world is on track to avoid the worst-case scenarios. A recent *New York Times Magazine* article on the subject said, "Just a few years ago, climate projections for this century looked quite apocalyptic, with most scientists warning that continuing 'business as usual' would bring the world four or even five degrees Celsius of warming. . . . Now, with the world already 1.2 degrees hotter, scientists believe that warming this century will most likely fall between two or three degrees."[31] To be clear, that doesn't refer to an *additional* two or three degrees; current estimates from the United Nations[32] and independent climate trackers[33] say the world is on track for a *total* of 2°C to 3°C warming above preindustrial temperatures by 2100.

So Nordhaus's estimate of a climate change cost of roughly 2 percent to global economic output is the prediction to focus on, pessimistically assuming three degrees of total warming. Other expert assessments agree. Koonin pointed out that the IPCC itself presents a chart of twenty published estimates of the economic damage of global warming, with most looking at warming up to 3°C and a couple assessing the cost of higher levels of warming. The IPCC summed the studies up by saying "Estimates agree on the size of the impact (small relative to economic growth), and 17 of the 20 impact estimates shown in Figure 10-1 are negative."[34] Three of its studies predicted that climate change would be neutral or positive for economic growth.

Koonin put the point more clearly: "global temperature rise of up to 3°C by 2100 would negatively impact the global economy by—wait for it—3% or less."[35]

The IPCC chart assesses climate damages in terms of income: thanks to climate change, people in 2100 are expected to earn about 3 percent less than they otherwise would, though they'll still be far more prosperous than they are today. In his review of Koonin's book *Unsettled: What Climate Science Tells Us, What It Doesn't, and Why It Matters*, the economist David R. Henderson helpfully spelled out the implication: "If world economic output increases by 2 per cent annually for the rest of the century, global warming of 3 degrees Celsius will cause GDP to increase annually by approximately 1.95 per cent instead. . . . So instead of world output in 2100 being 387.5 per cent higher than it is now, it would be 'only' 368.8 per cent higher."[36]

One recent paper examined the conclusions of eleven studies on the damage caused by 2.5°C of warming: "Researchers disagree on the sign of the net impact, but agree on the order of magnitude: the welfare loss (or gain) caused by climate change is equivalent to the welfare loss caused by an income drop of a few percent—a century of climate change is about as bad as losing a year of economic growth."[37]

So that's the realistic worst-case scenario about the cost of global warming, using pessimistic assumptions about both the extent of warming and the damage caused by it. That's a concern but is far from being apocalyptic.

There's the expected cost of climate change. Now for the other side of the equation: What's the cost of cutting emissions, and what is the optimal balance between the two costs? This is exactly the difficult question Nordhaus won a Nobel Prize in Economic Sciences for answering. Here's his model's answer about the level of acceptable warming that balances the costs of emissions with the costs of cutting them:

> In the DICE model, it is essentially infeasible to attain the stringent temperature target of 1.5°C, and the 2°C path requires negative emissions in the near term. Another finding, much more controversial, is that the cost-benefit optimum rises to over 3°C in 2100—much higher than the international policy targets. Even with the much more pessimistic alternative [climate change] damage function, the temperature path rises to 3°C in 2100.[38]

His answer is that letting emissions increase global warming much past 3°C would be bad and cutting emissions to limit global warming much below 3°C would be bad. It turns out that 3°C of global warming by 2100, which we appear to be roughly on track for in the years since he spoke, is a plausible balance between the cost of climate change and the cost of cutting emissions.

The studies by Nordhaus and the IPCC provide further evidence that the massive wave of $50 trillion to $100 trillion in ESG investments BlackRock half-heartedly predicts won't actually happen. To begin with, one trillion dollars' worth of investment over the last couple of decades is very weak evidence of $50 trillion to $100 trillion over the next couple of decades, especially considering that ESG funds are now experiencing outflows. Thanks to the evidence from scientists and economists, we now have a good explanation for why ESG investment is trending far below the level necessary to meet the Paris Accords' targets and why it will likely continue to do so. The ESG momentum thesis is, at best, based on a radical change *exponentially* raising ESG investments from current levels to suddenly meet ambitious international targets, but the economics of climate change suggests staying on our current *linear* path will lead to roughly the optimal outcome.

The prophesied tsunami of green investments will happen only if governments worldwide regulate fossil fuels into the ground, and governments will do so only once they have sufficient incentive. So far, they haven't found enough incentive, and there's no sign that they will. That's true for a couple of reasons: first, the most rigorous evidence available indicates that quickly and dramatically cutting emissions would cause more damage than it would prevent. The costs would fall most heavily on developing nations seeking to benefit from the cheap energy of fossil fuels, which have so far declined to destroy themselves to save themselves. In addition, even if some governments mistakenly believe that climate change is a greater threat than it is, they're not doing anything about it.

Nordhaus pointed out that the Paris Accords and other international agreements in the last thirty years have not resulted in massive emissions cuts. In fact, he said, once China is removed from the data, "the rate of decarbonization is virtually identical before and after 2000. The three landmark years (1994 for the Framework Convention, 1997 for Kyoto, and 2015 for Paris) show no breaks in the ex-China trend. . . . the trend definitely suggests that climate policies have not tilted the emissions curve down."[39]

Not only are we far from being on track to meeting the Paris Accords' targets, factoring in the cost of cutting emissions suggests that we won't and shouldn't even try to meet them. The math and historical evidence strongly disfavor betting on rapidly accelerating ESG investment. So those who bet the farm on it are likely to lose their clients' money.

The heart of the matter is that what you think of ESG is not all about money. The real reason so many people favor ESG investing is that they think it's necessary to save the planet, maybe even to save the human race. The argument that it's all about making money is something that US asset managers have to tack on to try to make ESG investing fit into the straitjacket of the sole interest rule. I have some sympathy for that motivation. It's hard to condemn someone for cutting corners to try to save the world. But financial considerations aside, the belief that climate change is an existential threat is misguided. We're talking about global GDP growing by 1.95 percent annually versus 2 percent. That compounds, so it matters, but you don't need to stock up on guns and ammo and stop having kids. And "Force ESG on investors at all costs to avoid extinction" is not a valid argument.

That is the implicit argument that lurks behind all discussions of ESG. Many environmentalists believe that climate change poses a catastrophic threat to humanity. In Europe, proponents of stakeholder capitalism are free to act directly on that alarm by directing the private sector to cut emissions. In the United States, for better or worse, "I'm trying to save the world" is not a legal justification for asset managers to ignore their clients' wishes. So firms such as the Big Three have invented the shared fiction that climate risk is investment risk and built a house of cards supporting it.

Notice something interesting: when ESG proponents make arguments about the supposed long-term profit of mitigating climate change, they never acknowledge that older investors have shorter time frames. It's rational for a 60-year-old saving for their impending retirement to care less about what happens in 2050 than a college student does. Yet not once have I heard an ESG supporter admit the importance of the fact that some investors will get to experience more of the long run than others. There's a reason for this willful blindness. Their true concern is climate risk, not investment risk. ESG's desire to save humanity from climate catastrophe is the love that dares not speak its name.

However, the truth is this is not a break-glass emergency where asset managers should feel free to violate the law in order to save the world. The conclusion that climate change will cause people in 2100 to earn up to 3 percent less than they otherwise would doesn't come from climate skeptics; it comes from twenty studies examined by the leading global body of climate scientists. It comes from the very same documents ESG proponents cite. Their panic was more understandable when it was plausible that global warming might reach 5°C or even 6°C, because the amount of damage rises exponentially along with warming. Since it's now clear that the world is on track for only 2°C to 3°C of total warming this century, any possible moral justification for an asset manager breaking the law and ignoring its clients' wishes has vanished.

The world doesn't need the Big Three to save it by using their clients' money to rob them of their votes as shareholders and citizens. It doesn't need Larry Fink to be its hero. There's no bat signal in the sky. The path that BlackRock's clients are choosing for themselves will not lead to disaster. Their own choices will do just fine. In the absence of an overwhelming catastrophic threat that only they can address, asset managers should stick to maximizing returns and leave climate policy where it belongs: in the hands of citizens and their elected representatives.

Chapter 4

TERRIBLE AT PICKING STOCKS, GREAT AT PICKING LAWS

J ack Bogle had a bad heart. I don't mean he was wicked; he was actually unusually benevolent. But he had a bum heart. The most influential investor in modern history, the man who epitomized the belief that you should buy the market and hold it for the long run, never knew if he was going to make it to the next day.

He suffered from a congenital heart defect and had at least six heart attacks throughout his life. He'd show up to his daily squash games carrying a defibrillator, joking half seriously that his opponent might have to revive him. His biographer, Eric Balchunas, speculated that Bogle's bad heart might partly explain his lack of greed—what's the point of spending your life stacking up money if you might die tomorrow?[1] Bogle wanted to build something that would last, something that would outlive him.

And he did. If you're reading this, chances are that he's made you a lot of money. If you're enjoying a comfortable retirement or looking forward to one, he's probably one of the main reasons why. This chapter tells the story of how Jack Bogle set out to make you money and succeeded. But it's also about how the creations that outlived him outgrew his vision and ended up stealing your power and voice even as they gave you wealth. It's not really a story about Jack Bogle; it's a story about you—the story of how you unwittingly traded autonomy for security.

Most people enter asset management to make money. Few people, to be honest, enter it primarily to make other people money. Sure, to get reliable inflows to your funds, you have to provide value to investors. But for most people, making money for their clients is a necessary means to the end of making money for themselves. A doctor doesn't dream of making himself healthy, but an asset manager dreams of making himself rich. Maybe that's because the doctor starts out healthy but the asset manager doesn't start out wealthy. His goal is to become rich by making other people money, not to make them money by becoming rich.

Jack Bogle was the exception that proved the rule. Here's the best way I can concisely explain who he was and what he did for you: imagine a version of Bernie Sanders who studied math at a young age and decided to infiltrate the asset management industry to redistribute its wealth. Bogle did more than anyone else in US history to fight wealth inequality. He created a revolution Bernie could only dream of, gradually and methodically rebuilding the financial system in his own image. He did it not through the government but from the inside.

Jack grew up during the Great Depression in the ruins of the Roaring Twenties. After the good times became too good and the market crashed, his family had to sell their house. His dad sank into depression and alcoholism. His parents divorced, and he lived with his mom. At age ten, he was scooping ice cream and selling newspapers to get by. He won a scholarship to a prestigious private high school, excelled in math, then studied economics at Princeton. His senior thesis laid out the beginnings of the argument he'd make for the rest of his life: that asset managers needed to become better stewards of their clients' interests.

The power of compound interest was well understood, but Jack Bogle understood it in reverse: he realized that if an asset manager charged each client a seemingly small fee each year, over decades, the magic of compounding would transfer vast wealth from the clients' pockets to the manager's. So he made it his lifelong mission to lower those fees across the entire industry.

The question was how, and Bogle stumbled upon the answer by accident. He'd been hired out of college by the Wellington Fund, where he worked his way up and eventually became chairman. But he made a big mistake: he made a merger that went bad. In the bitter aftermath, his partners all but exiled him from the firm. He was able to stay on only under the condition that he'd no longer manage any funds.

Bogle turned to an idea that academics such as the economist Paul Samuelson had bandied about, something called "passive investing," where you construct a kind of index of stocks that mirrors the market and hold it forever. It was based on Samuelson's theory that the market does a good job at quickly factoring all public information into an asset's price, so there aren't really any bargains available. Consequently, few, if any, people can beat the market in the long run.[2] Today, this theory is known as the *efficient markets hypothesis*. It's probably mostly true, but not entirely. However, it seemed likely at the time that the best the vast majority of people could do was to buy the market itself. In the early 1970s, there was no way for the average person to do that.

Bogle took the idea to his partners and argued that if he created such a market-tracking fund, he wouldn't really be managing anything—the results would all be up to the market, not him. He wouldn't be picking any stocks or trading them. Instead, his fund would just own the stocks and leave them alone, growing alongside the market, its massive diversification protecting it from volatility. And since Bogle didn't have to pay tons of commissions for trades or hire analysts to research companies, he could charge lower fees than other funds did. He created a new company to oversee the administration of his new mutual fund and gave it a fitting name: Vanguard. And so passive investing was born. One day it would conquer the world—first the financial world and eventually the rest of it.

It would take a long time. Vanguard didn't reach a 10 percent market share until twenty-five years after its creation. When Jack Bogle launched his index fund in 1976, no one was interested: it opened with $11 million under management, 95 percent short of its goal. Back then, no one wanted to match the market; the whole point of investing was to beat it. Edward Johnson, the head of Fidelity Investments, the largest asset manager at the time, summed up the fatal flaw in Bogle's idea: "I can't believe that the great mass of investors are going to be satisfied with just receiving average returns. The name of the game is to be the best."[3]

Bogle offered American investors mediocrity, but they each knew in their heart that they were exceptional. He called his creation the First Index Investment Trust, but the asset management community gave it a different name: Bogle's Folly.[4] The folly ended up being theirs in the long run, as the efficient markets hypothesis had foretold. There was no single factor behind the gradual rise of passive investing, but there were some significant moments, which tended to align with historic market crashes that made active investors rethink their exceptionalism.

For instance, the Dow Jones Industrial Average dropped a staggering 23 percent on Black Monday, October 19, 1987, due in part to new computerized portfolio insurance mechanisms backfiring as algorithms created a vicious cycle of selling that panicked human traders. Essentially, mutual funds automatically sold falling stocks just because they were falling. After that, at the SEC's suggestion, traders created a new financial instrument called an exchange-traded fund (ETF). The idea was that instead of investing with a mutual fund, investors could buy the stock of an ETF that was in the business of owning other stocks. If you wanted to bet on the whole market or against it, you could bet on or against the ETF. Random individual stocks wouldn't get caught up in huge automated portfolio rebalancing and the covering of short sales.

The ETF creators set their fees to match that of Bogle's Vanguard fund. What was the appeal? An ETF is basically the same as a mutual fund, except that you can get in and out more easily, and it has significant tax advantages.[5] So traders got in on index funds, blurring the line between active and passive investing: no stock picking but active trading.[6]

The line was blurred even more when some ETF makers had a bright idea: Why own the S&P 500 when you could get rid of the worst companies and instead own, say, the S&P 250? What if investors could own an index but pick the best parts? Thus was born the "smart beta" ETF, which is really just a fancy way of taking an index fund as a base and using algorithms to try to weed out the worst companies and identify the best—a blend of active and passive techniques. So people still talk of active and passive investing, but the two really exist on a spectrum, which is why it's hard to measure how much money is in either one.

The 2008 financial crisis delivered the death blow to Bogle's detractors; the safety-minded funds beat out the actively managed funds. After that, the ETF version of Bogle's idea took off like a rocket. As for the original, Vanguard's assets under management grew every month as the market shrank and investors fled to tried-and-true, boring Vanguard funds for safety. As Balchunas put it, bull markets are good for passive investing, but bear markets are great.

That was basically the ball game. After Vanguard's gains during the Great Recession, other asset managers had to copy its style or at least lower their fees to compete with it to attract inflows—after all, why would you pay active managers a lot more than Vanguard charged when they'd just performed worse than Vanguard had? So Bogle got the last laugh. After four decades, he'd finally taken from the rich and given to the poor, forcing the market to (begrudgingly) lower its fees.

These days, the majority of the money in the stock market is invested in some variation on what Jack Bogle started, no matter how it's labeled. The Vanguard Group now has more than $8 trillion in assets under management (AUM), almost twice Fidelity's. Jack Bogle's original index fund still exists under the name Vanguard 500 Index Fund; it hit a high of almost $700 billion total assets under management in 2021.[7]

But what's really impressive is its expense ratio, the fee that funds charge their investors: a paltry .04 percent, or four basis points. That's where the magic happens. Bogle had been patiently shaving that expense ratio down point by point for forty years as greater economies of scale gradually allowed him to lower his fees. That was what every other asset manager had to compete with. Gone are the days when hedge funds could charge 2 percent of AUM plus 20 percent of whatever profit they made. The same is true for all other asset managers. Over the last twenty-five years or so, expense ratios for equity mutual funds have dropped from an average of 1.04 percent to .5 percent.[8] Because all types of funds compete with one another on some level, when fees drop somewhere, they drop everywhere else as well.

That adds up to trillions of dollars retained in the pockets of workers and retirees instead of paid to asset managers. The fees keep inching lower, and the savings keep compounding. It may be the largest redistribution of wealth in history—a peaceful revolution. Bernie would be proud, if he understood it.

The Separation of Ownership from Ownership

The financial security provided by index funds and their ilk comes with a price that can't be measured in dollars. You may have money in a mutual fund, but you don't have the rights or responsibilities you would if you owned the stocks in it directly.

In theory, a shareholder has many rights: the right to vote on mergers and to elect members of the company's board of directors, the right to sue them to enforce their fiduciary duty, the right to receive information from the company, the right to govern it through making shareholder proposals, and the right to use the threat of all those actions to influence the company's officers. You may think you own shares of many companies through your passive investments, but you don't have any of these rights. Amazon and Microsoft won't take your calls; they don't owe you anything.

How can that be? Back in law school, my property professor drilled this mantra into my brain: "Property is a bundle of sticks." Laypeople think that the question of whether you own something is black and white, but the concept we call "property" is actually a collection of rights: for instance, the right to officially possess something, the right to use it, the right to stop other people from using it, the right to profit from the use of it, and the right to transfer those rights from yourself to other people. "Mine" is an intuitive notion we understand at a young age, but the law carves it up into very fine pieces.

When something belongs to you in the fullest sense, you might have all of those rights, but there are many times when the law allows society to peel some sticks away from the bundle and give them to others; for example, maybe you own a piece of land by the river, but other people have the right to walk on it to get to the water. Maybe you own an apartment, but you can't legally kick out a squatter who's lived there for five years. Maybe you own your body, but you can't transfer your ownership right over it to other people; you can't enslave yourself or sell your kidney, for example. Maybe you own the royalties from a song you wrote and sang, but someone else decides when and where it gets played.

And maybe you own an index fund and can gain dividends from the companies in it and sell it to realize a profit, but you don't have the voice or the vote that a real shareholder has. That's the end result of passive investing: you may think you own shares of a bunch of companies through an index fund, but in fact you maintain only the profit element of ownership and the ability to transfer that right to someone else by selling your shares of the fund. You lose the original power of owning a company's shares: the ability to tell that company what to do. You handed that ownership over to the index fund's manager. When every individual investor rushes to put money into index funds, a terrifying corollary emerges: a few giant asset managers suddenly gain the right to tell every public company in the United States what to do. Then they can use that vast authority to create policies you yourself would never support.

Technically, what you typically own are shares in an asset manager's trust, and the trust itself is the entity that owns shares in each company in an index. So you don't own any shares of Microsoft or Amazon; you have exposure only to their profit or loss. Microsoft doesn't have a fiduciary duty to you; it has a duty to your asset manager, which has a duty to you to manage its Microsoft shares responsibly. There is a vast distance between you and the company you profit from.

Former Delaware chief justice Leo E. Strine, Jr., named the new problem "the separation of ownership from ownership."[9] That's a nice way of putting it. If a share is a bundle of sticks, passive investing has created financial instruments that peel all the sticks except the right to share in a company's profits out of the hands of investors. They're left holding financial security, but nothing else. Somehow, most of the property rights end up in the hands of the asset managers that provide the financial instruments. The question is how they will use them.

Three Blind Giants

The truth is that until recently, enormous asset managers such as Black-Rock, Vanguard, and State Street didn't usually wield the awesome power of the shares they hold. Their stewardship teams were mostly content to sit back and let corporate executives do as they wished, trusting them to maximize their companies' profits.

But times are changing. You've seen ample examples of the kinds of policies the Big Three are throwing their weight behind: Scope 3 emissions requirements; climate impact audits; racial equity audits; diversity quotas in hiring; rubber-stamping almost anything that goes under the name "sustainability"; tying executive compensation to all of the above. The sleeping giants have awoken. What we see in these policies is that they are just beginning to stretch their limbs.

There is a tremendous irony in all this: asset managers such as the Big Three have amassed their power because society has accepted as common wisdom the claim that no one can reliably pick the right stocks. Yet the Big Three seem to have absolute faith that they can pick the right social policies.

Most asset managers believe that they have no ability to make wise choices within their area of expertise but exceptional insight outside it. They think that no one can beat the financial market but beating the political one is easy. Predicting the future performance of a stock? Impossible; foolish even to try. Predicting the future financial impact of boardroom diversity quotas or the state of the planet thirty years from now, along with environmental regulations twenty years from now? Easy. They've read a couple of good articles on the subject. They watch the news—when they have time.

Asset managers know that social and political issues are contentious. You don't have to be a rocket scientist to figure out that much of the country is not clamoring for racial equity audits. They know that at least half of their clients would not vote for the corporate policies they propose, vote for, and lobby for behind the scenes. But if anything, that makes companies such as the Big Three more determined to support those causes: if they themselves don't save the world by creating the right policies, their clients can't be trusted to do it on their own. If democratically elected governments cannot save the planet from climate change because of citizens' poor decisions, their asset managers must step up to the plate.

With great power comes great responsibility, and surely someone with both must also have great wisdom. Sometimes clients need to be protected from themselves. Are asset managers not charged to protect clients' interests? It is *because* clients are not clamoring for racial equity audits and Scope 3 emissions caps that index fund providers must make sure they happen.

Just as academic theorists anticipated and contributed to the rise of passive investing, contemporary academics have recognized its growing problems. The seminal article articulating the dangers of the wealth concentration that passive investing enables is Harvard law professor John C. Coates, IV's "The Future of Corporate Governance Part I: The Problem of Twelve." Writing in 2018, Coates documented the rise of the Big Three and argued that thanks to their growing dominance, we will soon enter a world in which twelve people control the majority of US companies. Five years later, his argument looks prescient.

Early in the article, he wrote, "The prospect of twelve people even potentially controlling most of the economy poses a legitimacy and accountability issue of the first order—one might even call it a small 'c' constitutional challenge."[10] That's a law professor's way of saying that the Big Three are becoming a threat to democracy. Their power, and their increasing willingness to use it, are becoming a greater factor in national affairs than whatever voters themselves do. This is especially true when voters are divided, and the Big Three speak with one voice.

According to Coates, we may already be living in a corporatocracy. When he wrote, the Big Three controlled more than 15 percent of the S&P 500, a far higher share of the market than any three investors had ever owned before.[11] Not only that, Coates pointed out, many shareholders never vote, making that 15 percent actually amount to 25 percent of likely votes in any contested vote. "That share of the vote will generally be pivotal," he wrote. "Add another few funds, and the votes of other funds that follow the advice of proxy advisory firms such as ISS and Glass-Lewis, and the collective vote of the group of index funds will almost always include the median vote in such fights. Hence, the Problem of Twelve."[12]

In the years since Coates's article, that base of 15 percent market control has already risen to almost 20 percent. The future is coming even faster than he feared. And since bear markets are boons for passive investment, the current market downturn will only further accelerate the concentration of wealth and power in the hands of a few asset managers. He argued that the implications for democracy are dire:

The bottom line of this influence is very different than what the term "passive" investment implies. . . .

A small number of unelected agents, operating largely behind closed doors, are increasingly important to the lives of millions who barely know of the existence much less the identity or inclinations of those agents.[13]

To be fair, academic experts don't speak with one voice on this subject. But even the disagreement provides additional cause for alarm. The most prominent objection to the view Coates and I share is that asset managers such as the Big Three actually do *too little* to discharge the great responsibility derived from their great power. This argument was given voice by Harvard's Lucian Bebchuk and Scott Hirst in a study titled "Index Funds and the Future of Corporate Governance: Theory, Evidence, and Policy," which came out shortly after Coates's paper.

The central point Bebchuk and Hirst made is that theory suggests that the Big Three don't have much incentive to make use of their massive voting power, and evidence from the past and present suggests that in fact, they haven't made much use of it. The paper weighs in at 118 pages, but the main insight motivating it is simple: spending resources on corporate governance doesn't provide an advantage to the Big Three over their competitors. In fact, if anything, it would be a disadvantage, because if they spend money to increase the value of their portfolio companies, all the index funds competing with them will reap the same benefits without having spent anything. Exercising the best possible stewardship over hundreds of companies would be very costly and time consuming, and only a small fraction of the benefits would flow to the Big Three themselves.[14]

In Bebchuk and Hirst's tale, this is where the minuscule fees of index funds come back to bite investors. The question is this: How would an asset manager make money by using their voice and vote to improve the companies in their portfolio? Even if it succeeded in increasing the companies' values, the asset manager doesn't make money directly from the appreciation of the stocks it holds; it makes money from that .04 percent fee it charges on the assets under its management. So even if its costly interventions succeed in raising the market value of its portfolio by 1 percent, the asset manager stands to claim only .04 percent of that increase for itself. Combined with the cost of stewardship, this generally recommends doing nothing, which Bebchuk and Hirst say the data bear out.

Coates says that the problem is that the Big Three have too much power; Bebchuk and Hirst say that the problem is that they do too little with it. What if both camps are right? It costs too much for BlackRock, Vanguard, and State Street to dig into details, researching which policies would increase the value of the companies they control, and they stand to gain far too little by doing so. The math doesn't work out. The main way they can make more money is by bringing more money into their funds, not by increasing the value of the companies in those funds. Doesn't it follow that the Big Three should wield their vast voting power in whatever ways will cheaply create good press and thus bring more money into their funds? It cost hardly anything to read the headlines after the George Floyd riots, notice that a vocal portion of the public is pushing for diversity above all else, and decide that more clients would be brought in if they voted for racial equity audits at every company in the S&P 500. And if such policies decrease the value of those companies by, say, 1 percent, that barely cuts into the Big Three's fees at all; any decrease in their fees due to losses in portfolio company value will easily be outweighed by additional client inflows.

Bebchuk and Hirst wrote that the Big Three may soon grow so much that they ought to be called the Giant Three instead. I fear that they haven't considered all the implications of their argument. They consider only how the Big Three lack the incentives to govern wisely; they overlook how their argument implies that they possess incentives to govern poorly. Both camps of academics are right; we have entered a world created by the staggering of three blind giants, groping about in the dark for truths they only half care to see.

Jack Bogle saw all this coming. After a heart transplant gave him a new lease on life in 1996, he again became active trying to lead the business he'd started all those years before. He became concerned that Vanguard's new leadership was prioritizing expansion at all costs above its fiduciary duty to its clients. He was quietly shown the door. Vanguard asked him to leave its board of directors due to his advanced age and set him up with a ceremonial research role in a nice office far away from everyone else.[15] As the years of his forced retirement passed, he grew more and more alarmed as he watched the industry he'd transformed grow far beyond his vision. His last act was to warn the world that the giants he'd created were growing too strong. He made his case in an article published in the *Wall Street Journal* a little over a month before he died.

> If historical trends continue, a handful of giant institutional investors will one day hold voting control of virtually every large U.S. corporation. Public policy cannot ignore this growing dominance, and consider its impact on the financial markets, corporate governance, and regulation. These will be major issues in the coming era.
>
> . . . Most observers expect that the share of corporate ownership by index funds will continue to grow over the next decade. It seems only a matter of time until index mutual funds cross the 50% mark. If that were to happen, the "Big Three" might own 30% or more of the U.S. stock market—effective control. I do not believe that such concentration would serve the national interest.[16]

Jack Bogle's last public words were soon proven correct. His financial revolution did an enormous amount of good. But it ended as so many revolutions before it had: in tyranny.

Chapter 5

NO MANAGER CAN SERVE TWO MASTERS

No manager can serve two masters. When forced to choose between ESG values, the interests of the businesses they invest in, and the clients who actually own the capital, an asset manager usually finds a way to serve itself. It's the same problem stakeholder capitalism faces: those who are accountable to everyone end up being accountable to no one. Opportunity knocks, and greed opens the door.

Sometimes managers act in their naked self-interest. Take the activist hedge fund Engine No. 1's ESG advocacy activities at Coca-Cola in 2022.[1] The fund pushed Coca-Cola to do a big deal with Republic Services for recycled bottles. It claimed it wanted to help Coca-Cola go green, but Engine No. 1 holds a much larger stake in Republic Services than it does in Coca-Cola, and one that is much more important. That's because Engine No. 1 holds Coca-Cola only in its generalized fund, which mimics the S&P 500 and charges a tiny fee, while it also holds Republic Services in its flagship net zero fund, which charges fifteen times as much. Thus a boon to Republic Services is a boon to Engine No. 1.

Or take State Street's women-in-leadership fund. This story is one I began in *Woke, Inc.*: To promote its new fund, State Street commissioned *Fearless Girl*, a statue of a young girl that suddenly appeared on Wall Street in New York City near the iconic bull. The placard at *Fearless Girl*'s feet read, KNOW THE POWER OF WOMEN IN LEADERSHIP. SHE MAKES A DIFFERENCE. SHE, of course, referred not just to women in general but to the ticker of State Street's new ESG-focused ETF. Even as State Street battled gender discrimination lawsuits in court, it put up a statue paying lip service to gender equity.

But SHE didn't keep her promises, even on her own terms. In 2019, Morningstar uncovered that SHE had routinely voted *against* gender equity proposals in the companies it held.[2] In fact, the fund had voted for such proposals just twice over the preceding few years. Much tinier gender-focused funds, such as the Glenmede Women in Leadership U.S. Equity portfolio and the Impax Ellevate Global Women's Leadership Fund, by contrast, voted for them every time.

Why doesn't State Street vote for all gender-related proposals and all female director nominees in its gender diversity ETF? It could always vote the other way in its other, non-gender-focused funds, right? Wrong. One of SHE's lead investors—the money behind the money behind *Fearless Girl*—was the California State Teachers' Retirement System (CalSTRS). It kicked off the fund with a $250 million investment,[3] increasing that to $500 million later on. And despite what CalSTRS says, as a pension fund, it is legally required to focus only on value maximization, not gender issues. This means that State Street *must* vote all the SHE shares the same way it votes the shares in its regular funds; if it voted differently on a gender-related proposal, it would be admitting that voting in favor of the proposal wouldn't really maximize value.

That conflict—running ESG funds that claim to care about the environment, water impact, or gender issues but then taking money from asset allocators that aren't allowed to care about such things—permeates ESG investing. It infects both ESG and non-ESG funds. Sometimes, as with SHE, ESG clients take a back seat to financially motivated investors.

But often it's the other way around. Anytime BlackRock, State Street, or Vanguard wants to prove its ESG bona fides—by voting for a climate proposal or racial equity audit or ousting a "nondiverse" director—it has to drag its non-ESG funds along for the ride.

That's not about to change. If State Street or BlackRock wanted the flexibility to do otherwise, it would have to purge pension funds and 401(k)s from its ESG funds—drop its biggest clients from its most lucrative products. It's not going to do that. So instead, asset managers issue a single voter guide that applies to all of their funds, ESG or not, that is a mishmash of ESG buzzwords brushed with a thin veneer of long-term value, and hope no one reads it too closely. BlackRock will pursue both making the world a better place and making you money. State Street will help both women in corporate leadership and teachers in retirement. Engine No. 1 will pursue both Coca-Cola's recycling ambitions and its own AUM ambitions. All unfulfillable promises to serve two masters.

ESG for Thee, but Not for Me

Sometimes the conflict is not between an ESG fund and a non-ESG fund but between the interests of US clients and governments abroad. BlackRock, for instance, pressures US companies to adopt ESG policies while remaining largely silent about ESG to its portfolio companies in China. The reason? It spent years trying to break into the $4.3 trillion Chinese asset management market and, having recently launched mutual funds there, is wary of criticizing its new CCP overlords.

In 2018, CEO Larry Fink described China as "a significant long-term opportunity for BlackRock" and said he hoped to do business there "if and when the market opens" to US companies.[4] As he surely knew, China was and remains one of the fastest-growing asset management markets in the world, with a middle class that exploded from just 3 percent of its population in 2000 to more than half in 2018.[5] There are now almost a billion potential new customers who are looking to save for retirement. The Swiss bank UBS has called China the "single largest growth opportunity" for global investment managers.[6]

So when Beijing's chief trade negotiator called a meeting of Wall Street executives at a Washington, DC, hotel in 2018, Mr. Fink answered. "We need your help," Vice Premier Liu He told guests, according to a *Wall Street Journal* report.[7] China was looking for allies to persuade the Trump administration to lower its proposed tariffs on China as part of the two countries' trade deal. In exchange, Mr. Liu promised to open Chinese financial markets to Wall Street firms—another arranged marriage, with each side holding its nose as they said their vows.

The reward was as swift as it was sweet. In August 2020, BlackRock became the first foreign company approved to offer mutual funds in China. But more favors came due. In the summer of 2021, at the height of the sell-off of Chinese stocks, China's securities regulators summoned Black-Rock executives to a meeting, after which BlackRock urged its investors to triple the amount of their assets allocated to Chinese companies. Two weeks later, BlackRock launched its Chinese mutual funds.

Now that it's gained entry, BlackRock doesn't want to be shown the door. It keeps encouraging investors to pour money into China, even though investing in China is as risky as it gets. The CCP regards all Chinese companies as instruments of its one-party state; there are no true "publicly owned" companies in Communist China. So when a Chinese company wants to raise capital from Western investors, it sets up a shell company in the Caribbean, enters into a fake "service contract" with a Caribbean entity called a *variable interest entity*, or VIE, and lets US investors invest in that. As a result, US investors who think they are investing in Alibaba, Tencent, or a Chinese solar panel company are really investing in a Cayman Islands shell company that the Chinese government doesn't recognize and has already held to be illegal. If US-China relations go south or President Xi Jinping wakes up and decides to engage in some anticapitalist shenanigans, China could simply declare that such entities don't exist and US investments would go poof.

The US Securities and Exchange Commission has repeatedly warned about this risk.[8] But BlackRock hasn't. Instead, its website has article after article with titles such as "Investing in China," and "Which Chinese Asset Do You Favor?" and "The Role of Chinese Assets," which inexplicably tells investors to buy more Chinese assets based on "China's commitment to a net-zero economy by 2060."[9] Then, on the thirty-eighth page of a legal document sixty-eight pages long, it uses soft language to inform its investors that "Intervention by the Chinese government with respect to VIEs could significantly affect the Chinese operating company's performance."[10]

I'm the CEO of an asset management firm who went to law school and is writing a book on this very topic, actively searching for this warning. And it was hard to find. You know what wasn't? BlackRock's warnings about the financial risk of having only one, rather than at least two, self-identified females on US companies' boards.

BlackRock also appears reluctant to advise investors on how to protect themselves against the financial fallout if China invades Taiwan.[11] Mr. Xi has unambiguously stated that reacquiring Taiwan is a pillar of his national rejuvenation platform and a vital national objective. Over the past year, he has increased pressure in the region. When it makes its move, Taiwan's largest company, the Taiwan Semiconductor Manufacturing Company, will go down. TSMC may not be a household name, but its products are. It manufactures more than half of the world's advanced semiconductors and 90 percent of the most advanced chips. These chips power every Apple iPhone, as well as many cars, refrigerators, computers, and household appliances. If TMSC can't produce chips, supply chains will break down and the global economy will tank.

There are ways for investors to protect themselves by, for example, investing in US semiconductor companies and asking them to build up their capabilities now. But BlackRock isn't giving that advice. Instead, it is loudly warning investors of hypothetical environmental risks that might occur if US companies don't align their business plans with anti–global warming policies that governments may or may not enact in the coming decades, while giving a lukewarm "medium" risk rating to what it calls "U.S.-China strategic competition," reassuring investors that "we do not see a military confrontation [with Taiwan] as likely in the short to medium term."[12]

When I called BlackRock out on downplaying this risk to please the CCP in the pages of the *Wall Street Journal*, the company claimed that its investment materials mentioned that "China [may] take steps to accelerate reunification with Taiwan."[13] Even in claiming that it's not beholden to China, BlackRock could not utter the word "invasion." Instead, it only obliquely referred to China's looming invasion of Taiwan as "reunification," a term that describes a child separated from a parent at a shopping mall, not the military invasion of a sovereign nation.

ESG for thee, but not for me. BlackRock hasn't exactly been vocal about its asymmetric social policies in the United States versus in China, but the differences are stark. It isn't entirely BlackRock's fault; it needs to take a different tack in China, because the CCP isn't about to let its corporations, much less foreign investors in its corporations, dictate its social policy. It recognizes that it is the role of government to determine political priorities. And so it has restrung ESG to play its own tune.

BlackRock is happy to lead the band. That's why it has an investor stewardship guide for China[14] that is very different from the one it has for the United States. Read them both carefully, and you'll see that the *E, S,* and *G* in ESG mean entirely different things.

In the US version, *E* is for "environment"; in China, it might as well stand for "energy supply." In 2022, for example, BlackRock threatened to oust US company board members unless they issued TCFD-aligned reduction targets for GHG emissions.[15] It also threatened to vote for climate-related shareholder proposals. In the Chinese version, these sections are absent.[16] BlackRock may make vague, aspirational statements about the importance of environmentalism in both documents, but it declines to back up those statements with the threats of concrete action in China. And in both documents, BlackRock asks companies to ensure a "just transition"—code for not being too fussy about net zero goals for developing nations that need fossil fuels for economic growth. China, of course, has long lobbied[17] to keep its "developing nation" status for just that reason—even though it is the world's second largest economy and by far its biggest polluter.

The S sections also differ. In the United States, BlackRock will vote out board members unless the board is 30 percent diverse. In China, the only request is a soft pitch for "at least one female" on the board. There's not even a hint that BlackRock will vote against boards that are not sufficiently racially and ethnically diverse, which might suggest that Uighurs, Muslims, Tibetans, and Mongolians would be fit to lead. Even the disclosure requirements are different; Chinese companies need only disclose demographic info such as gender, race/ethnicity, and age at the "aggregate level"—a concept that has been widely mocked by Western ESG proponents.

The G is the most fun. In the United States, good governance, at a minimum, means not being owned by a single autocratic dictator. That's sort of a given, so the ESG movement focuses on things such as making sure a company board has enough independence to oversee management, its members are reelected with some frequency, and maybe they have term limits, so they don't get too complacent. These are issues that presuppose a functioning board. In China, of course, good corporate governance and state governance are one and the same. "A local analyst would consider being a state-owned enterprise a good thing," one ESG expert in Beijing explained to Bloomberg. "There is culture and ideology involved."[18] But not to worry. "Markets like totalitarian governments," said Larry Fink. They are stable and predictable; democracy is "messy."[19] Okay, then.

Given these differences, you might reasonably think that it would be impossible for BlackRock to offer an ESG fund made up of Chinese companies. But it does. It's called the BGF China Impact Fund. But the "impact" is probably not the one its US ESG investors think. BlackRock's China Impact Fund defines its goal as helping to "address the PRC's social and environmental problems"[20]—the "problems" as the PRC sees them. It's unlikely that US investors in BlackRock's China Impact Fund are aware that the "impact" of their investments in China is to further the CCP's stranglehold on power and the population, but BlackRock needs to keep both Mr. Xi and ESG investors happy, so BlackRock publishes these disclosures in fine print.

China is probably the biggest beneficiary of BlackRock's conflicts, but it isn't alone. Look at Russia. It publicly claims to adhere to the Paris Agreement,[21] but in practice, it "focuses almost exclusively on promoting fossil fuel extraction, consumption, and export to the rest of the world."[22] As of 2021, the oil-and-gas sector accounted for 14 percent of GDP, 39 percent of federal budget revenues, and 60 percent of total exports.[23] Russia isn't about to "strand" its most valuable assets to save the environment. This is particularly true since, unlike most of the world, global warming will likely help Russia economically, as once impassible ice routes become navigable and frozen tundra thaws into arable farmland. Adaptation, more than prevention, is the Russian strategy. Suffice it to say that the race to net zero, a pillar of ESG, is not a priority for our Eurasian comrades.

There is one place where Russia is keenly interested in ESG: on American soil. For years, the US government has been concerned about Russia's financial ties to extremist US environmental groups that push to end fossil fuel, fracking, and pipelines. As Hillary Clinton explained in a private speech revealed by leaked emails, "We were even up against phony environmental groups, and I'm a big environmentalist, but these were funded by the Russians to stand against any effort, 'Oh that pipeline, that fracking, that whatever will be a problem for you,' and a lot of the money supporting that message was coming from Russia."[24] In March 2022, Republican congressmen wrote to prominent US environmental groups, including the Sierra Club and Natural Resources Defense Council, asking about their receipt of Russian dark money "to undermine US natural gas and oil production to Russia's benefit."[25] Democrats called the allegation "bogus"[26] despite their long track record of accusing the Russians of intervening in US politics.

The Sierra Club and NRDC aren't just environmentalist groups but ESG proponents as well. The Sierra Club has supported key ESG proposals at Chevron and ExxonMobil[27] and asked US banks to limit financing for fossil fuels.[28] Knowing it cannot pass such resolutions on its own, the Sierra Club has lobbied hard to get large asset managers such as Black-Rock to vote for its proposals[29] and threatened to pull its $12 million of endowment money if it does not.[30] The NRDC similarly wrote letters to Procter & Gamble's top shareholders imploring them to end P&G's deforestation.[31] Often such efforts work.

If we're going to follow the money, we need to ask: Where does it go? To Russia, Putin, and even more directly Gazprom, the Russian oil giant, which has become "too big to sanction"[32] and posted record half-year profits in August 2022.[33] As you'll read in Chapter 9, it funded Germany's fake climate foundation to complete Nord Stream 2. Among its top ten largest foreign shareholders are—you guessed it—Vanguard and Black-Rock.[34] The same firms that are telling US companies to drill less on US soil are cashing in on Russian projects.

Or let's take Brazil. In December 2020, the then CEO of Brazil's Petrobras called net zero a "fad"[35] as the company invested heavily in new fossil fuel development. That hasn't stopped BlackRock from being one of Petrobras's largest foreign shareholders. Notably, in its report on its engagement efforts with Petrobras, it noted that it had voted in favor of the board's nominee for chairman and praised the company for its efforts on reducing Scope 1 and 2 emissions, without mentioning the stricter Scope 3 emissions or net zero targets it imposes in the United States.[36]

Or look at Mexico, where BlackRock opened a private prison generating $65 million in revenue a year,[37] while it excluded prisons from its

US-based ESG funds.[38] Or Indonesia, where BlackRock declines to require that palm oil companies fully adopt sustainable practices because of "price sensitivities,"[39] while pressuring US companies to boycott those same nonsustainable palm oil suppliers over environmental concerns.[40]

It's a double standard: BlackRock loudly imposes ESG on US companies and profits handsomely from it; it quietly declines to impose ESG on non-US companies and profits handsomely from it. American companies lose. American investors lose. BlackRock wins.

Conflicts on American Soil

Sometimes the conflicts take place entirely on US soil. Take one of Black-Rock's more recent debacles: trying to position itself as a vocal ESG advocate, but one that is willing to voice both pro- and anti-ESG messages, depending on the client. It's simply not possible.

For years, asset managers didn't have this problem. Asset managers managed assets. It was complicated, but only in a financial-mathematical kind of way. A Trump supporter and an Alexandria Ocasio-Cortez supporter could both buy BlackRock's index funds through E*TRADE or their retirement accounts and never give it a second thought. A liberal state pension fund might have the same asset manager as a conservative state pension fund in the same way that the two states might buy from the same printer paper company or employ the same cafeteria operator. Politics simply didn't matter.

Then suddenly they did. With the rise of ESG, politics became central to an asset manager's mission. Larry Fink began calling for companies to "earn their social license to operate" and claiming that "the transition to a net zero world is the shared responsibility of every citizen, corporation, and government."[41]

BlackRock's sudden interest in ESG did not spring from quiet introspection. Democratic officials encouraged large asset managers to politicize their investment strategies and dangled the carrot of lucrative asset management fees in return. In 2017, for example, the largest public pension fund in the country—California Public Employees' Retirement System (CalPERS)—founded Climate Action 100+. The group works like this: Asset managers agree to collaborate to pressure the companies they invest in to adopt net zero goals. The more investors join, the more votes they control at shareholder meetings and the more heft the group has in ordering companies to decarbonize. State pension funds in New York, Connecticut, Illinois, Hawaii, New Jersey, Oregon, and Washington soon jumped in, as did university and nonprofit endowments. But to really have an impact, the group needed the largest private sector asset managers to get on board, too.

That was where BlackRock came in. In 2016, it was already making $7.2 million per year in fees from CalPERS.[42] So it's no surprise that it eagerly joined Climate Action 100+. CalPERS took note, issuing a statement that "CalPERS welcomes BlackRock as the newest signatory to Climate Action 100+" and saying it looked forward to working with BlackRock to get "the largest global emitters of greenhouse gases to limit global warming."[43] BlackRock's strategy appears to have paid off. From 2016 to 2021, its annual revenue from CalPERS increased by nearly 40 percent to almost $10 million per year.

Eventually, however, states with different priorities began to catch on. States such as Texas and West Virginia,[44] whose economies rely on coal, oil, and gas, introduced legislation intended to prevent banks and asset managers from targeting the fossil fuel industry. Their leaders spoke out against the "existential threat to our jobs, our economy, and our tax revenue."[45] Other conservative leaders, such as Ron DeSantis in Florida, were less concerned about the threat to home state industry sectors and more concerned about the threat that "holdings in Chinese companies" and "ideology-crazed investment funds" posed to their citizens' pension funds and retirement accounts.[46]

As those states began to push back, BlackRock scrambled to distance itself from its ESG commitments. One Texas official memorialized such a discussion in January 2022, saying that it was "nice to hear that BlackRock didn't mean—or no longer believes—many of the disagreeable things the company and . . . Mr. Fink have said."[47] In March, Texas comptroller Glenn Hegar launched a formal investigation into BlackRock and others, explaining that they were "telling us and other energy-producing states one thing, and then turning around and telling their liberal clients in other states another thing."[48]

As pressure mounted, BlackRock did damage control, sending letters to several Republican-led states downplaying its ESG commitments. Arizona attorney general Mark Brnovich summarized one such letter, stating that it claimed "that BlackRock focuses solely on its fiduciary duty, allows its clients to determine how to approach the 'energy transition,' and has joined climate organizations merely to 'dialogue.'"[49]

Many state leaders were not convinced. Republican states wanted more than empty assurances that BlackRock's climate talk was merely empty assurances. That was when the nineteen attorneys general wrote to BlackRock, accusing it of making "statements that appear to conflict with BlackRock's previous public statements and commitments."[50] The letter accused the company of using "the hard-earned money of our states' citizens to circumvent the best possible return on investment" by "pressuring companies to . . . force the phase-out of fossil fuels" and adopt ESG goals.[51] BlackRock again took a step back. It denied that it had boycotted energy companies and claimed that it considered climate-related risks only to maximize long-run financial returns.

This time, BlackRock's left-leaning clients had something to say. Eight days later, fourteen Democrat-led states, including New York and California, wrote an open letter stating that investment managers should challenge their portfolio companies to work "toward reducing their carbon footprint."[52] Then New York City's comptroller, Brad Lander, wrote an even more pointed letter, calling BlackRock's backtracking "alarming," and issuing a thinly veiled threat to pull New York City's pension fund money if the firm did not do more to combat climate change.[53]

The Texas comptroller responded the next day, citing the "concerning . . . use of doublespeak by some financial institutions as they engage in anti–oil and gas rhetoric publicly yet present a much different story behind closed doors." The comptroller similarly noted "a systemic lack of transparency that should concern every American regardless of political persuasion."[54] Finally, an ESG disclosure issue Democrats and Republicans could agree on.

As the debate reached a fever pitch, state pension funds hit BlackRock where it hurt. Between January and November 2022, treasurers in Missouri, South Carolina, Louisiana, Utah, Arkansas, and West Virginia announced the divestment of more than $3 billion in capital from BlackRock because of its ESG and net zero pledges.[55] BlackRock was left with little choice; it was forced to give back one of its prized possessions: the ability to vote its clients' shares. Amid the scrutiny, it promised that it will now allow state pension fund managers to vote their shares themselves.[56] How can it possibly have conflicts of interest if it lets its clients choose their investments and vote the way they want to? Problem solved.

As a practical matter, most state pension funds don't have the staff or expertise to cast informed votes at the shareholder meetings of portfolio companies. An analyst whose state pension fund is invested in Vanguard's total stock market index fund would have to cast tens of thousands of votes each spring for the stocks held in that fund alone. Multiply that by all of the funds and companies in which the pension fund is invested, and the task becomes unmanageable.

But even if pension funds were to cast their own votes, most of the action doesn't happen at the corporate ballot box; it happens in the engagements that happen well beforehand. BlackRock uses its "soft influence" to convince companies to go green or not; do racial equity audits or resist them; ensure that its supply chain doesn't deforest the rain forest or chooses the cheapest suppliers. It is impossible for BlackRock to be an advocate for both its blue-state and red-state clients.

BlackRock has a single engagement team making calls to the same companies. And when its team tells Chevron to reduce its emissions[57] or tells a Chinese coal company to stop mining in a First Nation heritage site in Australia,[58] it does so on behalf of all of its assets under management. BlackRock doesn't call up a portfolio company and say, "Hey, Apple, some of our clients feel strongly that you should do a racial equity audit. You better do it. [brief pause] But also, some of our other clients feel strongly that you should *not* do a racial equity audit, so you better not do it." It wouldn't make any sense.

The upshot is that, regardless of the Band-Aid approach to self-voting that BlackRock seeks to use, it can stop the hemorrhaging only one way: by picking a side—by being either an ESG advocate or a financial one—and attempting to regain the trust it has lost by trying to play both.

Pension Fund Managers Get into the Game

To the untrained eye, pension fund managers may look like good guys: trying to represent the political interests of the constituents who elected them. Liberal states want their money to go to liberal causes, and conservative states don't. Dig deeper, and you'll find that state pension fund leaders have conflicts all their own. That's because they often wear two hats: as state treasurer, they are the state's top financial officer, elected by citizens or appointed by the governor to manage the state's financial affairs; as the head of the pension fund, they're a fiduciary responsible for maximizing financial benefits alone. These two roles are often incompatible, at least since ESG entered the scene.

Often, they are incompatible in the usual way, when elected officials seek to politicize pension funds to do through the back door of corporate America what they would never be able to do through the legislative process. This motivation is most apparent when politicians with no responsibility for pension fund oversight, such as mayors, nonetheless leverage pension funds to enact their political priorities. New York mayor Bill de Blasio, for example, was quoted as planning "to use the pension funds to direct Corporate America to change its ways."[59] A pension fund becomes just another tool in politicians' toolboxes; providing financial security for retired public workers is an afterthought.

This conflict is also apparent in California, where CalPERS' thirteen-member pension fund board is split between seven politically-appointed officials and six elected by CalPERS members and retirees. Unsurprisingly, the actual members of CalPERS often elect ESG skeptics. In 2018, for example, CalPERS members elected Jason Perez, who campaigned on a #ProtectOurPension platform that criticized CalPERS for "put[ting] our retirement security at risk due in part to environmental, social, and governance investing priorities."[60] Once elected, he continued to criticize CalPERS for "extorting companies" through ESG initiatives and tried to reverse CalPERS' ban on tobacco stocks.[61] These efforts have proven fruitless, however, as the majority of CalPERS board are political appointees, and so are motivated to pursue political goals over financial return.

Sometimes, the conflicts are even more direct. One new G issue is "tax integrity," specifically, the idea that companies should voluntarily pay more in taxes than they legally owe. It's essentially asking companies to put more cash into their state's coffers. The additional funds enable additional social programs, which comptrollers can then tout to enhance their reelection prospects. It's essentially a pay-to-play scheme with extra steps.

Other times, pension fund managers seek to use their position to defund their political opponents, rather than fill their own party's piggy bank. Commonly, this is done through shareholder proposals requesting that companies align their political donations with the goals of the Paris Accords. That means that companies can keep donating to politicians, but only if those politicians promise to enact policies to fight global warming. Those politicians are exclusively Democrats. In 2022, ESG activists proposed twenty-one such proposals; sixteen companies, including well-known companies such as Amazon, Uber, and JPMorgan Chase, agreed to implement them without having put them to a vote.[62] Sometimes the request is even more direct. In 2021, for example, state pension fund managers in eight blue states demanded that BlackRock stop donating to any Republican congressmen who refused to certify the results of the 2020 presidential election—and instruct its portfolio companies to do the same.[63] The political donations to Democrats, of course, should keep flowing—including, presumably, to Stacey Abrams, who still refuses to accept the outcome of the 2016 Georgia governor's race, and the seven House Democrats that voted against certifying the 2016 presidential election.

These abuses reflect not only a political problem but a core flaw in the ESG ideology itself: it's undefined. "ESG" means little more than "goodness." And "goodness" is in the eye of the beholder. So it's no surprise that political actors—well-meaning or not—use ESG to advance their own party's goals. When those same political actors are also charged with investing their states' multibillion-dollar pension funds, trouble is guaranteed.

Conflicted Advisors

Asset managers and politicians aren't the only ones seeking a piece of the pie. As ESG has skyrocketed in popularity, various cottage industries have sprung up. Rating agencies, ESG advisors, consultants, regulators, and lawyers all seek to help asset allocators, managers, and the companies they invest in navigate this brave new world. But look close enough at many players in the ESG ecosystem, and you'll see the outlines of an old-fashioned protection racket.

Let's start with rating agencies. These companies—MSCI, Sustainalytics, and others—grade publicly traded companies on ESG issues. They claim to analyze hundreds, sometimes thousands, of factors behind the scenes, and then they award a score, denoted by globes, an A to F rating, or an AAA to D rating like credit scores. These scores are more than a badge of honor or scarlet letter. Banks use them to determine whether to loan money and at what rates. Insurance companies have pledged to use them to determine coverage and premiums.[64] Activists cite them to shame companies into action. And asset managers such as BlackRock use them to determine which companies get into their coveted ESG funds. The rating companies are built on the premise that they are objective. But they're not. They are rife with conflicts of interest.

For starters, many rating companies also offer advising services to help rated companies boost their scores. This "advice" surely helps since the rating criteria are opaque and vary tremendously from firm to firm. Facebook (before Meta), for example, is in the top 4 percent according to one ESG rating firm but the bottom 1 percent according to another.[65] The only people who know why are the raters themselves. A look behind the scenes is invaluable.

You might think that to meaningfully improve its ESG score, Nestlé would have to stop buying up water rights in drought-ridden California or Nike would have to stop using forced labor.[66] Not so. Instead, companies are told that they can boost their scores by circulating employee satisfaction questionnaires or updating their handbook to expressly forbid already illegal kickbacks—easy, check-the-box exercises to improve their ESG scores without improving their ESG outcomes. But they can't do it unless they know what boxes to check.

They also have to be willing to check them. At least one outspoken ESG critic is not. I'm talking, of course, about Elon Musk—one of the only business leaders rich enough and bold enough to openly criticize the ESG-industrial complex. He's called ESG "an outrageous scam" that's been "weaponized by phony social justice warriors."[67] ESG scores, to him, measure purely "how compliant your business is with the leftist agenda."[68]

Given Musk's propensity to comply with no agenda but his own, it's no surprise that in May 2022 a major ESG rater dropped Tesla—an electric car manufacturer—from its ESG index while keeping Exxon in the top ten.[69] Its reasoning was illuminating: Tesla's ESG score didn't change, but apparently its peers' scores did, "effectively pushing Tesla down the ranks."[70] The lesson is clear: If a company refuses to pay the ratings firms to figure out how to play the game, its competitors will.

There is also pressure to give a high score to everyone, regardless of merit: grade inflation on an economywide scale. Here's why. Many rating agencies make most of their money not from the scores themselves or even consulting but from their indexing business. Indexing just means creating a list of publicly traded companies, based on whatever characteristics an agency chooses. The S&P 500, for instance, is an index of the five hundred largest US companies. ESG ratings companies make indices of companies with good ESG scores. These indices are then licensed by asset managers such as BlackRock to create ESG funds.

It's a cash cow. MSCI, for example, gets a fee on every dollar of the funds that BlackRock manages—a take on trillions of dollars. Forever. The popular investment website Seeking Alpha describes MSCI as "the most attractive business in the world": "Imagine a business where you earned a royalty on the amount of wealth in the world, and as wealth increased you would automatically see your earnings increase as well."[71] That's MSCI.

BlackRock doesn't want MSCI to be too picky. What it really wants is to relabel its S&P 500 fund as an ESG fund with MSCI's stamp of approval. That way, it can offer a broadly diversified, market-tracking ESG fund without having to sacrifice returns. MSCI has been happy to oblige. That's why BlackRock's ESG funds include fossil fuel behemoths such as Chevron and ExxonMobil—and why almost 90 percent of the S&P 500 have wound up in ESG funds built with MSCI's ratings.[72] It also explains why, as ESG funds have skyrocketed in popularity, ESG scores have risen across the board, even though companies' ESG-related behavior has not improved.[73] Just as professors at for-profit colleges are pressured to give students better grades to increase graduation rates, MSCI gives nondiverse, carbon-spewing companies a pass. ESG rating firms are the new diploma mills.

There are also the teacher's pets, including BlackRock. MSCI rates BlackRock AA, calling it an ESG "leader," no doubt because BlackRock's partnership with MSCI demonstrates how seriously it takes ESG. Indeed, one of the biggest factors that goes into BlackRock's, and all other Wall Street firms', ESG rating is "the integration of ESG factors in the management of their own assets or the assets they manage on behalf of others."[74] The more a firm uses MSCI, the higher its ESG rating will go. The fact that MSCI generates 13 percent of its annual revenue from BlackRock is conspicuously absent from its reporting on BlackRock's AA score.[75]

Even better, rating firms sometimes rate their own corporate affiliates. Most rating firms are not independent businesses but members of large corporate families that are merged, spun off, bought, and sold by investors. Given this entanglement, researchers at the University of Hong Kong investigated whether ESG rating firms give sister companies higher scores than they do nonconnected firms.[76] They do—by a significant margin. The researchers also looked at how ESG firms scored new sister companies before and after they were acquired. Sister companies' scores jumped once they joined the clan. Of course, it is theoretically possible that the companies behaved better upon joining an ESG-focused corporate family. But the researchers considered that factor, too. After a merger, a new sister company got a boost in its ESG score, but its negative ESG incidents did not decrease. The authors concluded that the only explanation was an old-fashioned conflict of interest: the large shareholders who owned both the rating firms and the rated companies cared more about appearances than performance.

Outside advisors fare little better. Accenture, for instance, doesn't rate companies itself but offers consulting services to help companies boost their ESG scores.[77] This may make it seem less conflicted, but a look behind the curtain proves otherwise. Who are the largest investors in Accenture? BlackRock, Vanguard, and State Street. The same large asset managers manning the gates to their ESG funds are advising companies on how to get through the door.

Then there are the proxy advisory businesses. Proxy advisors tell asset managers how to vote their clients' shares. Two proxy advisory firms—Glass Lewis and ISS—have cornered the market, providing 97 percent of all services. They have enormous power: the two firms can sway up to 40 percent of all votes cast at shareholder meetings.[78] These two firms count large asset managers such as BlackRock as clients, but they advise small funds as well. These clients are critical to ISS's and Glass Lewis's stranglehold on corporate America: as many as half of all small index funds "robovote" their shares, meaning that they blindly follow ISS's and Glass Lewis's recommendations, without any independent evaluation at all.[79]

Why? One reason is that there is an overwhelming number of director nominations and shareholder proposals each year. Microsoft alone had twelve directors up for election and six shareholder proposals in 2022 on topics ranging from whether to hire ex-cons to climate change to whether to stop developing products for the military. Multiply that by the five hundred companies in the S&P 500 or the two thousand in the Russell 2000, and outsourcing begins to make a lot of sense.

The other reason is government regulation. In the wake of the Enron scandal in the early 2000s, the SEC enacted regulations that essentially forced asset managers to vote their clients' shares. The thinking was that the hands-off approach some asset managers had historically taken gave management too much freedom, which wasn't good for shareholders. But asset managers are not always trustworthy, either. To prevent asset managers' hands in the corporate cookie jar, the SEC said that asset managers could not have conflicts of interest when voting their clients' shares.

It seems straightforward enough, but asset managers are hugely conflicted, as they own thousands of different companies through many different funds on behalf of many different investors with potentially very different goals. Fortunately, there was a loophole: asset managers didn't have to worry about their own conflicts of interest if they outsourced voting to a third party, such as Glass Lewis or ISS. But unlike asset managers, proxy advisory firms do not owe fiduciary duties to anyone—other than the owners of ISS and Glass Lewis themselves. And as we will see, an interest in maximizing profits for Glass Lewis and ISS is not always the same as an interest in maximizing profits for public company shareholders. The rise of proxy advisory firms is a story of government regulation designed to prevent conflicts of interest instead giving rise to new ones—a classic American tale.

The conflicts aren't hypothetical. ISS, for example, provides consulting services to the same companies and boards whose fates it holds in its hands. Common sense dictates that ISS is more likely to recommend that shareholders vote in management-friendly ways—reelect existing board members, approve a CEO's compensation package—when management pays ISS handsome consulting fees. Research bears this out: a 2013 study showed that proxy advisory firms that also have consulting businesses show favoritism toward management, compared to firms that don't.[80] Of course they do.

ISS also sells its consulting and advisory services to universities, labor unions, pension funds, and ESG asset managers, who make shareholder proposals of their own and look to ISS for support. CalPERS, for example, one of the largest ESG activist funds in the nation, pays hundreds of thousands of dollars to both ISS and Glass Lewis every year.[81] Its number one priority in 2022 was to "create meaningful change at the companies in which we invest" on issues such as "corporate board diversity" and "climate change."[82] But as big as CalPERS is, it can't change corporate America on its own. It needs proxy advisors' support. ISS and Glass Lewis know where their bread is buttered, and they are happy to help.

Again, academic research bears this out. USC researchers found that because specialized ESG investors are willing to pay for high-quality voting advice, while most generic index fund investors are not, proxy advisors "compete for business" by "slant[ing]" advice toward ESG goals.[83]

This advice is then used by ESG and non-ESG funds alike. As a result, proxy advisors "[tilt] corporate elections toward minority shareholders that are willing to forego financial returns in order to advance social goals."[84] Since proxy advisory firms don't have any money at stake, forgoing other people's financial returns isn't a problem—especially if doing so keeps their largest customers happy. The numbers are staggering: In 2021, for example, ISS and Glass Lewis recommended voting in favor of environmental and social proposals 82 percent and 69 percent of the time, respectively; for its part, BlackRock voted that way 74 percent of the time.

Even proxy advisors without consulting side gigs are conflicted. To maximize their business, it behooves proxy advisory firms to make shareholder voting as frequent, complicated, and contentious as possible. So that's what they do. ISS and Glass Lewis have both pushed companies to hold say-on-pay votes (where shareholders vote on executive compensation packages) every year,[85] even though the law requires a vote only every third year. By doing so, they successfully created more work for themselves, even though a study out of Stanford University showed that the practice hurts shareholder value.[86]

Proxy advisors are also incentivized to come up with their recommendations as cheaply and quickly as possible. Proxy voting is invisible to most owners of capital, so accuracy doesn't matter. In fact, inaccuracies can themselves be profitable. Glass Lewis, for instance, charges companies to review their own reports—a precondition for seeing if anything is wrong. In one case, a company learned that Glass Lewis had recommended against its CEO's compensation because it had miscalculated how much the CEO was paid. But when the company asked for a correction, or at least to see the math, the company was told that it would have to pay $30,000 to become a full subscriber or $5,000 to see its own report.[87] Another company described the situation as a "hold up where we have to pay money simply to defend ourselves or know what has been said about us—if we don't pay we find ourselves shadow boxing in response to rumors that we hear piecemeal."[88] None of this helps shareholders. But it isn't designed to.

Recently, both ISS and Glass Lewis launched ESG rating businesses, meaning that they are no longer even pretending to be neutral arbiters.[89] Now that the voting advisors have openly donned activist hats, all semblance of objectivity has surely been lost. That means that although asset managers might once have been able to sidestep their conflicts of interest by relying on proxy advisory firms, such an approach can no longer be taken.

Certain asset managers have recognized these issues and have tried to avoid such conflicts by uniformly voting with the company's board. This doesn't work. First, blindly voting with a company's board presents the same abdication of responsibility as not voting at all—the very problem that post-Enron government regulators were trying to address. For that reason, voting with the board may itself violate an asset manager's oversight duties. Second, the strategy may not even work. ESG activists are no longer simply offering ESG policy proposals to existing boards but replacing those financially minded boards with ones that are more ESG compliant. Once they recruit ISS and Glass Lewis for this mission, the coup will be complete. At that point, voting with those boards' recommendations will be no different from voting with ISS and Glass Lewis, or with ESG activists for that matter.

Proxy advisors and rating firms are the largest recipients of the ESG largesse, but there are others. CEOs have managed to snag compensation packages that give them extra cash if they meet ESG metrics. "Hire more diverse employees" or "Reduce our carbon footprint," their company plans say. The practice incentivizes absurd conduct: a company's management may buy a carbon sink, go on a year-end hiring spree, or forgo an acquisition that would be good for shareholders, all to ensure a fat bonus check. More broadly, these packages turn the very purpose of incentive compensation on its head; a system designed to ensure that CEOs' personal financial interests were aligned with those of shareholders is now being used to decouple the two. ESG activists have intentionally created a conflict of interest, incentivizing CEOs to take ESG-driven steps that lose money for shareholders by offering them more money for themselves.

Lawyers, as always, have been eager to get their share. In the past few years, ESG groups at major law firms have exploded, including lawyers who advise companies how to fight shareholder activism, how to manage the antitrust risks associated with joining groups such as Climate Action 100+, how to lobby for or against or comply with or dodge ESG government regulation. They also do racial equity audits, for which they are paid huge sums by the very clients they are "independently" investigating. And they defend companies, such as Starbucks, that are inevitably sued when those same racial equity audits impose race-based hiring in violation of the Civil Rights Act.[90] Accounting firms, too, have joined the cause, with Ernst & Young providing "sustainability services" and PwC offering to help businesses with "climate change reporting." There are ESG PR firms, ESG marketing agencies, and ESG government lobbyists. There's even a company that helps dentists adopt ESG practices[91]—whatever that means. If someone can dream it, they've figured out a way to profit from it. In each instance, the ESG lawyer, consultant, lobbyist, PR specialist, proxy advisor, or rating agency is purporting to serve a company's interests; they're really serving their own.

Sometimes ESG's critics claim that ESG is exploiting the separation of ownership from ownership, by which they usually mean that asset managers are taking money from investors and diverting it from profit-seeking investments and toward ESG goals. But only a small portion of that money, if any, makes it to that destination. Instead, it is pilfered by self-interested actors in the ESG ecosystem along the way.

Chapter 6

TOO BIG TO COMPETE

I n late 2022, the Investor Advisory Group of the International Sustainability Standards Board (ISSB), a nonprofit dedicated to "integrat[ing] ESG considerations into investment and stewardship decisions across global portfolios,"[1] held a "climate finance" meeting.[2] Members of the Advisory Group include behemoths of finance such as BlackRock, State Street, Vanguard, Goldman Sachs, JP Morgan, and the Carlyle Group.[3] There was nothing unusual about such a meeting—just another ESG get-together among Wall Street giants committed to saving the planet. One thing was peculiar, though: no one was allowed to speak until a lawyer read out a disclaimer stating that the group was "not a cartel."[4]

Why the legal disclaimer? Because cartels are a serious problem in antitrust law, and ESG has a serious antitrust problem. As any antitrust lawyer will tell you, the fact that a conclave of firms says it's not a cartel doesn't mean it's not a cartel.

In an ideal free market, firms act independently. They may react to one another's production and pricing decisions, but they don't coordinate their decisions with one another. Instead, they compete, and their competition maximizes social welfare resulting in better products at lower prices.

Consumers benefit from competition, but firms tend to hate it. Lower prices mean lower profits. As a result, firms often look for clever ways to evade competition. The purpose of antitrust law is to prohibit them from doing so. The easiest way for firms to eliminate competition is to form a cartel—to collude. All their executives have to do is pick up the phone and agree, for example, to charge the same high price for a product. That's why the first section of the United States' first antitrust law—the Sherman Antitrust Act of 1890—bars firms from entering into anticompetitive agreements (or, in the words of the statute, from "combin[ing]" to "restrain trade").

OPEC is a classic cartel; its members collude instead of competing. Their favored tactic is not to fix prices but to agree to pump less oil. By the ironclad laws of supply and demand, reduced production increases prices. If OPEC were governed by US antitrust law, which it is not, its members would be in jail.

Imagine now that the billionaire owners of the United States' largest oil and gas companies get together behind closed doors. Imagine that they decide to do what OPEC does, jointly agreeing to reduce production. Their agreement would be unlawful under Section 1 of the Sherman Act. If discovered, they'd be subject to prosecution and treble damages.

That could never happen, right? Wrong. BlackRock, State Street, and Vanguard are the billionaire owners—actually, the trillionaire owners—of the United States' largest oil and gas companies, and they work together to reduce production at those companies.

Who Owns Big Oil?

ExxonMobil is the biggest of the Big Oil companies in the United States. In fact, it's the largest investor-owned oil and gas company in the world;

only state-owned enterprises in Saudi Arabia and China are larger. ExxonMobil is the descendant of one of the original monopolies that the Sherman Act was passed to break up: John D. Rockefeller's Standard Oil. Who owns ExxonMobil today? The largest shareholder is Vanguard, which owns 8.95 percent of the company. BlackRock is second, with 6.82 percent of the company, and State Street is third, with 5.59 percent.[5] Collectively, that's more than 21 percent of the company.

Meanwhile, Vanguard owns 8.24 percent of Chevron, the second largest US oil and gas company, with BlackRock holding 6.72 percent and State Street 6.70 percent.[6] Again, that's more than 21 percent in all. At the same time, the Big Three own about 22 percent of ConocoPhillips common stock (as well as some 40 to 50 percent of preferred stock) and almost 28 percent of Marathon.[7]

Twenty percent ownership is often regarded as the threshold for a control share or a change of control in a publicly held company.[8] Both the New York Stock Exchange and Nasdaq presume that there is a change in control resulting from certain transactions that put an entity over the 20 percent threshold. Under Nasdaq's rules, "Generally, if a transaction results in an investor or group of investors obtaining a 20% interest or a right to acquire that interest in the issuer on a post-transaction basis, and that ownership position would be the largest position in the issuer, the transaction may be presumed to be a change of control."[9]

With their combined 20 percent–plus ownership, the Big Three can and do exert considerable power over the major US oil producers. And they use that power to lower production. Glance at any of the Big Three's glossy ESG sections on their websites, and you'll encounter head-spinningly vaporous corporate copy pledging allegiance to the world's climate. BlackRock: "We believe that the transition to a net zero world is the shared responsibility of every citizen, corporation, and government."[10] State Street: "We believe that there is an urgent need to accelerate the transition towards global net zero emissions."[11] Vanguard: "Our efforts to inform and safeguard investors on climate change include . . . seek[ing] to facilitate an effective transition to a low-carbon economy."[12] Translated into plain English: the Big Three are committed to reducing their portfolio companies' production of oil and gas.

What does this policy look like in practice? In May 2021, a brand-new, tiny investment firm called Engine No. 1 accomplished the unthinkable: it won a proxy fight against ExxonMobil's management. At a publicly traded company, open seats on the board of directors must be filled by shareholder vote. In practice, shareholder ratification of management's preferred candidates is pro forma; contested elections are rare, and management's preferred candidates losing is rarer still. But Engine No. 1 succeeded in installing three directors it had chosen over the objections of management. Its goal: the "near elimination of conventional fossil fuels," as a document accompanying its investor outreach put it.[13]

To pull it off, Engine No. 1 must have wielded overwhelming voting power, right? Wrong. It held only .02 percent of ExxonMobil's outstanding shares. It achieved that stunning victory with the help of powerful friends. All of the Big Three supported Engine No. 1's slate of directors.[14] Before the proxy fight started, ExxonMobil had announced plans to increase oil and gas production by 25 percent over the following five years—but Engine No. 1 had other ideas,[15] and once the heavyweights threw their lot in with the climate activists, ExxonMobil's fate was sealed. Immediately after the proxy fight, ExxonMobil ditched its long-term production increase targets and resolved to keep oil output at the lowest level in two decades through 2025—a 25 percent decline from previous forecasts. "That was a good kind of early win," commented Engine No. 1's CEO, Jennifer Grancio.[16]

The ExxonMobil proxy fight is a particularly high-profile example, but the Big Three, along with other asset managers, have used their enormous financial clout to drive down fossil fuel production throughout the US energy sector. According to the Federal Reserve Bank of Dallas, pressure from investors to divest from fossil fuel production has driven underinvestment in extraction and refinement capacity.[17] In 2022, probably fearful of suffering their own ExxonMobil-like board of directors debacle, three other major US oil companies announced that they were joining the Oil & Gas Methane Partnership 2.0, an international UN-backed organization working to reduce greenhouse gas emissions—a move "brokered" by Engine No. 1, as the *Wall Street Journal* reported.[18] The result: an artificial and anticompetitive reduction of supply. Throughout 2022, despite record high oil prices, US output stubbornly remained below prepandemic levels, with oil executives citing, among other factors, ESG pressure and the "vilification" of the oil industry by Wall Street.[19]

Ms. Grancio was right: all of that was certainly a "win"—for climate activists and for non–fossil fuel energy companies. But not so much for consumers, who faced crisis-level energy shortages and soaring prices at the pump.

Concerted Action

If the Big Three asset managers were each independently pushing the ESG agenda on America's oil companies, they wouldn't have anywhere near the power that they achieve by acting in concert, and arguably there might not even be an antitrust problem, since Section 1 of the Sherman Act applies only when firms collude. But they aren't acting independently.

A 2017 analysis of proxy voting records found "that the Big Three do utilize coordinated voting strategies and hence follow a centralized corporate governance strategy."[20] The same study found that "the Big Three may exert 'hidden power'" through "private engagements with management of invested companies." Moreover, when it comes to ESG, collusion among the Big Three is not in fact "hidden"; it's in plain sight.

Along with hundreds of other asset managers, the Big Three have joined numerous international investor organizations whose members collaborate to push ESG environmental activism onto their portfolio companies. Although there are perhaps a dozen of these organizations, two are the most prominent.

The first is the Net Zero Asset Managers initiative, which has some 300 signatories with approximately $60 trillion in assets under management.[21] The organization is, in its own words, "an international group of asset managers committed to supporting the goal of net zero greenhouse gas emissions by 2050 or sooner."[22] Signatories commit to "an immediate cancellation of all new thermal coal projects, including thermal coal plant, coal mines and related infrastructure" and a "phase-out of all unabated existing coal-fired electricity generation in accordance with 1.5° Celsius pathways."[23] Outside of coal, each member commits to reaching "net zero emissions by 2050 or sooner across all assets under management" and to "collaborate with each other and other investors . . . to deliver these commitments."[24] They further commit to using their proxy voting power to force company directors to adopt net zero policies or face expulsion.

This is an open declaration of concerted action, and Net Zero Asset Managers isn't even the largest ESG investor organization. That title belongs to Climate Action 100+ (CA100+), an "investor-led initiative to ensure the world's largest corporate greenhouse gas emitters take necessary action on climate change." The organization boasts more than seven hundred investors representing more than $68 trillion in assets under management—"over 50 percent of all global assets under management."[25] The CA100+ "focus[es] on 166 companies that are critical to the net-zero emissions transition"[26]—prominently including oil, gas, coal, and energy utility companies—making investment in such companies depend on the "company's decarbonisation strategy" and its commitment to "decarbonis[ing] its future capital expenditures."[27] Translation: our members won't invest in you unless you agree to reduce fossil fuel output.

The CA100+ is a centralized hub of coordinated decision making. The organization is overseen "by a global steering committee that establishes . . . strategic priorities, governance, and infrastructure."[28] According to its website, "Climate Action 100+ has established a common high-level agenda for company engagement to achieve clear commitments to cut emissions."[29] Signatories agree to conduct "direct engagements with focus companies,"[30] working "cooperatively with a number of collaborating investors,"[31] to cause those companies to "reduce greenhouse-gas emissions."[32] In other words, like the Net Zero Asset Managers initiative, Climate Action 100+ openly boasts of its members' agreement to work in concert to reduce production of fossil fuels.

Nevertheless, both groups maintain, in lengthy legal disclaimers, that they do not coordinate the behavior of their members.[33] Individual participants, such as BlackRock, similarly maintain that their participation signifies no coordinated action of any kind.[34] But saying so does not make it true. In one breath, these groups disclaim coordination and simultaneously advertise their ability to "ensure strong and concerted action" from their members.[35] Participating investors in both these organizations agree to a set of common steps to reduce their portfolio companies' production of, consumption of, and investment in fossil fuels. That transforms their individual actions into concerted activity, and the Sherman Act does not contain an ESG exception.

In December 2022, Vanguard abruptly pulled out of the Net Zero Asset Managers initiative, stating that it needed to "speak independently."[36] (BlackRock and State Street remain members.) Vanguard's action was almost certainly motivated by fear of legal exposure. Its withdrawal was a devastating admission that membership in organizations such as the Net Zero Asset Managers initiative involves concerted conduct.

Climate Finance

Forcing ESG policies onto US oil companies is not the only way deep-pocketed Wall Street firms are colluding to reduce fossil fuel production. Major banks are denying financing to oil and gas companies in the name of ESG. As a result, the all-important cost of capital has skyrocketed for US oil producers, while the cost of capital for renewable energy projects has not.[37]

Consider the Arctic National Wildlife Refuge (ANWR) in Alaska. A long-prized target for oil exploration, the region is believed to contain the largest untapped onshore oil reserves remaining in North America.[38] In 2017, Congress lifted a decades-long ban on oil and gas drilling in the ANWR, authorizing the Department of the Interior to lease new lands for oil exploration.[39] In response, Wall Street organized to oppose new drilling. When the Bureau of Land Management issued a call to oil companies to identify favorable ANWR lands for leasing in 2020, the largest US banks—Morgan Stanley, Wells Fargo, Goldman Sachs, JPMorgan Chase, and Citigroup—pressured by environmentalists and ESG advocates, all announced their refusal to finance any new oil and gas exploration in the Arctic.[40] Bank of America signed on to this de facto boycott a few months later.[41] Starved of capital, Arctic drilling, which is expensive, is a nonstarter, and all of the major oil companies retreated from their plans to pursue new claims.[42]

Of greater consequence to antitrust law, the boycott of drilling in the ANWR implies collusion. If each bank were truly acting independently, its refusal to finance oil and gas projects in the Arctic would be both economically self-destructive and pointless. It would simply be handing the projects and the profits on a silver platter to its competitors. Each bank's decision makes sense only if it knows that its competitors will also join the boycott.

How do the Big Three fit into the banks' climate finance game? The same way they fit into ExxonMobil's lowering of production. The Big Three not only own Big Oil; they own the banks.

Actually, State Street is itself a bank—one of the fifteen largest in the United States.* And the "Big Three collectively hold controlling shares of 13 of the 14 others—with their directly controlled ownership shares ranging from about 17% to 25%, and their indirectly controlled ownership

---

*As of September 30, 2022, State Street was the twelfth largest US commercial bank by total assets.

shares ranging from about 24% to 45%."[43] Not coincidentally, many of the major US banks with significant ownership stakes held by the Big Three are also members of the Net Zero Banking Alliance, the banking counterpart of the Net Zero Asset Managers initiative.[44] As a result of this collective ownership and control, the Big Three can get the United States' major banks to do something that would be economically self-destructive for any one bank to do on its own: refuse to finance (at competitive rates) lucrative oil and gas production.

Legally speaking, any company, on its own, may refuse to deal with any other firm. However, there appears to be a collaborative effort among the Big Three and the major banks to deny capital to oil and gas producers or make it prohibitively expensive. This is another potential antitrust violation. The Sherman Act does not permit "group boycotts"—concerted efforts by competitor firms to deny critical facilities (such as bank loans) to other, rival companies. Several state treasurers, including those of Texas and West Virginia, have already concluded that the major US asset managers and US banks are engaged in precisely such a boycott of fossil fuel companies;[45] other states are investigating the issue.[46]

Group boycott law is complicated. Some group boycotts are automatically illegal; others are reviewed more carefully under a standard called the "rule of reason." Even under rule of reason analysis, however, the concerted effort to deny or restrict capital to oil and gas companies looks to be illegal. It plainly has anticompetitive effects (because it is aimed at reducing supply), and it lacks any apparent pro-competitive justifications. Moreover, notwithstanding the banks' planet-saving declarations, the boycott is undergirded by good old-fashioned economic motivations.

Creating Growth Opportunities in Renewables

Why are the Big Three and the major banks colluding to kill oil drilling? Their stated explanation, of course, is that they're concerned about the environment. More recently, ESG advocates have been emphasizing the notion that Big Oil is a bad investment on the circular ground that the ESG movement will convince governments around the world to ban fossil fuels. A more plausible answer might be that Wall Street stands to make a fortune from the "great energy transition."

A massive Wall Street payday will be a by-product of any large-scale transition from fossil fuels to renewable energy. The scale of the project is vast and will require trillions in "green financing" from Wall Street to accomplish. There will have to be construction of new wind and solar farms as well as manufacturing plants for the batteries, solar panels, and other basic materials of renewable energy generation; the retrofitting of existing power plants; and the development of as-yet-untested technologies. All of this will require financing, and that's how Wall Street makes its money: by collecting billions of dollars in fees by underwriting such projects.

Brian Moynihan, the CEO of Bank of America, was uncharacteristically blunt about this state of affairs. He said that the great energy transition is a "big business opportunity" for the bank.[47] According to an OECD report, the clean energy transition is worth nearly *$7 trillion annually*.[48] If Wall Street bankers base their fees on that total sum, as they traditionally do, it's easy to see why they are so excited about ESG.

But as long as extracting energy from fossil fuels stays cheaper than using renewable energy sources, renewables will not significantly displace traditional energy sources. The only way to achieve cost competitiveness is by raising the cost of fossil fuel production. No Wall Street asset manager or bank could achieve that result on its own. But through collective action, they can, thereby jump-starting a colossal ESG money pump.

The economics behind ESG help explain another vexing puzzle: Why do ESG advocates reject nuclear energy? From a sustainability perspective, nuclear power should be an ESG darling. Nuclear energy production is nearly limitless and carbon free. Moreover, nuclear energy is reliable: it works even when there's no sun or wind. Nuclear energy has a comparatively small environmental footprint: rather than damming rivers or blanketing picturesque landscapes in unsightly solar panels or wind turbines, it can be housed in a traditional power plant. Most important, nuclear power works *today*. It is the only clean energy source that has been successfully adopted on a large scale; France, for example, has relied on nuclear power for the majority of its electricity generation for decades.

Yet the anti–climate change Left has long opposed nuclear energy. Germany, for example, is on track to spend €500 billion by 2025 on phasing out its existing power generation sources—including shutting down nuclear power plants, which at their peak in the 1990s produced about one-third of Germany's electricity supply.[49] The country's reward: higher electricity prices.[50] Even at the end of 2022, when Russia's war in Ukraine reduced fossil fuel production, and a brutal winter resulted in soaring energy prices and energy shortages across the European continent, Germany announced it would stick to its plan to decommission its nuclear power plants by April 2023.[51] Nuclear energy continues to largely be shunned by ratings associations and investors responsible for investing ESG-designated assets.[52]

Unlike unproven technology such as wind and solar power generation, nuclear power generation does not require the same massive revamp of existing energy infrastructure to scale up. But if nuclear power is shut down, there's a fortune to be made on Wall Street from underwriting trillion-dollar bets on renewable energy boondoggles that may or may not pan out.

Illegal Even If No Collusion

So far, I have been discussing antitrust violations under Section 1 of the Sherman Antitrust Act. These violations are predicated on collusion. But there is another key provision of antitrust law—Section 7 of the Clayton Antitrust Act of 1914—that does not require collusion. Section 7 prohibits the acquisition or holding of shares in publicly traded companies where the effect "may be substantially to lessen competition."[53] Though it is ordinarily applied to mergers and acquisitions, Section 7 of the Clayton Act sweeps much further, and leading antitrust experts have recently concluded that it applies to horizontal shareholding by the Big Three even in the absence of any agreements or collaboration among them.[54]

"Horizontal ownership" or "horizontal shareholding" refers to the phenomenon we've already seen with respect to the Big Three's ownership of the United States' major oil companies and banks. When all the major competitors in a given market have common owners, that's horizontal ownership. To economists and antitrust experts, the explosion of horizontal shareholding by the Big Three is of ground-shifting importance. According to Harvard Law School professor Einer Elhauge, such horizontal ownership is an "economic blockbuster" and a violation of Section 7 of the Clayton Act.[55]

The legal mechanics of Section 7 are simple: it prohibits an investor from buying or holding the stock of a publicly traded company when doing so would produce substantial anticompetitive effects.[56] The number of shares held need not be a majority; the test is simply whether the holding of the shares in question substantially lessens competition.[57]

Horizontal ownership negates firms' incentives to compete. The classic example postulates that there are only two restaurants in a given town, each competing with the other. So far, so good. Competition keeps their prices down and their quality up. Now suppose that the owner of one of these restaurants buys the other. Now the restaurants have no incentive to compete. If an increase in price at the first restaurant were to drive some customers to the second, the owner wouldn't mind at all—since he owns both.[58] Every dollar lost from one pocket goes into the other pocket of the same owner.

The same anticompetitive effects occur when publicly owned companies have common shareholders with significant stakes, at least in sectors with high market concentration. In a seminal study of the airline industry—where, once again, the Big Three collectively hold more than

20 percent of the major competitors—researchers found that greater horizontal shareholding was positively correlated with higher airline ticket prices. On average, airline tickets were 3 to 7 percent more expensive than they would have been absent horizontal shareholding—a large effect in an otherwise deeply competitive industry with an average net profit margin of 4 percent.[59] Similar results hold for the banking industry, where increased horizontal shareholding correlates with higher fees and lower interest rates provided on customer deposits.[60] In the pharmaceutical industry, when branded and generic drug manufacturers have a high degree of horizontal shareholding, manufacturers are less likely to introduce a lower-cost generic product at the close of a branded drug's exclusivity period.[61] Horizontal ownership appears, predictably, to cause an industry to become less competitive. This is the very ill that Section 7 of the Clayton Act was designed to address.

Some scholars have theorized that the sharp rise in the level of horizontal ownership since 1980 is responsible, in part, for the rise in income inequality in the United States over the same period.[62] Horizontal shareholding results in inflated returns on capital—or stock held by shareholders—and deflated returns on labor. Since wealthy people disproportionately derive their income from capital and poorer people from wages, the theory holds, horizontal shareholding increases inequality between the rich and the poor. Decades of artificially high prices can transfer a lot of revenue from normal people to stockholders. Aggressive antitrust enforcement under Section 7 of the Clayton Act thus may not only fight accumulated corporate power but also help lessen class inequality.

The kicker? The Big Three *also own one another*. Vanguard is the single largest owner of BlackRock and State Street. "Taken together," noted the *Wall Street Journal*, "the Big Three directly own about 19% of BlackRock and 22% of State Street. The companies also own controlling shares of many of the other institutional stockholders holding the Big Three's shares. After including those holdings, the Big Three cumulatively control—if indirectly—no less than about 32% of BlackRock's equity and 42% of State Street's."[63]

This entanglement further compounds the anticompetitive effects of horizontal ownership. The Big Three benefit when their portfolio companies work to reduce output and raise prices—and the Big Three are themselves among those very portfolio companies. Squint a little, and this mare's nest begins to resemble the famous cartoon of Standard Oil as an octopus. Like the great trusts of the robber baron era, the Big Three are really one creature, with tentacles reaching into every sector of the US economy.

Too Big to Disclose

Beyond antitrust violations, the Big Three's massive holdings put them into potential violation of federal securities disclosure requirements. In the main, US securities law does not mandate what companies can and cannot do. Rather, it is structured around disclosure, and a key threshold is crossed when a person or entity acquires more than 5 percent of any publicly traded company.

The Big Three cross this threshold with abandon. As stated earlier, BlackRock alone has at least a 5 percent share of 95 percent of the firms in the S&P 500.[64] A federal securities law provision—Section 13(d) of the Exchange Act—is supposed to kick in at this threshold. Under Section 13(d), any investor owning more than 5 percent of a company has to file a disclosure statement outlining any steps they have taken or intend to take to control that company. Most investors fully comply with Section 13(d). Thousands of 13(d) forms are filed yearly, including by some of the world's most sophisticated institutional investors, such as Warren Buffett and Carl Icahn. But the Big Three refuse to comply with it.

BlackRock, like the other behemoth asset managers, claims that it is exempt from Section 13(d), instead reporting its ownership stakes on Schedule 13G, an alternative and much less demanding disclosure form. Schedule 13G, however, is available to a firm only if its shareholding has neither "the purpose nor the effect of changing or influencing the control of the issuer."[65] The SEC defines control as "the possession, *direct or indirect*, of the power to direct or cause the direction of the *management and policies* of a [company], whether through *the ownership of voting securities, by contract, or otherwise*" (emphasis added).[66] Under this definition, the pro-ESG activities of asset management firms such as BlackRock almost certainly have both the purpose and the effect of changing or influencing control.

BlackRock can't say that its votes for Engine No. 1's activist directors against the recommendation of ExxonMobil's own management had no impact on the company's policies. The vote was a deliberate effort to change ExxonMobil's management and policies. Indeed, that's the express purpose of all of BlackRock's ESG initiatives at its portfolio companies, whether through proxy voting or so-called shareholder engagement, including at BlackRock's supposedly passive index funds.

Recently, SEC commissioner Mark T. Uyeda stunned Wall Street by pointing out in a public address in Washington, DC, that the ESG policies of the Big Three seem to put them in breach of Section 13(d). He cited the SEC's definition of control, and he wondered how the systematic effort by the Big Three to pressure company directors and executives into adopting ESG policies did not count as an attempt to alter the "direction of the management and policies of a company."[67]

The Big Three refuse to make public what they say to company executives in their pro-ESG communications with those executives. Even as they demand ESG transparency from their portfolio companies—requiring those companies to disclose a laundry list of ESG information such as emissions data, plans to achieve carbon neutrality, racial equity audit results, and other diversity, equity, and inclusion (DEI) measures—the Big Three refuse to disclose their own ESG "engagement" communications and refuse to comply with Section 13(d). Apparently, it's disclosure for thee, but not for me.

Through their massive size and horizontal shareholding, the Big Three have recreated the old monopoly trusts of days past. As Harvard Law School professor Elhauge put it:

> The reason that the Sherman Act was called an anti*trust* law was that it aimed to prohibit certain trusts, and those trusts were horizontal shareholders. These pre–Sherman Act trusts were formed by having the stockholders of the competing firms transfer their stock to the trust, in exchange for a trust certificate entitling each stockholder to a share of the trust's income. The trusts then used their horizontal shareholdings to elect directors of each firm that would refrain from competition. . . . Indeed, many ETFs with horizontal shareholdings are literally trusts.[68]

The Sherman Act was passed to bust these horizontal shareholding trusts. It's time to apply that statute to today's rebirth of the very evil that antitrust laws were enacted to abolish.

Chapter 7

GOVERNMENT CONSCRIPTS EMPLOYEES INTO ESG WARFARE

A nun, a rabbi, and the head of New York City's pension funds walk into a shareholder meeting. "I'm speaking on behalf of all the Catholics invested in your company," says the nun. "I'm speaking on behalf of all the Jewish investors," says the rabbi. "And I'm speaking on behalf of every teacher, firefighter, police officer, and city worker," says the pension fund manager. Yet they're all delivering the same sermon: telling American businesses to marshal their financial resources to pursue the greater social "good," as these leaders see it, rather than long-term financial value. It sounds like the setup for a joke, but it's not. It's happening every year across corporate America. And it's not comedy but tragedy—at least as far as the First Amendment is concerned.

As you know by now, legal scrutiny of ESG has come from many directions. It's a breach of fiduciary duty. It enables unethical money managers to exploit conflicts that enrich themselves at the expense of others. It allows unelected monopolists to engage in social engineering with other people's money. But there's a deeper problem: states that use retirees' money to make social proclamations and cast politicized proxy votes commit a cardinal constitutional sin.

The First Amendment's free speech clause prevents the government from forcing citizens to espouse views they disagree with. We typically think of "free speech" as the right to say what we want to, but it also prevents the government from forcing us to say things we don't want to. A 1943 decision (*West Virginia State Board of Education v. Barnette*), for instance, ruled that schoolchildren could not be forced to recite the Pledge of Allegiance. A 1977 decision (*Wooley v. Maynard*) held that New Hampshire drivers couldn't be forced to display the state motto, "Live Free or Die," on their license plates. More recently, this has meant that public universities can't force professors to profess a belief in microaggressions.[1] Forcing public employees to agree with diversity statements, join the climate fight, or affirm transgender rights would all also be of dubious constitutional accord.

A corollary of this principle is that the government cannot force citizens to pay for speech they disagree with. The Supreme Court has held that California cannot force lawyers to pay for a state bar's expression of ideological beliefs (*Keller v. State Bar of California*, 1990) and that Illinois cannot force teachers to pay for the union's exposition of political views (*Janus v. American Federation of State, County, and Municipal Employees Council*, 2018). So why can a state force public workers to pay for a pension fund's social advocacy? Answer: it can't. The "compelled subsidization of speech" doctrine prevents the state from doing so.

"To compel a man to furnish contributions of money for the propagation of opinions which he disbelieves and abhors, is sinful and tyrannical," Thomas Jefferson wrote nearly 250 years ago. As the *Janus* decision more recently explained, "Forcing free and independent individuals to endorse ideas they find objectionable is always demeaning." If it's illegal to force public teachers and lawyers to financially subsidize the advancement of political ideas they find objectionable, it's illegal to force firefighters, transit workers, and other pension fund members to do so, too.

Sweeney v. Illinois Municipal Retirement Fund (2019) addressed the pension fund elephant in the post-*Janus* room. Workers sued their pension fund, the Illinois Municipal Retirement Fund (IMRF), for investing in the stock market, because publicly traded companies sometimes took political positions with which the workers disagreed. The workers lost. But the district court explained that the reason they had lost was because the "speech" that the workers objected to was too "attenuated" from their contributions: "all IMRF does is purchase stock in publicly held private companies." Critically, the pension fund's investment strategy had been "designed to provide benefits to municipal workers" rather than to advance partisan goals. But the court warned that its ruling would be different had that plaintiffs alleged that "defendants' investment strategy [was] not viewpoint neutral."

Today the behaviors of many pension fund managers are decidedly viewpoint infused. In 2018, the head of Connecticut's pension fund told gun manufacturers in its investment portfolio to "aggressively . . . [adopt] the Sandy Hook Principles—a set of measures aimed at curbing gun violence."[2] In 2019, the New York State Common Retirement Fund (NYSCRF) waged a crusade against YouTube, complaining that it did not remove hate speech or misogynistic content quickly enough.[3] In 2021, CalPERS railed against Berkshire Hathaway for failing to adopt Climate Action 100+'s emission reduction targets.[4] In 2022, Massachusetts' state pension fund created an ESG committee to "leverage the Fund to be a force that promotes worker safety, fosters diversity, [and] fights against climate change."[5] Not to be outdone, New York City's comptroller used funds from the city's five largest pensions to launch a campaign against Amazon, replete with its own #DeliverAccountability hashtag, demanding that the company focus more on diversity, equity, and inclusion, among other things.[6]

The constitutional problem is even more pronounced in red states, where such behaviors depart more sharply from the views of plan participants. A Texas pension fund, for example, touts its use of ESG factors in its investment decisions, including "Prioritizing a 'green' Covid-19 recovery" and fighting "systemic racism."[7] Florida likewise told portfolio companies to focus on "diversity in gender [and] race" and "environmental solutions."[8] These statements go beyond mere window dressing. In 2022, the Employees Retirement System of Texas voted to limit fossil fuel financing at Bank of America, Citigroup, Goldman Sachs, and Wells Fargo.[9] In 2021, Florida's pension fund voted for racial equity audits at Amazon, Bank of America, Goldman Sachs, and JPMorgan Chase—all over the objections of those companies' respective boards. Florida also voted to replace four ExxonMobil board members with climate change activists; even BlackRock voted for only three.

Red states also risk constitutional scrutiny if they invest to support conservative values. There is little evidence that this has happened so far, but it's not out of the realm of possibility. For example, in late 2022, a new, conservative-themed God Bless America ETF launched, promising to invest in companies "with a track record of creating American jobs" and excluding companies that "have emphasized politically left and/or liberal political activism."[10] There are also now investment products that promote "biblical values" (New York Stock Exchange: BIBL) and "Republican political beliefs" (New York Stock Exchange: MAGA). That's a fine way for individuals to invest, but if a conservative-leaning pension fund manager were to decide to use public workers' money to support these views, the First Amendment might cry foul.

Fund managers sometimes claim that they pursue social causes only for financial gain. The New York State Common Retirement Fund (NYSCRF), for example, claims that it considers ESG only to "enhance and protect the Fund's long-term value."[11] Its behavior suggests otherwise. In 2022, it supported a proposal made by the Benedictine Sisters of Mount St. Scholastica asking Denny's to increase wages for tipped employees to reduce poverty, despite the fact that the Denny's board opposed it.[12] Similarly, it supported a Sierra Club proposal asking Morgan Stanley to stop financing fossil fuel projects to achieve net zero, even though its passage would have cost the company its ability to do business with Texas.[13] In this case, both the advocate (Sierra Club) and the opponent (Morgan Stanley) apparently agreed that the proposal advanced a noncommercial purpose. It strains credulity to believe that the NYSCRF voted for it based on financial considerations alone.

Some people may argue that politicized proxy voting is action, not speech, because votes can be cast at shareholder meetings with little to no actual speaking involved. They may therefore argue that the First Amendment's compelled speech protections do not apply. I offer two responses to this critique. First, in practice, pension fund managers do not limit their political activities to depositing a ballot in the corporate ballot box. They shame companies on their websites.[14] They write open letters to businesses.[15] They tweet encouragement to other shareholders to sway their votes.[16] These are all examples of "speech" in the truest form.

Second, the First Amendment protects not just "speech" but "expressive conduct." That's why the Supreme Court held, in *Tinker v. Des Moines Independent Community School District* (1969), that public school students have the right to wear black armbands to protest the Vietnam War and, in *Texas v. Johnson* (1989), that protesters have the right to burn the American flag. Pension fund managers routinely claim their votes are designed to express a specific view, regardless of whether checking a box on a proxy form requires uttering any phrases or writing any words. Connecticut's treasurer, for example, explained that he opposed compensation packages for executives at pharmaceutical companies that contributed to the opioid crisis in part because he wanted to hold those executives accountable for the "significant pain and suffering" the opioid crisis caused.[17] New York City's comptroller similarly explained that the city's pension fund had voted against a board member at JPMorgan Chase to "send a message that we will not allow fossil fuel's old guard [to] dictate our future."[18] When votes are designed to send a message, rather than maximize shareholder value, the First Amendment applies.

Other analysts, such as the law professors Eugene Volokh and William

Baude, have argued that being forced to pay for speech is not speech; it's payment.[19] But the Supreme Court has said otherwise. Not just in *Janus*— in which the Supreme Court held that payments to a union violated the compelled speech doctrine—but in cases such as *Buckley v. Valeo* (1976) and *Citizens United v. FEC* (2010), in which the Supreme Court recognized that because money facilitates speech, restrictions on spending money to speak restrict speech. And sometimes the compelled payment can make all the difference. In one case, for instance, a court found that the state could force abortion clinics to distribute pro-life literature to their clients but that forcing the abortion clinic to *pay* for the literature was a constitutional bridge too far.[20]

It's true that our tax dollars can be used to support public broadcasting and that universities can charge students activity fees even when they host controversial speakers.[21] The Supreme Court held in *Southworth v. Board of Regents* (2000) that such funds could be used to support a forum for "facilitating the free and open exchange of ideas." But pension funds that use their dollars to vote for political agendas aren't hosting a debate; they're taking sides in the debate.

Courts have similarly held that when the government speaks in its own voice, it is free to say almost anything; that's why the Centers for Disease Control and Prevention (CDC) can recommend that Americans get vaccinated, for example. But this is not so when a small subset of Americans is forced to contribute to an organization that purports to speak on their behalf. That was why *Keller* found a First Amendment violation even though the speaker, the state bar, was a government agency. That agency, like pension funds, exists to represent its members, so its speech counts as the speech of the members themselves; if California cannot legally force every firefighter it employs to write a letter to Berkshire Hathaway imploring it to cut greenhouse gas emissions, it cannot force every firefighter to pay into CalPERS to write the same on their behalf.

This type of co-opting of public servants' voices goes to the heart of the First Amendment, because the speech is so political. Under the legal framework established under the First Amendment, there are different tiers of protection given to different kinds of speech. Commercial speech typically enjoys the lowest amount of protection; that's why the government can compel cigarette manufacturers to put health warnings on their packages, even though it is a form of compelled speech. It's also why, at least in the view of certain legal scholars, the Supreme Court has allowed the government to force cattle ranchers and farmers to fund advertisements they disagreed with.[22] Political speech is on the other end of the spectrum. The Supreme Court has explained, "advocacy of a politically controversial viewpoint is the essence of First Amendment protection."[23] Our democracy depends on it. Political speech therefore gets the most First Amendment protection. Any infringements on political speech are thus "subject to strict scrutiny"; at times, the Supreme Court has suggested that there can be no restrictions on political speech at all.[24] And pension fund advocacy—from racial equity audits to aligning lobbying with the Paris Accords to defunding political opponents—is openly political.

First Amendment jurisprudence suggests that the compelled speech problem may be cured in various ways. Fund managers could allow employees to opt out of paying for political speech, similar to the way a Massachusetts baker who objects to joining the United Food and Commercial Workers International Union (UFCW) can be charged only 88 percent of full union dues, because the other 12 percent is earmarked for political action.[25] Alternatively, a pension fund can refund dissenters after the fact, just as the Oregon State Bar refunded $1.15 to each member who objected to its "Statement on White Nationalism and Normalization of Violence."[26]

Such solutions aren't easy to implement. The administrative burdens would be enormous—prohibitive, even. A pension fund manager would have to notify every pension fund participant and beneficiary of every politically motivated ESG statement he intends to make, determine how much that statement would cost the beneficiaries (in terms of both hard costs, such as resources devoted to making the statement, and conse- quential costs, such as the negative impact on return), and then compen- sate each pensioner who dissents individually. There would have to be nine fingers manning the administrative buttons to keep just one on the Twitter button. That's not easy to do, even if it were politically palatable.

Which, to be clear, it isn't. State pension funds haven't even tried to disaggregate political speech from their investment pools. And there's a clear reason why: they love being able to throw around the weight of their millions of members and billions of dollars in capital and profess to speak with one voice. They *want* to represent the school nurses, the sanitation workers, and the little old ladies who help kids cross the street to get to school, to co-opt their voices and their reputations, to send a stronger message to corporate America to fall into line with a politician's political views. New York City's Brad Lander, for example, recently spoke at a webinar denouncing "abusive" practices at Amazon. How did he start? By claiming "I'm sitting here representing teachers and firefighters and school crossing guards and the whole set of hundreds of thousands of New York City workers."[27] That gave him credibility. It's a compelled speech problem of the highest order.

Another idea, proposed by University of Richmond assistant law professor Da Lin, is to make the pension system voluntary, so that pen- sion fund managers can engage in political grandstanding without forc- ing dissenters to contribute.[28] But voluntary or not, a pension is still a benefit that public employers would offer to employees. And requiring public employees to give up their constitutional rights to receive that benefit—particularly one that has historically been part of their ordinary compensation—would likely present constitutional problems of its own. The Constitution is not so easily circumvented.

More broadly, all of the potential constitutional "solutions" run head- long into violations of pension fund managers' fiduciary duties, as fund managers would essentially be admitting that they are investing for polit- ical, rather than financial, reasons. But the First Amendment problem is much larger than the fiduciary duty problem—and more consequential. A fiduciary duty problem, after all, can be resolved by passing new laws. California's constitution, for example, expressly allows its state legislature to "prohibit certain investments by a retirement board where it is in the public interest,"[29] even when such prohibition may cause financial harm. And the California legislature has exercised this power, passing statutes prohibiting the pension funds from investing in Sudanese companies that have been complicit in the Darfur genocide[30] and Iranian companies complicit in terrorism.[31] In more recent years, the legislature has introduced bills requiring divestment from fossil fuel companies and Russian companies following Russia's invasion of Ukraine. There's no constitutional right to have your investments managed with your best financial interest in mind, as prudent and well founded as the laws that mandate it may be. But allowing the government to force citizens to subsidize beliefs with which they disagree is exactly the kind of compelled speech violation that Jefferson warned against 250 years ago. And the only way to change that is by constitutional amendment—an outcome that is as unlikely as it is unwise.

The Tyranny of Compelled Association

There's another significant—and often overlooked—constitutional protection on which ESG elephants are trampling: freedom of association. Unlike freedom of speech, religion, press, and assembly, freedom of association isn't explicitly listed in the text of the First Amendment. But the Supreme Court has said it's there. The Court first recognized this right in the 1958 case *National Association for the Advancement of Colored People v. Alabama*, in which it held that members of a civil rights group had the right to associate with one another free from state interference. Alabama wanted the NAACP to produce a list of names and addresses of all of its members; the NAACP refused. The Supreme Court wasn't about to aid and abet Alabama's shenanigans, so it recognized a new right, sometimes called the right of expressive association. In his majority opinion, Justice John Marshall Harlan II wrote, "It is beyond debate that freedom to engage in association for the advancement of beliefs and ideas is an inseparable aspect of the 'liberty'" assured by the Constitution. And so freedom of association was born.

Just as freedom of speech includes freedom from compelled speech and freedom of religion includes freedom from compelled religion, the right of free association includes the right to be free from compelled association. That's why the Supreme Court held, in *Boy Scouts of America v. Dale* (2000), that the Boy Scouts have a constitutional right to exclude gay men as scoutmasters and, in *Hurley v. Irish-American Gay, Lesbian, and Bisexual Group of Boston, Inc.* (1995), why a Boston veterans group organizing a Saint Patrick's Day parade had a constitutional right to exclude an LGBTQ group (and the Ku Klux Klan) from marching in its parade. These groups exist for an expressive purpose, to send a message, and requiring them to accept members who do not align with their views would dilute that expressive purpose. Such groups are allowed to be choosy.

The right to be free from compelled association prevents the government from forcing individuals to join groups. That means that the government cannot force an employee to join a group, such as a pension fund organization, that stands for something with which the individual disagrees. This right is related to the right to be free from compelled subsidization of speech, but it's distinct. That's because even if the government refunds all of the money going to political causes or even makes membership free, it still can't force individuals to associate with a group that espouses social or political views with which they disagree.

Extreme examples may help to highlight the point. The Biden administration could not, for example, make every government employee enroll as a member of Planned Parenthood as a condition of employment. So, too, the Trump administration could not make every civil servant join the National Rifle Association. Even if the organizations were on board with such a plan, it would infringe on employees' rights as American citizens. It's true that it would be worse if the government said that it was going to enforce a new, mandatory payroll deduction from every employee's paycheck for membership dues—which is essentially what pension funds do. But even if the membership fees were waived, the constitutional infringement of the right to be free from compelled association would remain.

Most Americans bristle at these extreme examples. As it turns out, though, they may not be so extreme. Take the Oregon State Bar example mentioned above in which the state bar association capitulated after members complained about its "Statement on White Nationalism and Normalization of Violence," and gave dissenters a $1.15 refund. The court found that there was no compelled speech violation, because the refund meant that the dissenting lawyers weren't forced to pay for the speech. But the Court nonetheless allowed the compelled association claim to proceed, because the state cannot force individuals to be members of a bar association that espouses views they disagree with, even if the bar doesn't use their money to do so.

The same was true of the State Bar of Texas.[32] The association did not limit its activities to those germane to its mission of regulating the legal profession but also did things such as lobby the Texas legislature to change the definition of marriage and create civil unions. Given those activities, a Texas appellate court held that it was unconstitutional for the state to force lawyers to join the bar association, regardless of whether dissenting members funded those lobbying activities or not.

The right to be free from compelled association is also why joining a public sector union is optional. In *Janus*, for example, the Supreme Court explained that individuals have a "right to eschew association for expressive purposes." And because being a member of a union is inherently political, public sector workers have a constitutional right to opt out.

Despite this rule, many public sector pension funds are mandatory— not just in financial terms but in the fact that every public worker is required to be a member. For example, there is "mandatory membership" in the New York State Teachers' Retirement System for every full-time public school teacher in New York.[33] Likewise for police officers, at least after they've served a minimum amount of time.[34] These employees are forced to join as a condition of their employment contract and have no way to opt out.

Such a requirement may pass constitutional muster when membership just means being part of a politically neutral financial system that is paying benefits to workers, just as a public sector employer might automatically enroll you as an Aetna "member" for medical insurance purposes or require you to be a "member" of a participating bank to enroll in direct deposit services. But when a public pension fund decides to embark on a political mission that is not germane to its core mission of providing financial benefits for retirees, forced membership presents very different concerns.

The politicized nature of these missions is beyond serious dispute. New York City Pension Funds, for example, filed forty-eight different shareholder proposals in 2021. It is so active and so brazen that it issues an annual "postseason report" of "shareowner initiatives" it has supported. The document reads like a Democratic Party primary debate cheat sheet. There's a section with the relatively innocuous title "Diversity, Equity, and Inclusion" whose first sentence reads "High-profile killings of Black men and women in 2020 highlighted the grave consequences of systemic racism in society." It goes on to explain that "NYCRS [New York City Retirement Systems] launched a national campaign calling on 67 companies to match their public statements with concrete actions" to fix the problem. A section entitled "Climate Change" touts the way the fund was "driving GHG reductions forward at Ford" and convinced GM to "[curb] its emissions." There is a section on the way NYCRS pressured Chipotle to end its mandatory arbitration clauses because such clauses tend to "favor companies and discourage employee claims"—a problem, of course, only if you are not on the side of the company. There is even a section on the way NYCRS fought for farmworkers at Wendy's, who apparently had suffered "the dire consequences of COVID-19 and of systemic racism on farmworkers of color."[35]

A teacher, firefighter, or police officer who has a different view of whether systemic racism exists, and against which groups, has no way to opt out of the pension fund he or she has been forced to join. Indeed, in some retirement systems, even quitting your job will not allow you to terminate your membership in the retirement system that administers the pension fund.[36] In this dystopian marriage, it really is "till death do you part."

The potential constitutional remedies here are much more limited, since refunding money or allocating funds won't solve the problem. But the solutions are also straightforward: pension fund managers must stay out of politics altogether and focus on investing exclusively for pecuniary purposes. This approach solves not only the compelled association problem but the compelled speech and fiduciary breach problems. That may be bad news for the nuns and rabbis who have been counting on public sector pension funds to support their religiously motivated social proposals, but it is good news for pension fund members who rely on this income for financial security in retirement—and even better news for the Constitution, which rejoices at the decoupling of the political from the financial, of the social from the corporate, of the Church from the state.

If ESG was the product of an arranged marriage brokered by Wall Street and social justice activists, the Constitution may end up being the party arranging the divorce.

Chapter 8

THE POWER OF THE PRESIDENTIAL PEN

t's no surprise that liberal politicians have been some of ESG's strongest proponents. ESG-friendly politicians often co-opt pension fund money for political ends. However, that's not the only power they have. Elected officials can also wield influence through executive orders, agency directives, and letter writing to pave the way for ESG asset managers to access the back door of corporate America and sometimes even shove those managers through.

That's exactly what President Joseph R. Biden, Jr., has done. The first thing he did when he took office was pick up his executive order pen. He used it to direct his federal agencies to revisit their rules with an eye toward making them more ESG friendly. There was no need for messy bipartisanship, congressional compromises, or involving the legislative branch at all. Why bother with the tedious, constitutionally approved method of making new laws when there is an army of federal bureaucrats at your disposal?

On day one of his presidency, he lamented "the unbearable human costs of systemic racism" and mandated an "ambitious whole-of-government equity agenda." To that end, he instructed every federal agency to "assess whether, and to what extent, its programs and policies perpetuate systemic barriers to opportunities and benefits for people of color," among other things. He gave the agencies two hundred days to do so and report back.[1]

The same day, he rejoined the Paris Agreement.[2] He simultaneously issued another order, directing that all federal agencies "immediately commence work to confront the climate crisis." This time, the agencies had thirty days to respond. Within a week, he issued yet another order, promising "bold, progressive action that combines the full capacity of the Federal Government with efforts from every corner of our Nation, every level of government, and every sector of our economy."[3] He charged every federal agency with appointing an "Agency Chief Sustainability Officer" and announced that the United States would be "promoting the flow of capital toward climate-aligned investments and away from high-carbon investments."[4] By May, his executive orders became even more specific, focusing federal climate efforts on the financial sector in particular.[5] Through strokes of the executive pen, a Green New Deal that would never be approved by Congress would be pushed on corporate America through Wall Street, guided by the heavy hand of federal agencies at every turn.

Following the orders of the new climate commander in chief, the government joined the ESG battle. For the most part, federal agencies were pleased to be conscripted into service.

Heigh-Ho, Heigh-Ho, It's Off to Woke We Go

The Department of Labor was one of the first agencies to respond. At the time President Biden took office, the department had regulations that made it harder for retirement fund managers to do ESG investing. The existing Trump-era rule memorialized the DOL's longstanding requirement that private pension fund managers consider only pecuniary factors when making investment, engagement, and proxy voting decisions.[6] Less than two months after President Biden took office, the department announced that it would not enforce the rule. As a department representative explained at the time, the DOL sought to replace the existing financially focused rules with ones that "better recognize the important role that environmental, social and governance integration can play in the evaluation and management of plan investments."[7]

And replace the rules it did. In October 2021, the Biden administration proposed a new regulation that repealed the Trump-era rules and replaced them with one that encouraged ESG investing with retirement and pension fund money.[8] The proposed rule pushed retirement fund managers to consider ESG factors such as "climate change" and "collateral benefits other than investment returns" when investing employees' money. Indeed, it said that consideration of ESG factors was "often require[d]."[9] The enacted version was slightly less radical; it says that investment managers "may" consider ESG factors, rather than requiring them.[10] The overall message is still pro-ESG. It still represented a departure from the strict financial focus of the Trump-era rules.

The Department of Labor, of course, is not supposed to be in the business of making environmental policy; it's supposed to be protecting workers—their working conditions, their safety, their wages, and, in this instance, their retirement funds. The very reason Congress had asked the Department of Labor to oversee pension and retirement accounts was to ensure that the funds would have as much money as possible—not just because American workers are depending on it but because taxpayers will end up on the short end if the funds fall short. The statute that gives the Department of Labor the power to regulate private retirement funds, the Employee Retirement Income Security Act (ERISA) of 1974, was passed because when the carmaker Studebaker had gone belly up in the 1960s, its pension had gone bust.[11] Assembly-line workers who had spent forty years at the company ended up penniless in retirement. Congress passed ERISA to create federal insurance for pension funds so that workers wouldn't lose out. That means that if a company's pensions are underfunded or a company goes bankrupt, taxpayers will make up the shortfall. But in return, companies providing retirement benefits are required to fund their pensions and invest the assets "solely in the interest of the participants and beneficiaries."[12] Allowing plan managers to invest for "collateral benefits" doesn't just run afoul of this statutory language; it runs counter to the justification for allowing the Department of Labor to regulate pension funds in the first place.

That's not just my opinion, but the opinion of twenty-five state attorneys general. In January 2023, a coalition of twenty-five states and a handful of private businesses sued the Department of Labor.[13] They alleged that the rule change allows large asset managers to "leverag[e] ERISA plans assets for nonpecuniary ESG purposes," which violates ERISA and exceeds the department's authority. In this case, the rule change isn't just bad, but likely illegal. Only time will tell if the Texas court decides to use the Wite-Out on the presidential pen.

The Securities and "Environmental" Commission

The Securities and Exchange Commission (SEC) has been marching to the Biden administration's ESG drum, proposing a bevy of new rules on climate and ESG issues. These rules, though couched largely in terms of "disclosures," will not only create new burdens on corporate America but direct the flow of money to particular favored causes. The SEC has moved from being an agency that oversees investors and the companies they invest in to taking the wheel on how companies should behave and investors should invest.

Take its proposed climate disclosure rule. The proposal—a staggering 534 pages long—would require publicly traded companies to disclose information on greenhouse gas emissions and risks related to climate change.[14] Companies now have to do financial accounting; soon they will have to do climate accounting, too. The *Wall Street Journal* called it "one of the Biden Administration's potentially most significant environmental actions to date."[15]

There's a lot in there. Every company must disclose its own GHG emissions and that of the energy it consumes. Many companies would also have to disclose the emissions of every supplier, vendor, employee, and worker across its "value chain," even if the company does not believe that such emissions are financially material. More specifically, the proposed rule would require any company that has pledged net zero goals to disclose its Scope 3 emissions and report on them in SEC filings such as its annual report.

It's the same clever two-step we've seen over and again: Step one, as we've seen, is for activist groups to pressure public companies to make high-level commitments to reducing their carbon footprint, reaching net zero twenty-five years from now, setting GHG targets, and so on. Step two is for the government to say, "Now that you, public company, have 'voluntarily' committed yourself to net zero, you need to make good on that promise by issuing detailed statements on every source of emissions connected in any way to your business." When companies were making those pledges, they had no idea they were signing up for this level of scrutiny or potential liability. As the lone dissenting SEC commissioner, Hester Peirce, explained, companies will be in for a "rude awakening" once they learn that "they are going to be playing an entirely different game, at far higher stakes."[16]

The rule also requires companies to disclose whether climate change may affect more than 1 percent of any line item, such as revenue or debt, and explain the impact.[17] Such requirements are not just burdensome but impossible to determine. Doing so requires speculation piled on top of speculation to guess what the climate trajectory will be, what the resulting regulatory landscape will look like in the United States and abroad, how third-party customers and suppliers are likely to react to such changes, and what the impact on any individual line item to a company's business might hypothetically be. Is 1 percent of our customers in coastal areas, and might they cut back on their discretionary spending if the cost of flood insurance goes up? Will a property management company be forced to increase its costs by 1 percent for more frequent lawn mowing to help prevent wildfires? Will the EPA pass a regulation that increases fuel costs, therefore increasing my delivery costs? The resulting disclosures will have the appearance of being reliable, quantitative, data-driven figures but will really be little more than guesswork.

That's not the only regulation the SEC has been working on. It also proposed a rule requiring mutual funds to categorize their proxy votes into buckets including environmental justice; diversity, equity and inclusion; gender pay gap; and "other social matters."[18] The SEC claimed that the new categories were meant to help investors, but, as Commissioner Peirce explained, "The real interest in this kind of detailed voting information seems to come from activists and the ever-expanding population of 'stakeholders,' for whom proxy voting seems to be the fund's highest purpose."[19] Commissioner Peirce noted that until 2003, proxy voting was by secret ballot; mutual funds did not have to disclose how they voted. Though there are pros and cons to this approach, at the time the original disclosure rule was pending, the heads of the two largest asset managers, Fidelity and Vanguard, jointly penned a *Wall Street Journal* piece raising at least one legitimate concern:

> Requiring mutual-fund managers to disclose their votes on corporate proxies would politicize proxy voting. In case after case, it would open mutual-fund voting decisions to thinly veiled intimidation from activist groups whose agendas may have nothing to do with maximizing our clients' returns.[20]

Commissioner Peirce called this prediction "prescient," explaining that since the original disclosure rule was enacted, "activists of every stripe can use the fact that funds have to publish their votes to increase their leverage through intimidation and negative publicity."[21] She warned that additional disclosures would serve only to give these activists more ammunition to further politicize the corporate ballot box. The SEC enacted the rule anyway.[22] President Biden is no doubt pleased.

In 2022, the SEC also proposed a pair of new rules imposing new disclosure and naming requirements for ESG funds.[23] The rules are meant to combat greenwashing and make sure that funds that are capitalizing on the coveted ESG marketing moniker are doing enough to push ESG goals. They require any sustainable fund to disclose the GHG emissions of its portfolio and any impact fund to detail its progress toward achieving its goals. The rules also contain what Commissioner Peirce termed the "nag rule," requiring funds that want to use the ESG label but do not screen their investments to engage in a sufficient amount of "nagging" of corporate America; such funds would be required to advocate for "one or more specific ESG goals to be accomplished over a given time period," ensure that the goals are "measurable," and initiate an "ongoing dialogue with the issuer regarding this goal."[24]

The SEC has justified this new wave of pro-ESG regulations by claiming that it is merely responding to investor demand.[25] But it's not; it's driving behavior. Take the climate disclosure rules, for example. Businesses will be forced to "disclose" board oversight of climate-related risks, including identifying specific board members or committees responsible for overseeing climate issues, detailing board members' expertise, describing the process and frequency of discussions about climate risk, explaining whether it considers climate issues as part of its business strategy, and on and on. There are similar "disclosure" requirements for management. As Commissioner Peirce explained, these requirements "almost certainly will affect the substance of what companies do" and shift companies' focus away from their business and toward climate-related goals.[26] That's the point.

The same is true of the rules requiring asset managers to categorize votes by ESG issue, make fund-level GHG disclosures, and make detailed disclosures about corporate engagements. No fund will want to end up on the "wrong" side of history and expose itself to activists, so it will vote in favor of ESG proposals knowing that its vote will be disclosed. No ESG fund will want to check the "no" box when answering whether it has a specific engagement strategy, so it will create one. According to Commissioner Peirce, it's all part of a "troubling trend of not-so-subtle coercion through disclosure mandates."[27]

The SEC has also promoted ESG in more informal ways. Shortly after President Biden took office, it launched an enforcement task force "focused on climate and ESG issues."[28] It also issued a bulletin for investors, highlighting the popularity of ESG funds and offering advice on how to invest in them.[29] And it issued a legal bulletin making it easier for activist shareholders to get proposals onto the ballot: the existing rules did not allow shareholders to propose resolutions related to ordinary business operations; the new one allows shareholders to do so if the proposal focuses on a "significant social policy."[30] All of these efforts have opened the floodgates for ESG activists and ESG-aligned asset managers to accrue funds and then use them to impose their worldview on corporate America.

This activism has taken a toll on the agency. If it sounds like a lot of rule making, it's because it is. As of October 2022, the SEC had more than fifty proposed rules on its agenda.[31] It proposed twenty-nine new rules in 2022 alone, more than twice the previous year and more than it had in any of the previous five years.[32] As a result, an SEC Office of the Inspector General report warned that SEC staff were having trouble keeping up with the breakneck pace and raised concerns about their ability to do other "mission-related work," such as protecting investors from fraud, "because of the increase in the SEC's rulemaking activities."[33] The SEC, it turns out, was so focused on climate change rules and ESG regulations that it didn't notice SBF's multibillion-dollar crypto fraud happening right under its nose.[34]

The problem is not just with the SEC. Every government agency is now tasked with fighting climate change and systemic racism as part of its agency mission statement, just as every corporation in America is tasked with amending its corporate charter to do the same. The result is similar: just as the calls for all corporations to advance ESG goals have resulted in a kind of bland corporate sameness where every corporation issues the same PR statement every time a social injustice occurs, every federal agency must now march uniformly toward net zero and social justice goals. Whereas the Department of Veterans Affairs was once tasked with "car[ing] for those 'who shall have borne the battle,'" it must now care for veterans *and* fight climate change *and* support women-owned businesses.[35] Whereas the US Patent Office once awarded patents to "foster innovation, competitiveness, and economic growth," it must now work to foster innovation *and* advance equity *and* fight climate change.[36]

By requiring every agency to be a mini-EPA, the Biden administration has not only undermined the EPA itself but has diluted all of the other agency's missions and prevented it from carrying out the missions Congress created it to do. "We Are Not the Securities and Environment Commission," Commissioner Peirce titled one of her recent remarks, "At Least Not Yet."[37]

He Who Regulates the Gold Makes the Rules

There's another little-known federal agency that is playing a big role in allowing ESG to go unchecked: the Office of the Comptroller of the Currency (OCC). The agency is tucked inside the Department of the Treasury and is tasked with regulating US banks.[38] Per the Dodd-Frank Wall Street Reform and Consumer Protection Act of 2010, the OCC's mission is, among other things, to ensure "fair access to financial services."[39] Like many other laws, it lets the agency concerned make specific rules and take enforcement actions to carry out its mission.

In the waning days of the Trump administration, the OCC did just that. The agency passed a rule preventing banks from refusing to serve entire categories of customers they found politically or morally unsavory.[40] It said that "fair access" means that banks have to evaluate customers individually, not make blanket refusals to serve, say, coal-mining companies, gun manufacturers, or whatever the socially unfashionable cause du jour may be.[41]

It was meant to end what the Electronic Frontier Foundation has called "financial censorship," which is the ability of behemoth banks to use their financial power to impose their social mores on US businesses.[42] The regulation, it should be noted, applied only to banks with $100 billion or more in assets. These are the banks with major power in financial markets. As ESG proponents know, access to banking services from major financial institutions is a critical part of any business—if a business can't open a bank account, process credit card payments, or get lines of credit, it can't exist. Last winter, the Girl Scout who knocked on my door to sell cookies told me I could pay via app; we're long past the days when an entrepreneur or small business can survive using cash alone. Cutting off banking services is a death blow, and one that can be delivered without political or market accountability.

Indeed, to the extent that there is accountability, it is pressuring banks to act in the other direction—to deny fair access to banking services through politicized banking policies. That's because banks are rewarded for politically biased lending, since refusing to do business with "unethical" companies raises their own ESG scores, regardless of whether the customer would have been profitable for the bank and its shareholders or not.

This was not a hypothetical concern. As the rule makers noted, both for-profit and nonprofit activists had been pressuring banks to cut off disfavored businesses on both sides of the political divide. Abortion clinic operators, adult entertainers, and condom-manufacturing start-ups, for instance, had reportedly been refused banking services due to the nature of their businesses.[43] On the other side, ESG activists pressured banks to debank rifle makers, private prison operators, large agricultural businesses, and, of course, the US fossil fuel industry. In many instances, the banks complied.

The rule makers were particularly concerned because the banks didn't just cut off lending—which could theoretically be justified as a concern about mitigating financial "risk"—but *all* banking services, including advisory services. The goal was to punish certain businesses, to deprive them of the banking services their businesses needed. Sometimes, at least in the energy industry, a bank would make an exception—but only if the customer convinced it that it would control carbon emissions sufficiently or was located in a jurisdiction committed to international climate agreements. The OCC was having none of it.

> Climate change is a real risk, but so is the risk of foreign wars caused in part by US energy dependence and the risk of blackouts caused by energy shortages. Furthermore, balancing these risks is the purview of Congress and Federal energy and environmental regulators. It is one thing for a bank not to lend to oil companies because it lacks the expertise to value or manage the associated collateral rights; it is another for a bank to make that decision because it believes the United States should abide by the standards set in an international climate treaty. Organizations involved in politically controversial but lawful businesses—whether family planning organizations, energy companies, or otherwise—are entitled to fair access to financial services under the law.[44]

The drafters also expressed concern that once banks were allowed to engage in political discrimination, the temptation for self-interested politicians to push them to do so would prove too great. They pointed to the now-discredited 2013 "Operation Choke Point," through which the Department of Justice had pressured banks to close the accounts of disfavored businesses—firearms dealers, payday lenders, telemarketers—on a sweeping, industrywide basis, without any proof of individual wrongdoing.[45] It's much easier to ask big banks to drop customers as a "favor" to the DOJ, after all, than it is to prosecute individual cases of alleged fraud. And so long as the private sector is acting "voluntarily," government can conscript it into doing its dirty work without having to worry about tedious notions such as due process, constitutional rights, or even letting customers know the real reason their account was closed. Eventually, the DOJ shut the operation down, acknowledging that it had been "a misguided initiative."[46] But so long as banks remained free to discriminate, the temptation for politicians to use banks as a political sledgehammer remained. The new rule put an end to that possibility.

But the new rule did so by taking the sledgehammer away from everybody—not just politicians, but ESG activists, too. They were outraged. Leveraging the enormous power of banks—through corporate engagements, shareholder proposals, and organizations such as the Net-Zero Banking Alliance—was critical to their strategy of directing the flow of capital toward their social goals. The public submitted thirty-five thousand comments on the rule; more than thirty-two thousand of them were negative. The OCC enacted it anyway.

But after President Biden's executive orders, that all changed. Less than two weeks after Biden was sworn into office, the OCC reversed course. It announced that it had "paused" the rule, allegedly to "allow the next confirmed Comptroller of the Currency to review the final rule and the public comments the OCC received, as part of an orderly transition."[47] The agency cautioned banks that its toothless "supervisory guidance" requiring fair access to banking services remained in effect, but many in the banking industry understood the decision as an indication that the rule would be reversed.[48] Since then, the OCC has released new guidance that not only allows but encourages banks to "consider climate-related financial risks as part of the underwriting and ongoing monitoring of portfolios."[49] That's bank regulator speak for "charge higher interest rates to businesses that aren't environmentally friendly enough."

And so ESG activists have continued to pressure big banks to censor and discriminate, and censor and discriminate they have. The impact has been felt. In 2021, for example, the website OnlyFans announced that it would start banning sexually explicit content in response to pressure from "banking partners" and "payout processors," only to reverse the decision days later following a massive backlash.[50] (As an aside, given the ESG movement's generally leftist bent, you'd be forgiven for thinking that porn companies would not be at the top of the ESG movement's naughty list. But that belief would be wrong. "Porn Is Worse than Pollution in Ethical Investing Portfolios," according to a Bloomberg report.[51] ESG funds sometimes even screen out abortion providers. There really is no standard definition of what's in and what's out, even within the world of ESG.[52])

Of course, the bank censorship hasn't been limited to the adult industry. In September 2022, the *Wall Street Journal* reported that Black Rifle Coffee Company had been prevented from opening an account at Chase because of its controversial pro-veteran, pro–Second Amendment messaging and that several major banks had refused to help it arrange an initial public offering—despite its $233 million in annual revenue.[53] The following month, PayPal made headlines after it updated its terms of service to prohibit transactions that involved the "sending, posting, or publication of any messages, content, or materials" that PayPal, at its sole discretion, finds objectionable.[54] The penalty was a $2,500 fine, which PayPal could take directly from users' accounts. After public backlash, it backtracked on the fine when it came to "misinformation" but stood by its policy of fining users for speech it deems intolerant.[55] And there's nothing stopping PayPal, Wells Fargo, or Bank of America from slipping such language back into its fine print once the spotlight dims.

So through the OCC's somewhat obscure rule-making and guidance-issuing process, the Biden administration has handed ESG activists their sledgehammer back. Banks, like asset managers, are simply one more tool that politicians can manipulate to further political agendas that Congress would never enact. "He who has the gold makes the rules," I wrote in *Woke, Inc.* That might have been an oversimplification; the banks have the gold, but it's the OCC that writes the rules. And when it decides not to enforce them—or, worse, to coerce the banks into doing their political bidding—the big banks truly wield the power to enact the social policies that all of us must follow.

He Who Can Deny Insurance Coverage Makes the Rules

Banking, of course, is just one aspect of running a business. Another is insurance. That's also highly regulated—there's a Federal Insurance Office (FIO)—so the government already has its fingerprints all over it. The Biden administration took note. As with banking, the administration has enlisted the Federal Insurance Office to push insurance companies to discriminate against politically disfavored industries. The difference is that the FIO has been even more open about its ambitions.

When it came to pulling the plug on the OCC's fair access rules, the Biden administration didn't expressly say that it wanted banks to discriminate against coal companies, private prisons, or conservative coffee chains. It didn't have to. It simply paused the rule that would have prevented it. Even its climate-specific guidance document—the one that tells banks to charge more to fossil fuel producers—is couched largely in terms of "financial risk" and justifies its policies in terms of the risk that climate change poses to banks, rather than the other way around.

The FIO, by contrast, has been bolder. Shortly after President Biden took office, he instructed the FIO to "assess climate-related issues." And assess it did. A few months later, the FIO announced its "initial climate-related priorities." Among them was a plan to "leverage the insurance sector's ability to help achieve climate-related goals." The FIO explained that "the insurance sector has the ability to shape industries, products, and practices" and "can influence climate-related activity of other sectors of the U.S. economy." The Biden administration therefore sought to use insurance companies to "help achieve national climate-related goals," including through underwriting activities—i.e., by asking insurance companies to deny (or charge more for) insurance of blacklisted, high-carbon industries.[56] As one commentator explained, "It may be that the FIO will seek to have insurers serve as private regulators (similar to private attorneys general)" who could enforce the administration's priorities across corporate America by granting or denying coverage to favored or disfavored businesses[57]—except that these private regulators would operate behind the scenes, under a standardless regime, elected by no one and accountable only to themselves. Sounds great, right?

The insurance industry got the memo. Two months after the Biden administration asked the FIO to make climate assessments, eight major insurers created the Net-Zero Insurance Alliance.[58] The goal of the organization, according to its leader, the CEO of the French underwriting firm AXA, is to have "all the insurers applying a methodology to only underwrite companies directed toward climate transition and not to the dark ages of burning coal."[59]

Initially, the Net-Zero Insurance Alliance and its promises to underwrite society's way out of climate catastrophe didn't appeal to US insurance companies. So naturally, ESG activists sought to force the issue. They filed shareholder proposals at the Travelers Insurance Company, Chubb, and The Hartford to deter the companies from covering new fossil fuel projects.[60] The companies objected to putting those proposals onto the ballot, but, aided by the SEC's new guidance allowing proposals that focus on a "significant social policy," the SEC forced them through.[61] Although the proposals were ultimately voted down by shareholders, other climate proposals have gained more traction.[62]

The FIO has been advancing similar goals in parallel. In 2022, the FIO announced that it had joined the Network of Central Banks and Supervisors for Greening the Financial System (NGFS), an organization comprised of government entities "committed to . . . mobilising mainstream finance to support the transition toward a sustainable economy."[63] Its entire purpose is to use financial institutions and insurance companies to fight climate change; it's not to crunch numbers in a politically neutral way to ensure that insurance companies stay solvent, have enough liquidity to pay claims, or avoid taking on too much risk. When the federal insurance regulator announces its intent to "green" the sector, insurance companies know what they're supposed to do.

All this pressure has been working. Peabody Energy, the largest coal company in the United States, told its investors that "insurance companies and large investors are curtailing or ending their financial relationships with fossil fuel–related companies," which has had "adverse impacts" on coal producers.[64] In 2020, one survey estimated that coal companies were facing insurance hikes of 40 percent.[65] A 2022 report found that new coal-mining projects are "'effectively uninsurable' outside China" because so many insurance companies are refusing to provide coverage.[66]

Fossil fuel producers aren't the only ones feeling the pinch. Insurance companies have also threatened to pull coverage from contractors such as construction companies and shipping companies unless those companies promise that they will not use their trucks to transport coal, do construction work on a mine, or otherwise provide services for the fossil fuel industry.[67] Companies are now guilty by association, rendered uninsurable unless they recant their affiliation with any client connected to the fossil fuel industry and pledge fealty to net zero goals.

What's next? Should Caterpillar refuse to sell bulldozers to mining companies (or lose its banking services)? Should Kroger refuse to buy produce from farmers who use fertilizer (or be charged a higher interest rate)? Should McDonald's refuse to sell a Big Mac to an oil rig worker (or lose its property insurance)? If Madison Square Garden can use facial recognition technology to deny entry to law firm workers who are suing the company, it can use that same technology to deny entry to executives or workers associated with fossil fuels, private prisons, debt collectors, Comcast, Facebook, or whoever.[68] We're one creative ESG proposal away from coercing companies to blacklist any potential vendor, customer, or supplier the proponent dislikes. And the government isn't merely turning a blind eye to this radical perversion of democracy but using its power to make sure ESG proponents get the job done.

Major Questions Deserve Major Deliberation

The current scenario is bleak, but there is reason for hope. All of these executive orders, agency announcements, bulletins, guidance, and rules are not legislation; they are workarounds to avoid having to pass legislation. But that also means that they're subject to greater scrutiny, particularly after the Supreme Court decided *West Virginia v. Environmental Protection Agency et al.* in June 2022.[69]

Here's what happened: the Clean Air Act of 1963, a statute passed by Congress, gives the EPA the power to make rules to limit pollution from power plants. Since its passage fifty years ago, the EPA has understood this to mean that it can set standards to make power plants operate more cleanly. Under the Obama administration, however, the EPA decided to go a step farther: it passed rules that set the emissions standards for coal plants so low that they couldn't meet them, even with the best possible technology. Instead, the plants would have had to transition to natural gas or renewables, shut down, or purchase emissions "credits." The White House stated that the rule would "drive . . . aggressive transformation in the domestic energy industry."[70] It would have cost billions of dollars in compliance costs, increased electricity rates by 10 percent, and reduced US GDP by a trillion dollars by 2040. It was a big deal.

The Supreme Court struck the rule down. It did so based on what's called the "major questions doctrine." That doctrine says that major policy questions—the type that have "vast economic and political significance"—are reserved for Congress, for actual legislation, subject to the deliberative process and checks and balances—at least unless Congress "clearly" states otherwise. The doctrine has long-standing roots: As Chief Justice John Marshall explained in 1825 in *Wayman v. Southard*, "important subjects . . . must be entirely regulated by the legislature it-self"; Congress can allow executive agencies only to "fill up the details" of provisions Congress itself enacts. In *West Virginia v. EPA*, the EPA wasn't just "filling up the details" when it decided that coal plants needed to move to renewables, it was forcing a radical transformation of the entire US energy industry. There was certainly no "clear statement" granting the EPA that authority. Therefore the regulation was invalid. An agency cannot "'work around' the legislative process" when it comes to "a ques-tion of great political significance," Justice Neil Gorsuch explained in his concurring opinion.

Under this reasoning, many, if not all, of the executive actions in this chapter are likely invalid, too. When Congress created the Federal Insur-ance Office, it gave it the power to "monitor all aspects of the insurance industry" to identify issues "that could contribute to a systemic crisis in the insurance industry or the United States financial system."[71] There's no reason to think that it intended to allow the FIO to use insurers as its climate goons, granting and denying insurance coverage to unofficially enact the sitting president's political goals. There's equally no reason to think that Congress's grant of power to the SEC to make rules "for the protection of investors" included the power to transform itself into the climate change police.[72] Think about it this way: if even the EPA is not allowed to regulate outside the bounds of a broad environment-related statute in the name of fighting climate change, there is little doubt that the SEC, OCC, FIO, and DOL can do so instead.

In some ways, the irony is palpable: the very reasons President Biden has invoked to justify enlisting federal agencies to further his political agenda—that the climate crisis is profound and potentially catastrophic, that not "closing racial gaps" would cost the United States "$5 trillion in gross domestic product over the next five years"—are the very reasons that he isn't allowed to do so.[73] But the principles exist for good reason. The issues are too big, too consequential. Political issues of this magni-tude are supposed to be reserved for Congress, for the people we elect to high office through a process in which every citizen, rich or poor, has one vote. Big policy issues aren't supposed to be decided by agency bureaucrats, spurred into ping-ponging administrative rule making by presidents of varying political persuasions or by the private financial actors they nudge into action. And after *West Virginia v. EPA*, it looks as though the Supreme Court may be the institution that ensures it will stay that way.

Chapter 9

HOW ESG'S EFFORTS TO SAVE
THE WORLD ARE HURTING IT

feel bad for those who get fucked by it. By this dumb game we woke westerners play where we say all the right shiboleths [*sic*] and so everyone likes us."

I didn't know it at the time, but when I was writing *Woke, Inc.* a couple of years ago, I was writing about Sam Bankman-Fried, otherwise known as SBF. He wrote those words to explain to a Vox reporter how he had built a cryptocurrency empire on empty promises of virtue and wealth.[1]

What you are about to read is not a story about hypocrisy, it is a story about fraud—one that was made possible by ESG-infused virtue signaling. For a movement that was born to contain negative externalities— meaning the harm that one's economic actions impose on others—this is one of the great harms that it instead perpetuates: widespread fraud.

One well-known ESG rating firm,[2] Truvalue Labs, owned by FactSet, gave FTX a higher governance score than ExxonMobil.[3] However, the CEO who replaced Bankman-Fried, John J. Ray III, said that the company had had more problems than when he had taken over Enron after its collapse:

"Never in my career have I seen such a complete failure of corporate controls and such a complete absence of trustworthy financial information as occurred."[4] How a once-in-a-generation financial catastrophe waiting to happen could be praised for its high ESG scores is a puzzle worth diving deeper into.

SBF was the face of a philosophy called *effective altruism*, which is basically extreme utilitarianism: religiously pursuing whatever maximizes the world's long-term happiness. He grew up studying thinkers such as Jeremy Bentham and Peter Singer. As a young grad student at MIT, he met the philosopher William MacAskill, who convinced him that instead of pursuing a career in animal welfare, he ought to make as much money as possible so he could give it all away.[5] SBF married that theory with another about mixing moral and financial value. He and his cryptocurrency exchange, FTX, brought ESG values to crypto, legitimizing a lawless industry and propelling it into the mainstream.

The Miami Heat played in the FTX Arena. Larry David promoted the company in a Super Bowl ad.[6] FTX sponsored a crypto conference attended by stars such as Katy Perry and Orlando Bloom; SBF moderated a panel on regulation featuring Bill Clinton and Tony Blair. FTX stood for the "governance" part of ESG—it was the good guy, the one pushing for responsible regulation, civilizing the Wild West of cryptocurrency; the one you could trust. NBA superstar Steph Curry affirmed that in a commercial, saying "I'm not an expert and I don't need to be. With FTX, I have everything I need to buy, sell, and trade crypto safely."[7]

Wasn't there an environmental problem with branding a crypto exchange as an ESG darling? Crypto mining burns a massive amount of energy, accounting for up to 1.7 percent of all electricity usage in the United States.[8] FTX found the perfect solution: supermodel Gisele Bündchen signed on as its top ESG advisor. In an interview with *Forbes*, Bündchen spoke about how crypto would give everyone access to the financial system: "If this can make investing more inclusive, I think that's great." "We're giving millions each year to launch sustainability related initiatives both through carbon offsets but also through research and development on new technologies that can help mitigate climate change," SBF added, throwing in a few lines about inclusivity for good measure.

The interviewer got the point: "It's great that you're building this company with the environmental impact and inclusion in mind." She wrote that FTX was working to provide solar energy in the Amazon.[9] Its efforts to promote inclusion extended even to racial equity. FTX established its US headquarters in Chicago, contributed to guaranteed basic income programs, and gave underserved minorities access to the riches of crypto. Mayor Lori Lightfoot was ecstatic: "This is a mechanism and a tool to bring traditionally underrepresented and ignored populations into the world of crypto so they can take ownership and control of their own financial destiny. I think the sky is the limit."[10] Everyone's conscience was appeased, and greed was free to take over. Bündchen and her then husband, Tom Brady, filmed a commercial calling their celebrity friends and asking "Are you in?"[11] Shaq made one revealing that he, too, was all in—"Are you?" he asked the viewer.[12]

For too many, the answer was "Yes." Lured by big names and pretty words, millions of people trusted FTX with their money. And then, as SBF assessed the situation, they got fucked.

FTX went bankrupt overnight, and more than $8 billion of customer funds went missing. The collapse began when CoinDesk reported on a leaked document revealing alarmingly close connections between FTX, SBF's crypto exchange, and Alameda Research, his crypto-trading hedge fund run by his girlfriend. More than half of Alameda's $14.6 billion in assets consisted of coins FTX had minted, such as FTT—Monopoly money that had value only because Alameda had bought most of it and assigned it a value.[13] Essentially, it turned out that both of SBF's crypto firms were worth a lot only because each said the other was worth a lot.

The CEO of a rival crypto exchange, Binance, suddenly announced that he was liquidating his entire $529 million holding of FTX's proprietary coin.[14] Then everyone else realized that the currency was in free fall and rushed to dump it at any price. FTT cratered. FTX and Alameda had both borrowed real money, heavily using FTT as collateral. By the time everyone else saw what was happening and tried to withdraw their funds from FTX, there was no money left.

Where did the missing $8 billion go? After all, FTX was supposed to be holding its customers' money, not gambling with it; banks are allowed to lend out clients' money, but exchanges are supposed to hold on to it. To call what happened a run on the bank overlooks the crucial fact that FTX was not a bank. For it to lend or invest its customers' money was simply theft.[15] The day before the collapse, SBF had tweeted investors to assure them that the money was there: "We don't invest client assets."[16] Afterward, in an overly candid interview with a Vox reporter with whom he'd assumed he was having a friendly chat, he revealed that FTX had lent its clients' funds to Alameda, which had then gambled with it and lost. Alameda had also loaned $4.1 billion to FTX executives.[17] "Sometimes life creeps up on you," he observed philosophically.[18]

Reuters reported that FTX employees and SBF's parents had bought more than $300 million worth of property in the Bahamas, often in their personal names.[19] His parents, professors at Stanford Law School, had been heavily involved in his environmental efforts and other charitable work. That charity extended to politics: SBF and other FTX executives had donated at least $40 million to Democrats during the 2022 midterm campaigns and $23 million to Republicans.[20] SBF claimed that he had made additional "dark money" donations to GOP candidates that he had hidden from the media to avoid upsetting reporters.[21]

Basically, he tried to buy everybody. He even funded a program at Vox. That was why he revealed so much to its reporter; he must have thought she was on his payroll. SBF did interviews with all his media friends to try to talk his way out of prison, painting himself as a naive young idealist who simply couldn't keep track of all the big numbers.[22] Then he was arrested.

You have to understand that SBF isn't a *hypocrite*; he is a *fraud*. His cynical recitation of ESG truisms was an essential part of his fraud. It allowed him to position FTX as the face of crypto good governance when the company didn't even have a board of directors and had never been audited.[23] Meanwhile, much of his lobbying for crypto regulation was really about burdening his competitors in decentralized finance (DeFi); in an exchange that uses the blockchain to exercise group control over transactions instead of centralized control, it would actually have been impossible for a middleman like SBF to steal his clients' money. When a captain of industry calls for regulation of himself, always read the fine print.[24]

But the details didn't matter; only the appearance of virtue, the aura of sustainability and governance that FTX wrapped itself in like a cloak, mattered. SBF realized that we now inhabit a world in which if he chanted enough trendy buzzwords such as *sustainability*, *inclusivity*, and *equity*, it didn't matter whether his company actually had any good governance practices; the words are all many people are looking for, and their meanings are often vague and subjective anyway. In fact, that was how he got his governance rating from Truvalue, which brags that it "applies AI-driven technology to over 100,000 unstructured text sources . . . to provide daily signals that identify positive and negative ESG behavior."[25] SBF's pleasing patter about ESG was literally all that mattered to the rater. He reduced the game to its essence.

It was the exact same game I talked about in *Woke, Inc.*: *Pretend you care about something other than profit and power, precisely to gain more of each.*[26] At the time, many people told me I was stating the obvious. Yet more than enough people still fell for the ruse under the name ESG and lost their life savings with FTX, so the point bears repeating.

"ESG has been perverted beyond all recognition," SBF told Vox. The natural reaction is to think "Yeah, and guys like you did that." But that misses the point. SBF saw everyone else playing the ESG game and decided he might as well play it, too. So he studied the game, distilled it to its central principles, and ruthlessly applied them to maximum effect. He didn't just exploit ESG; he was its product. The two perverted each other beyond all recognition. Sam Bankman-Fried saw the moral emptiness of woke capitalism and decided that in the absence of meaning, there was nothing left but the pursuit of power. In another life he might have spent his days fighting factory farming and debating the fine points of Bentham's felicific calculus. In a better system, he might have come to possess some of the goodness he pretended to; in this one, he became a nihilist.

Economists have a technical term for what everyone else thinks of as "That's not a me problem. That's a you problem." It's called *negative externalities*, harm your actions impose on others without any cost to yourself. SBF both became a negative externality of ESG and passed negative externalities on to all his customers. At their best, that's the kind of thing stakeholder capitalism and its incarnation as ESG are trying to prevent.

I know that many supporters of ESG are sincere. That very sincerity prevents them from seeing that many people who mouth the same words are insincere, that there are countless parasites using the true believers as cover. The true believers count their numbers and calculate how much good they'll do, but they have only half the equation; they can never reliably identify all the frauds in their midst and measure their cost. And the more power their cause gains, the more frauds flock to it and the more frauds it creates.

What's worse, the ESG movement has installed a system that incentivizes virtue signaling, making it trivially easy for wolves in sheep's clothing to rise to the top. ESG faces a paradox: the most virtuous people are the least likely to advertise it, so a financial system that focuses on rewarding virtue will really just funnel resources toward those who master self-promotion.

The central claim of ESG advocates is that companies will be rewarded in the future for their investments in ESG now. What they fail to see in stories such as that of FTX are the reasons companies might be punished for it.

The ESG Energy Crisis

The writers of the Will Smith movie *I Am Legend* decided that a good way to convey a postapocalyptic setting would be to set gas prices just below $7 per gallon. In March 2022, the price in some parts of California exceeded that,[27] then soared even higher during the summer. This is not the apocalypse, I think, but we may be hearing the hoofbeats of one of its horsemen in the distance. Whether Famine arrives is up to us.

ESG policies that attempt to accelerate the "energy transition" have strangled fossil fuel production without providing any reliable replacements, meaning that the world is simply transitioning from having energy to not having it. We have jumped off an energy cliff hoping that the fall will give us an incentive to build the perfect parachute. Now the ground's coming up fast. The tough question we face is whether to pull all the parachutes we already have—ones with ugly names such as oil, nuclear energy, and natural gas.

I don't need to give you stats to tell you that we're in an energy crisis. You're aware of that. You saw it every time you went to the gas station in 2022; you see it every time you pay your electricity bill. I can't predict the short-term future; maybe there'll be a recession that'll temporarily lower demand for oil and therefore its price. But the likely trend for the next couple of decades is that energy prices will go up as the world's appetite for energy outstrips its supply.

As I pointed out in a letter to Chevron's CEO, global energy consumption has grown by 2 percent per year over the last decade, yet fossil fuel production is not keeping pace even though fossil fuels still meet 82 percent of the world's energy demands; thanks to ESG pressure, capital expenditure on them has been cut in half since 2014. Leading analysts argue that we must increase oil and gas expenditures by at least $1.2 trillion by 2030 to support global economic growth. In the absence of proper investment in our main energy sources, with too many mouths to feed, prices must go up.[28]

That trend has been partially masked recently by President Biden's liberal use of the Strategic Petroleum Reserve, but that day has passed, as have the midterm elections. When he took office, the reserve held 638 million barrels of crude oil. Now, two years later, it has plunged below 389 million barrels—about a 40 percent decrease, the vast majority of that in 2022.[29] This is, in terms that ESG supporters might appreciate, not sustainable. If market conditions remain similar and our reserves are empty, prices must go back up. A bullet wound can't be treated with a Band-Aid.

Recognizing the problem, the White House has said it hopes to refill the Strategic Petroleum Reserve if the price of crude oil falls to around $70 per barrel.[30] A couple of years earlier, Senate Democrats blocked President Donald J. Trump's attempt to fill the reserve at $24 per barrel, bragging that they had stopped a "$3 billion bailout for big oil."[31] The ESG movement trumpeted that victory over the fossil fuel industry back then, but now that it's clear to everyone that it was a Pyrrhic victory, it has been forgiven and forgotten. Buying oil when the price was low would actually have been a bailout for our near-future selves, but ESG-colored glasses prevented too many people from seeing the obvious. ESG has created a rigid rule that any expansion in the production or purchase of fossil fuels is automatically bad, and, like most rigid rules incapable of responding to specific circumstances, it has terrible consequences when it meets reality.

Of course, ESG advocates will say that I've placed the blame for the world's energy woes at the feet of environmentalists, Biden, everywhere but where it really belongs: Vladimir Putin. The proximate cause of the spike in global energy prices in 2022 was obviously Russia's invasion of Ukraine, which destabilized oil and gas supply chains around the world. Russia is the third largest oil producer in the world, responsible for 12 percent of the global crude oil supply.[32] It's the largest exporter of natural gas by a wide margin, and its biggest customer is Europe: in 2021, 45 percent of the natural gas the European Union imported came from Russia.[33] When the West imposed punishing sanctions on Russian energy, it punished itself equally.

That was why President Biden took care to dub high gasoline prices "Putin's price hike." But it was everyone's price hike, since the world had knowingly put itself at Putin's mercy. The war was not a black swan event, quite the opposite: Putin had been invading Ukraine for seven years, beginning by taking Crimea and parts of the Donbas with soldiers in unmarked uniforms. The world had dubbed them "little green men"; Putin had even admitted that they were Russian soldiers after annexing Crimea.[34] This time he simply sent a lot of reinforcements and had them wear Russian uniforms. ESG advocates insist that the current energy crisis is a black swan event caused by an unpredictable madman, yet Vladimir Putin is an entirely predictable madman.

There's a deeper problem that's even worse: not only did the West fail to account for the possibility that Russia would renew its assault on Ukraine, but its addiction to Russian energy played a role in *causing* that new invasion.

Putin knew how reliant Europe was on Russian oil and gas and therefore knew he would wield great leverage over the entire West if he started a war, enabling him to limit NATO's military and economic intervention. That gave him some of the confidence necessary to pull the trigger on the 2022 invasion. This is not armchair speculation. German justice minister Marco Buschmann recently said, "Knowing what we do today, the decision to pursue Nord Stream 2 following the annexation of Crimea in 2014 was Germany's contribution to the outbreak of the war in Ukraine." By continuing to build the Nord Stream 2 pipeline after Russia's first invasion, Germany sent an unmistakable signal that it was desperate enough for Russian gas to overlook an attack, clearing the way for war. As Buschmann put it, Germany—along with other Western nations, I'd add—must confront this truth directly and draw the right conclusions from it.[35]

What are the right conclusions? They vary depending on the eye of the beholder. ESG advocates will argue that we should have shunned fossil fuels in favor of renewables even sooner to prevent the global energy supply from being held hostage by a warmongering dictator. One weakness of that approach is that it would have just moved the West's window of vulnerability sooner, prompting an earlier assault. But more fundamentally, the fact of the matter is that wind and solar energy sources aren't ready to replace fossil fuels anytime soon.

Germany is a prime example. It provides a good extended case study, an object lesson of ESG's negative externalities. In 2010, it embarked on the world's most ambitious plan to transition to renewable energy: the *Energiewende*, or energy turnaround. Germany spent about €200 billion on renewable energy sources between 2013 and 2020.[36] Since the start of its effort, solar and wind power's contribution to its electricity supply has risen from 8 percent to 31 percent.[37]

But the wind doesn't always blow, and the sun doesn't always shine. Modern battery technology falls miserably short of being able to store enough renewable energy during the upswings to fill in during the downturns; we're maybe ten years away from being able to do that, in the same sense that we're always ten years away from developing fusion. To meet baseload energy requirements to provide a firm backdrop for consumers, countries that depend on wind and solar power turn to natural gas, the cleanest fossil fuel by far. That led Germany right into Russia's hands. Germany is the forty-eighth largest producer of natural gas but the eighth largest consumer.[38] Nord Stream 1 was the Russian lifeline propping up Germany's dreams of renewables. To keep the dream alive, it had to approve the construction of Nord Stream 2 in spite of Russia's first invasion of Ukraine.

The Trump administration placed sanctions on the Russian companies building Nord Stream 2 as it neared completion. Germany and Russia found a creative way around them: a German state government set up a foundation through which the Russian energy giant Gazprom could reroute more than €165 million to finish the pipeline. Not only was the new money launderer sheltered by the aegis of the German government, but it also had an impressive name: the Foundation for the Protection of the Climate and Environment.[39]

Vladimir Putin gave ESG a new meaning: Export Soviet Gas. Europe's reliance on that gas gave him the leverage to invade Ukraine a second time with more force.

Germany is belatedly weaning itself off Russian energy. After much debate, the country begrudgingly extended the life span of three nuclear plants that had been due to be shut down, over many Green Party members' vocal objections.[40] But that's a drop in the bucket. So the world leader in the green transition is now achieving its baseload energy requirements by burning lots of coal and cutting down forests to burn trees.[41] More than twenty coal-fired power plants have been reopened to help Germany keep the lights on.[42] And though timber is technically classified as a renewable energy source, not only is leveling forests hard to square with environmentalism, but burning wood emits more carbon dioxide than does any fossil fuel.[43] The energy turnaround has turned around again and lunged backward.

Russia's war on Ukraine has dashed Germany's green transition hopes. Perhaps it should've remembered that lesson from the nineteenth-century Prussian military strategist Helmuth von Moltke: "No battle plan survives contact with the enemy." Or as Mike Tyson put it, "Everyone has a plan until they get punched in the mouth."

The dreams of ESG are brittle; they opened the world up to being punched in the mouth, and there was no Plan B. The plan revolved around wishful thinking. ESG idealists told themselves that any energy crisis would only accelerate the switch to renewables, as if workable batteries could suddenly be invented to make it possible.[44] Some people in the "degrowth" movement even imagined that instead of resorting to fossil fuels, humanity would embrace their vision of rejecting industrialization, limiting our energy consumption to live in peaceful harmony with the cycles of wind and sun.[45] But when the energy crisis arrived, the ESG realists who actually make decisions and answer to the public were forced to cut down forests and burn more coal. Before they could crash to the ground, they pulled every imperfect parachute they had, as most people would. The ESG idealists had misunderstood human nature.

For its part, the United States did indeed react to the energy crisis by increasing its investments in renewable energy; Congress passed the Inflation Reduction Act (IRA), which included hundreds of billions of dollars to develop renewable energy production and storage. The IRA subsidized solar energy by extending the tax credit for installing solar energy systems by ten years and increasing it to 30 percent.[46] But here, too, a dictator entered the ESG story: Xi Jinping.

We risk recreating Germany's reliance on Russian energy with our own main geopolitical rival. China controls every step of the solar supply chain: "at least 75% of every single key stage of solar photovoltaic panel manufacturing and processing."[47] And much of the work is done with Uighur forced labor; even as the United States incentivizes solar energy generation with one hand, with the other it holds up hundreds of millions of dollars' worth of solar components in ports because of a law banning Chinese imports made by slaves.[48] Civil rights groups are already warning that increased investments in solar energy will increase the use of slave labor.[49] This is a direct consequence of the fact that US companies take stands on human rights issues at home but turn a blind eye to China's abuses: we may end up using Uighur slave labor to produce solar panels in the name of sustainability.

We may also end up cutting down trees and killing wildlife in the name of environmentalism. Clean energy's dirty secret is that it takes up an immense amount of space, space currently occupied by flora and fauna. A recent study from Princeton University and Bloomberg News quantified this: "Expanding wind and solar by 10% annually until 2030 would require a chunk of land equal to the state of South Dakota. . . . By 2050, when Biden wants the entire economy to be carbon free, the U.S. would need up to four additional South Dakotas to develop enough clean power to run all the electric vehicles, factories and more."[50] Nuclear power generation, on the other hand, is emission free and takes up virtually no space. If we'd built more nuclear power plants decades ago, we'd already be at net zero and the world would have plenty of energy to continue economic growth; sometimes I wonder if that's why it hasn't happened. If anyone wants to solve the climate crisis and the energy crisis in one blow, nuclear power's the obvious answer.*

For some reason, the United States is going mostly with renewables. At best, the IRA's investments in renewable energy are long-term plays and partial bets on technology that hasn't yet been invented. Like Germany, in 2022, we had to address our short-term crisis. For that, President Biden emptied the Strategic Petroleum Reserve and then flew to Saudi Arabia to beg its ruler, Crown Prince Mohammed bin Salman, familiarly known as MBS, for oil.

In 2018, the CIA had accused the crown prince of ordering the brutal murder of *Washington Post* contributor Jamal Khashoggi that year; in retaliation, Biden had vowed to make Saudi Arabia a pariah state. But desperate times called for a fist bump of forgiveness between the two leaders.[51] After Saudi Arabia broadcast the photo to the world, the United States believed it had at least extracted a secret promise to produce more oil. But the fist bump came to naught; a few months later, MBS reneged on his promise and OPEC joined Russia to cut oil production instead.[52] He wanted more than a photo op. Less than a month later, the news came out that the Biden administration had determined that MBS was entitled to sovereign immunity in a case brought by Khashoggi's fiancée.[53] The district court judge dutifully dismissed the case, noting that despite his uneasiness his hands were tied by the executive branch's decision.[54]

Biden received no discernible return on his investment; as of this writing, Saudi Arabia and Russia are again discussing cutting oil production, partly in response to new EU sanctions, including a proposed price cap

---

*Michael Shellenberger has written extensively on this topic.

on Russian oil.[55] Who knows what's left in the negotiating arsenal? Next, MBS may make President Biden call him "Uncle." Or Vladimir Putin may ask Biden and the European Union to nudge Ukraine toward territorial concessions, using the energy war to make up for Russia's dismal performance on the battlefield.

The Western world has not truly ended fossil fuel expansion; it has simply outsourced most of it to appease internal critics. There's also a domestic version of outsourcing: a growing tactic called *brownspinning*, in which public energy companies placate ESG supporters by selling oil and gas projects to private companies. The drilling and fracking continue, but the public is entitled to no information about them and has no ability to invest in them. The public company's ESG stats improve, but nothing truly changes, other than the rich getting richer.[56]

Beneath the grand gestures toward ESG and renewable energy, there are always fossil fuels making them possible, quietly shouldering the load. And they usually come from dictator-ruled countries that produce them less cleanly than the West would in both a moral and an environmental sense. Russia, for instance, leaks massive amounts of methane during its fossil fuel production and distribution; methane "is about 80 times more powerful as a greenhouse gas than carbon dioxide, though it degrades in the atmosphere over about 20 years."[57]

When Western countries meet emissions targets by relying on foreign dictatorships to increase fossil fuel production, they actually harm the environment by having the same energy be produced in a dirtier way. ESG's *E* defeats its own environmental goals. It's possible that environmentalists, human rights activists, *and* consumers who are tired of paying the price for energy inflation could all turn their backs on ESG.

But the biggest problem comes with the *S*, its social cost. That's why I've saved it for last. The greatest negative externality of the ESG movement is that when elites force their values onto everyone else by cramming it into every institution, they make ordinary people trust every institution less. And that, in turn, makes society fall apart.

The Great Uprising

I will not eat the bugs. Not even to save the planet.

The phrase "I will not eat the bugs" has become a meme closely associated with "You'll own nothing and be happy"; both are related to the World Economic Forum's proposed Great Reset.[58] The Great Reset is the WEF's name for the idea that the covid-19 pandemic, though tragic, has given the world a unique opportunity to rebuild and transform its way of life to become more sustainable and equitable. WEF chairman Klaus Schwab says that there are three pillars to this reset of capitalism: stakeholder capitalism, ESG, and technology.[59]

The Great Reset has become controversial, to put it mildly. To many who oppose stakeholder capitalism, ESG, and rule by Davos, the Great Reset is a blatant power grab by elites, a brazen attempt to remake the world as they see fit, no matter what everyone else wants. People aren't just cogs in a system, and they don't like their lives being rearranged by business elites. That's the objection the rallying cries "I will not eat the bugs" and "You'll own nothing and be happy" express. In 2016, the WEF published eight predictions of what the world would look like in 2030. Its video starts by saying "You'll own nothing. And you'll be happy. Whatever you want, you'll rent. And it'll be delivered by drone."[60] The "bugs" part refers to the growing number of articles in liberal media sources encouraging people to eat insects instead of meat to lower their carbon footprint. Michael Shellenberger and Noah Blum[61] have documented dozens of cases of mainstream media outlets that are desperately trying to sell the world on eating bugs to fight climate change: "It sounds like a conspiracy theory, but it's not: they really *do* want you to eat bugs," Shellenberger has written.[62] See for yourself.

I won't eat the bugs because I'm a vegetarian. Truthfully, I don't think anyone takes the bug thing seriously; it's just a catchy way for people to say that they don't want to be force-fed ESG. Memes aside, technocrats worldwide are looking for ever more ways to nudge the rest of us into line, including ESG.

There are now critics of the Great Reset who call it by the same name as its proponent Klaus Schwab does. The conservative instigator Alex Jones wrote a book called *The Great Reset*. The conservative commentator Glenn Beck also wrote a book called *The Great Reset*. It's probably the only thing the two of them have in common with Schwab, but now that conservatives have started using Schwab's chosen term, progressives are calling critics who use the phrase conspiracy theorists. It's a familiar move, akin to the way progressives now look down their noses at those who use the once popular progressive term *woke*.

But the Great Reset is a worldview, and the labeling of its critics by its proponents shouldn't obfuscate *everyone's* understanding of that worldview. The Great Reset calls for the dissolution of boundaries between the different spheres of our lives. It calls for business leaders and government leaders to work together to address shared global challenges that neither group of actors can address on their own. That's what the World Economic Forum in Davos is really about—not just according to its critics but according to its founders and attendees. The Great Reset calls for the dissolution of boundaries between nations and for leaders of countries to work together to address global challenges.

At the heart of this worldview is a deep-rooted skepticism that "ordinary" citizens can be trusted to sort out the answers to challenging global questions without elite intervention. What's the point of having a democratic self-governing nation if the voters select public policies that result in the uninhabitability of the planet, for example? The Great Reset calls for the dissolution of boundaries to enable the elite leaders of various institutions to work together more effectively to solve the problems that the citizens of self-governing democracies are demonstrably unable to solve.

America's Founding Fathers rejected this worldview in 1776. They took exception to the Old World view that Church leaders, labor leaders, and business leaders should determine the "right" answers to normative questions and impose them on the rest of society at large. But the American view is the anomaly in human history. So it's no surprise that the Old World view is rearing its head again, most prominently on the ski slopes of an old Swiss mountain town.

But people in democratic nations don't like it. The Great Reset defies the basic premise that citizens in democratic nations were taught to believe about their own agency. And that's why the Great Reset is now being met by the Great Uprising. As many observers have noted, populist revolts of varying degrees are rearing their heads around the world. Antilockdown protests and packed school board meetings across the United States. Trucker convoys protesting in Canada. Yellow vest protests in France. A right-wing populist elected prime minister of Italy. Dutch farmers conducting mass protests over ESG policies that would threaten their livelihoods by halving their livestock production. A foiled coup in Germany. And most seriously, massive unrest in Sri Lanka after its government attempted to meet ESG goals by banning chemical fertilizers, resulting in an economic crisis, violence, and revolution.

This is the greatest negative externality of ESG: *when people see it being force-fed to them by being crammed into every possible institution, they lose faith in all those institutions.* When asset managers and corporations insert ESG considerations into their financial decisions, people lose faith that they care about wealth. When public health professionals say that mass protests for racial justice are a necessity during a pandemic, people lose faith that they care about health. When the media publish and censor stories based on how much they contribute to equity, people lose faith that they care about truth. When the military holds diversity training and assigns readings on antiracism, people lose faith that it cares about strength. When academics force job applicants to write statements pledging their commitment to diversity, equity, and inclusion, people lose faith that they care about education. And when a government cripples its economy by chasing half-baked sustainability initiatives, people lose faith that it cares about their well-being.

When any institution veers from its central purpose, people trust it less. The fundamental flaw of the Great Reset is this: when elites use their power to carve ESG principles into the core of every institution, every single one of the institutions holding civil society together loses its central purpose. And as people lose their trust in everything binding society together, it falls apart. They don't trust pharmaceutical companies. They believe the opposite of what news sources tell them—if they read or watch them at all. They don't join the army; there's nothing worth fighting for. They don't go to college; it would only brainwash them. They don't trust people with degrees. They don't believe that their government serves them, which means that it has to be replaced, by peaceful means or, if necessary, by violence.

I've lost some faith in most of society's institutions, too, which is why I have sympathy for those who have lost all of it. It's a terrible thing, to lose one's faith and have nothing to replace it with. It's a path to nihilism.

The path out is to remember that many of our core institutions worked before things such as the Great Reset and ESG redefined and distorted them. The castle has been infested, and the longer we fail to clean it, the more appealing the solution to burn the whole thing down will be.

But we still have an opportunity to clean the castle. Between the managerial class and everyday citizens rests a third category of actors: creators, people who build things that previously did not exist. These creators now have an opportunity to channel the energy of the Great Uprising into defeating the Great Reset, without burning the whole thing down but by replacing it with something new.

That was what Elon Musk seemed to be doing by buying Twitter and operating it as a free speech platform. As this book goes to print, despite the histrionics that Twitter would "break" under his ownership, the platform appears to be operating as well as it ever did, despite the fact that he rid the company of most of its workforce, including many members of its censorious managerial class.

This is what I am doing by building Strive to compete head-on with BlackRock—by offering investment products that provide everyday citizens a way to invest in index funds without promoting ESG principles in corporate America's boardrooms. Strive's assets under management exceeded $500 million less than four months after the launch of its first fund in the second half of 2022, and that asset base is continuing to grow as this book goes to print.

In late 2022, following Strive's headline-grabbing launch, BlackRock, State Street, and Vanguard started to slowly change some of their behaviors from prior years: offering proxy voter choice programs and, in Vanguard's case, withdrawing from industry associations such as the Net Zero Asset Managers initiative. Will Facebook and Google slowly start to change their censorship practices as well? Maybe the castle can be saved by building new ones to take its place.

Chapter 10

SOLUTIONS

I n early 2022, I sat down for lunch with the CEO of a megascale household-brand asset management firm that manages more than a trillion dollars. His public declarations were unambiguous: "Asset managers have a crucial role to play in supporting investment aligned with global efforts to reduce the impact of climate change on our planet"; "We're well down the path of embedding ESG in everything we do"; "We also share our views regarding the importance of racial equity."[1] His firm hosts a "global employee self-identification campaign" and is "committed to reducing our impact on the environment." In 2020, he proclaimed that his firm had "recently signed the Net Zero Asset Managers initiative, joining other asset managers to support the global goal of reaching net zero greenhouse gas emissions by 2050 or sooner." He publicly committed to "deliver an investment experience that enhances quality of life with both people and our planet in mind."[2]

Though these proclamations are eerily similar to those made by Black-Rock CEO Larry Fink, my lunch was not with Fink. Nor was it with the CEO of State Street or Vanguard. Instead, it was with Marty Flanagan, the

CEO of Invesco, the fourth largest passive asset manager in the United States. Public records show that he is a Republican donor. The two individuals who had connected me with Mr. Flanagan—one was a senior executive at the firm, another was a former board member of Invesco—had both encouraged me to meet him directly. They told me that he was actually quite sympathetic to my perspective on stakeholder capitalism, which was a bit of a mystery to me given his public statements. So I decided that it was worthwhile to have a mutually respectful lunch to figure it out.

I was also in the very early stages of getting Strive off the ground. My partner and I were still figuring out our business model. Our thought was that Strive would partner with an existing asset manager, outside the Big Three, to create funds that would provide alternatives to ESG. If what my mutual acquaintances with Mr. Flanagan told me were true, I thought Invesco might be a suitable candidate. I didn't expect him to abandon his ESG commitments, but I wondered whether he might be interested in starting a parallel business line within Invesco—one that would offer funds to clients that would allow them to opt out of their "main" funds, which use ESG-linked proxy voting and shareholder engagement guidelines. If I had been in Marty's shoes, I would have seen that as a business opportunity—a way to differentiate his company from its bigger competitors rather than merely copy them.

We sat down to lunch in a Thai restaurant, exchanged pleasantries, and ordered food. I opened the conversation by giving him a signed copy of my first book, *Woke, Inc.*—but before I could even share my views, he went out of his way to explain how much he agreed with me. He was a soft-spoken man but at moments expressed near anger at the nonsensical spread of ESG. That was surprising to me, given his public declarations, but I listened very carefully. The bottom line was that he had to say the things he said publicly not because he believed them but because he was *expected* to do so.

I proposed my idea: perhaps Invesco would want to partner with Strive. We would generate the intellectual property, including proxy voting and shareholder engagement that did not advance ESG in the board-room, and Invesco could create and distribute funds to clients whose desires matched such an offering. Clients who wanted to stick with exist-ing ESG-promoting Invesco products could do so, but those who didn't would no longer be forced to do so.

Marty grew visibly uncomfortable at the suggestion. He said that it would be very difficult for his company to even consider doing any-thing like it, and he explained why: large existing clients such as CalPERS would not look kindly upon its entering into such a partnership. Initially, I thought that he misunderstood my proposal: I clarified that CalPERS could still have its money invested—and its shares voted—*exactly* the same way they were now; the new option would apply only to clients who wanted it. But Marty had understood what I had said the first time, and his concern was that CalPERS and other large clients would no longer wish to do business with Invesco *as a firm* if Invesco were to entertain such an option with Strive. He ended the lunch shortly thereafter and asked me to follow up and stay in touch. I wrote him a note but never heard back. I later heard from his subordinate who had set up the meeting that Marty had appreciated the lunch but it would be a good idea if I didn't follow up with him on any business-related proposals.

A few months later, in June, I cowrote an op-ed in the *Wall Street Jour-nal* in which I criticized a number of asset managers for their supportive statements and commitments in favor of ESG. They included BlackRock, State Street, and Vanguard, but I also included Invesco as one of the firms cited in the piece—though less prominently than the other three. Within a day of its publication, one of Flanagan's subordinates called me to let me know that Marty was "livid" that Invesco had been named—even though the piece had contained nothing more than direct quotations of exactly what Marty himself had previously said. It turned out that he had wanted to gain private credit with me for being anti-ESG while enjoying public credit for being pro-ESG. Sounds like a typical corporate donor to the Republican Party, in my experience.

Marty may be one of those people who made donations to Republicans for the same reason that he issues paeans to ESG: he does what he thinks he's supposed to do instead of doing what he thinks is right. It feels impolite to include the specifics of the story in this book, but I'm doing it anyway because conversations such as these need to be exposed. The ESG scam is a scam because the things that its greatest proponents say behind closed doors are not the same things that they say out in the open. They feel compelled to coordinate with their competitors to exclude new entries into the marketplace of ideas. And that's exactly why the principal solutions to the problem rely on a few simple principles: more information, more transparency, more disclosure, and more competition. With those, there would be fewer finance leaders talking about diversity while wielding as much power as possible for themselves.

Investors: Self-Education

It's *your* right to know how your money is being used. You can start by asking your financial advisor—and also your 401(k) plan administrator if you have a 401(k) plan or your pension fund board if you have a pension—some simple questions. Here are a few to start with.

- At any time in the last five years, have I invested in any funds that voted my shares in favor of racial equity audits?

- At any time in the last five years, have I invested in any funds that voted my shares in favor of emissions reduction plans or executive compensation tied to environmental and social goals?

- At any time in the last five years, have I invested in any funds that systematically underweight companies in any of the following sectors: coal, mining, oil and gas exploration, defense, or firearms?

- Do you use ESG factors in your external fund evaluation process, internal operations, or client portfolio optimization strategies?

There are countless other questions you could ask, but these four will be revealing. Be prepared for some rude surprises. One is that your financial representatives almost certainly won't know the answers. The good news is that you can give them a mandate: find out. You're on a strong legal footing to do so.

Directors of corporations owe a fiduciary duty to their shareholders, but they enjoy broad discretion on how to run the business—and shareholders cannot simply demand information at whim. By contrast, wealth managers, pension funds, and asset managers are not merely fiduciaries but also *trustees*.

If your wealth manager—or the HR manager or pension rep—tells you that it would be too much trouble to find out, consider printing out the Supreme Court's opinion in *Fifth Third Bancorp v. Dudenhoeffer*. Leave a copy on their desk, along with legal opinions issued by attorneys general of the states of Kentucky, Indiana, Louisiana, or others about legal violations raised by ESG. That should be enough to convince them to at least do their homework. You may learn that some of these financial intermediaries were less sophisticated than you thought, in which case you can help them get a head start in their hunt for information.

Three of the largest index funds in the world are those that track the S&P 500; IVV is the ticker symbol for the one offered by BlackRock, SPY is State Street's, and VOO is Vanguard's. These three firms—and the fourth largest US passive fund manager in the United States behind them, Invesco—also provide countless other growth funds, value funds, and dividend funds that hold shares in large companies such as Apple, Home Depot, ExxonMobil, Chevron, Citigroup, Amazon, and the Walt Disney Company. Ask them to share with you a list of funds that hold any of just those seven companies.

That's something that any half-competent financial representative can do. Those seven companies alone have faced immense pressure, including shareholder proposals, to adopt ESG mandates ranging from racial equity audits to emissions caps. Some of the largest fund managers in the world voted for those proposals. And they didn't simply use *their* "ESG funds" to do so; they used *all* of them. Find out if that included yours.

Chances are that it did. If you wish to advocate for the environmental and social policies advanced by these funds, there is absolutely no problem; you are free to decide how your capital is invested. It is perfectly legitimate to advance environmental, social, liberal, conservative, or socialist agendas *with your own money* or to ask your financial representatives to do so for you. But if you don't want this to happen, you can follow up with two more questions:

- Why didn't I know this before?

- What other investment funds can offer me similar alternatives from a financial standpoint but without advocating for nonfinancial policies that I disagree with?

If you ask these questions, the answers may be illuminating—a light at the end of the tunnel that you were unknowingly stuck in.

As you know, the largest asset managers all use proxy voting and shareholder engagement to promote ESG principles. They do so very effectively, and they do so in *all* their portfolios, including their nominally "ordinary" non-ESG index funds. This is where the greatest risk of green-smuggling exists.

The problem can also be solved through disclosure and consent. It's not "smuggling," after all, if asset managers declare their intentions and the customs agent lets them through. Some of this disclosure is slowly starting to happen. As you read in Chapter 5, in the wake of backlash in 2022, large asset managers started to become more transparent as pension fund clients pressed them on their ESG practices. Regulators also started to demand greater transparency. Recall that in November 2022, the Securities and Exchange Commission enacted a new rule requiring asset managers not just to disclose proxy votes but to categorize them in buckets such as environment or climate; diversity, equity, and inclusion;

or "other social issues." And the Big Three all issue "stewardship guides" that disclose, at least in general terms, how they engage with companies and vote clients' shares.

Legislators who are concerned about the use of ESG in capital markets need not resort to banning it. Letting sunlight in on the problem can do the job. They should simply require that representatives inform capital owners that they intend to invest their money in an ESG-promoting fund and obtain the owners' express consent. Some capital owners will say yes, others no, but no one's dollars will be used to vote for social policies that they don't support. Wealth managers won't like it, and neither will pension plan professionals or 401(k) plan administrators. The reason for that is simple: most human beings don't like doing extra work if they can avoid it. They will surely grouse about the burdens of added "regulation."

Lawmakers shouldn't fall for that trick. The financial services industry, including asset management, is one of the most tightly regulated industries. There are countless byzantine rules that make little sense and others that require disclosure of the smallest minutiae that are far less relevant to individual investors than the fact that their dollars are being used to advance social and political goals that they find repugnant—and that may cause them to *make less money*. If legislators need to retire some outdated regulations to accommodate this new pro-disclosure requirement, they should do so. All told, asset allocators cannot escape their requirement as trustees to do their due diligence and obtain the consent of their clients before the clients' assets are used to support ESG objectives. If asset allocators are upset about the added burden, they should direct it at the ESG-promoting asset managers who have abused client funds over the last decade—not at lawmakers who bring greater transparency to the problem.

Lawmakers must also be clear that "ESG" means any nonpecuniary factor, objective or strategy, regardless of what it's called. Already, the Big Three have signaled an attempt to distance themselves from the "ESG" nomenclature. BlackRock, for instance, has renamed one of its funds not once, but twice in six years, from "impact," to "ESG," to "sustainable," all in a bid to chase the freshest buzzword while dodging scrutiny.[3] Others have been even more candid. At the most recent World Economic Forum meeting in Davos, Coca-Cola's CEO admitted that "ESG" has become "toxic" in the United States. His solution? To continue to use his position as CEO to "fix societal problems" but "stop saying 'ESG.'"[4] His comments drew applause from his fellow CEOs but should draw alarm from regulators.

Private and Public Attorneys General: Litigation

In states such as New York and California, where public pension plans have jumped headlong into activist ESG investing, plan participants may be able to sue their pension boards to vindicate both their rights under trust law's sole interest rule and their First Amendment right not to have their retirement money be devoted to political objectives with which they disagree. Even where public pension plans simply allocate capital to Big Three index funds, the managers of those plans risk legal liability. In August 2022, Indiana attorney general Todd Rokita stated in a formal opinion that public pension plans violate trust law when they put money into funds controlled by asset managers who use proxy voting or shareholder engagement to push the ESG agenda—which the Big Three all acknowledge that they do. Yet in virtually every state, public pension plans still inject vast sums of money into Big Three index funds, allowing their retirees' savings to be used to promote ESG objectives.

Suit could also be brought against the Big Three themselves. The collusive ESG activism engaged in by BlackRock, Vanguard, State Street, and dozens of other asset managers and banks is a massive antitrust violation. In addition, as SEC commissioner Mark T. Uyeda recently pointed out, it may put them in violation of the disclosure provisions of Section 13(d) of the Exchange Act, which both federal and state securities officials can sue to enforce. At the same time, BlackRock has profound conflicts of interest that it has never owned up to when it pushes environmental activism on US energy companies. As the owner of a huge stake in PetroChina, it stands to profit if and when China's oil company picks up exploration or production projects that the Big Three are forcing US energy companies to give up.

Litigation to promote disclosure and consent is another promising strategy. All over the country, investment advisors such as wealth managers place billions of dollars of clients' money into funds whose managers—unbeknown to their clients—vote their proxies to push racial equity audits and other ideologically motivated, nonpecuniary ESG objectives. That's material information that every client has a right to know and that every investment advisor, under both state and federal law, has a duty to disclose. Lawsuits to stop this blatant violation of basic fiduciary disclosure law can and should be brought immediately, both by state attorneys general and by private individuals. Capital owners have a legal right to be told of, and say yes or no to, the use of their investment dollars to promote the ESG agenda.

The damages could be staggering. One potential remedy is for investors to ask for a refund for the fees they've paid. Why should investment advisors and asset managers get to keep their ill-gotten fees? They shouldn't. The legal term for this is *disgorgement*, and courts have recognized it as a possible remedy for fiduciary breaches. "Courts may fashion equitable remedies such as profit disgorgement and fee forfeiture to remedy a breach of fiduciary duty," the Texas Supreme Court has ruled.[5] This remedy may be available even if investors cannot demonstrate financial loss.[6] That makes a lot of sense: if I hired a personal assistant to handle my finances and I asked her to donate to Planned Parenthood, and she decided to secretly donate to the National Right to Life Committee instead, I wouldn't be out any money, but I'd be pretty mad. And if I had paid her 1 percent of my donation amount as compensation for her services, I would certainly expect to get it back.

It's no different here. The Big Three, and many financial advisors, have been telling their clients one thing and then doing another. For investors who can show that they lost money because of this deception—because, for instance, they lost out on the gains the fossil fuel industry saw in 2022—they could almost certainly ask to be fully compensated for the loss. But even if they didn't, there is no universe in which these money managers and allocators should be entitled to keep their cut. Litigation may thus be useful not just so the Supreme Court can tell BlackRock and others to clean up their act going forward but to compensate those who have been taken advantage of in the past.

Competitors: Market Alternatives

Until 2022, asset allocators had a sympathetic defense of their own: even if they *wanted* to direct client funds to asset managers who didn't promote ESG, they didn't have alternatives. The good news is that that's no longer the case.

The first category of market alternatives includes funds that promote alternative *values* to the environmental and social agendas advanced by ESG-promoting industry titans. The simplest way to achieve this goal is to do it in the same way that ESG funds do: by excluding "sin stocks" and other securities that misalign with the investor's own values. Devout Catholics may wish to invest in funds that exclude companies that donate to, for example, Planned Parenthood (Nasdaq: CATH); a Muslim nation's sovereign wealth fund may systematically exclude companies whose practices violate Shariah law (Nasdaq: HLAL); a pro-American investor may wish to invest in funds excluding companies that offshore US jobs (e.g., New York Stock Exchange: YALL).

The principal challenge for new funds that screen out or underweight certain kinds of companies is the same challenge associated with ESG funds: it's not rational to think that such funds will outperform the market or even match it if the goal in choosing stocks was something other than value maximization.

To be sure, some investors are fine with sacrificing investment return to ensure that they do not hold securities in companies that are antithetical to their values. But this represents a very small minority of people, which raises a fundamental challenge for such investors: even if they succeed at penalizing the companies in undesired sectors a little bit, that simply creates an opportunity for other investors to buy that security at a lower price. That's part of the reason why values-promoting asset managers should, all else equal, expect to underperform investors who are not subject to the same constraint. But even more, it's a reason to believe that values-promoting asset managers will not be successful at achieving their intended social goals, because the underlying companies are not dependent upon them for capital or support. As one ESG skeptic put it, Middle Eastern investors may say, "We're against drinking; we don't want to own alcohol companies." But they don't think that by not owning them, they will stop people in France from drinking wine.[7]

Alternatively, such investors can use proxy voting and shareholder engagement as their tool of choice: instead of divesting from "woke" companies, they can *invest* in those same companies and help change the undesired behaviors at the corporate level. They can take a page from the ESG playbook but use it to score points for the other team. Counterintuitively, this may even be a path back to neutrality in the boardroom. If CEOs feel pressure from certain investors to pursue left-wing values and pressure from other investors to pursue right-wing values, those CEOs may feel empowered to ignore both sets of investors equally and to focus on doing what they feel is best for the business overall.

To date, the impact of "conservative" shareholder engagement has been limited, simply because there are no major asset managers pushing these values. The Free Enterprise Project[8] (FEP), housed at the nonprofit National Center for Public Policy Research, has been a conservative shareholder advocate for more than a decade. It has filed hundreds of shareholder resolutions on issues such as increasing viewpoint diversity, pushing back against the green agenda, and challenging questionable DEI practices. But its proposals tend to attract low shareholder support. That's in part because the proxy advisory firms ISS and Glass Lewis recommended voting against the FEP's proposals. Additionally, Broadridge Financial Solutions, which maintains a widely used proxy voting platform, regularly labels FEP proposals "antisocial" without providing a definition of that term. The FEP also publishes two free annual voter guides for right-of-center investors, but it's up to individual investors to navigate the complex and sometimes impenetrable process of actually voting their own shares.

A nonprofit is just that: a nonprofit. And the for-profit enterprises working on these issues aren't very big. The largest Catholic asset management fund in the world, Ave Maria Mutual Funds, has just $3 billion in assets under management.[9] That's nothing to sneeze at, but it amounts to approximately .03 percent of the amount managed by BlackRock. Due to the lack of capital scale of such asset managers and proxy voting options, they have not yet had a material impact on increasing the diversity of competing values in the boardroom.

But what if investors want to focus on maximizing *value* instead of promoting any values at all? The easiest thing that return-hungry investors can do is capitalize on the market dislocations created by ESG investors. Suppose a large swath of investors divests from alcoholic beverage producers (or coal producers or oil producers and so on). That would create an opportunity for other investors to buy those assets at a lower price. Call it a form of ESG arbitrage. Some firms are already quietly engaged in this kind of behavior, though fewer than one might expect because behemoths such as CalPERS and others also invest in these funds and demand that they adopt the ESG objectives that created the price dislocations in the first place.

This means it's harder for asset managers who use this strategy to find clients willing to invest. If an asset manager cannot raise money from large asset allocators such as CalPERS, which imposes ESG mandates on its investment strategy, that necessarily means that it has a smaller set of investors who can provide capital. But that's the truth of finding a unique way to make money: it's hard for a reason, or else someone would've done it already.

The reality is that most large asset allocators require a track record—often an extensive one—before they will invest with a new fund manager. But there's a simpler strategy for getting started: don't try to beat the market, just replicate the market with index funds and then use pro-value proxy voting and shareholder engagement to drive corporate behavioral change. Here the theory of victory over ESG is different from *values*-promoting shareholder engagement—by exclusively promoting *value* instead.

This model is the simplest of all: just replicate the index funds offered by large asset managers such as BlackRock, State Street, and Vanguard. No fund will meaningfully outperform the others, but the point of a new family of funds would be to deliver a different mandate to portfolio companies—namely, to focus exclusively on value maximization rather than on promoting anyone's values, be they progressive ESG values or Christian-conservative values. If scaled up over the long run, these funds have the potential to drive changes in corporate behavior that should, at least in theory, improve the value of all index funds—even those offered by the Big Three.

Another model is to drive a similar kind of change by disrupting the duopoly of ISS and Glass Lewis, which today wield a greater than 95 percent duopoly in the marketplace for proxy advisory services. As you will recall from chapter 5, in recent years, these firms have almost uniformly supported ESG-promoting shareholder proposals and corporate actions. Yet investors who wish to vote their shares exclusively based on value maximization can choose an alternative that provides precisely that.

I founded Strive to pursue these latter two approaches: providing index funds that differ from those offered by the Big Three in terms of proxy voting and shareholder engagement, as well as providing a proxy voting advisory option that competes with ISS and Glass Lewis. Strive's mandate to underlying companies is simple: focus on excellence over politics; provide excellent products and services to your customers; and maximize value for your shareholders by doing that rather than advancing any particular social or political agenda.

As this book goes to print, Strive has publicly engaged with some of the United States' largest companies, from Chevron to ExxonMobil to Disney to Apple. Speaking as a proprietor, I feel it would probably be best if other competitors didn't pop up to offer the exact same products—but in reality, the barrier to entry is relatively low. From my vantage point as a citizen, that's a good thing. I hope that by the time you read this book, there will already be new competitors to Strive aiming to do something similar—and that in due course the new Big Three asset managers will not be three financial institutions that together advance a monolithic social agenda but will include at least one or two major alternatives whose sole objective is to promote value maximization. If that materializes, the market solution will be the most potent one of all—and one that can end the ESG debate for good.

State Pension Funds: Proxy Vote Banking

States that are hungry to take action against ESG are weighing a wide range of legislative proposals. As I argued above, the simplest approach for legislators and regulators to take isn't to ban ESG per se but simply to require affirmative disclosure to—and express consent from—the capital owners whose funds are used to advance ESG objectives.

But many of these states forget that they are not only regulators but market participants. State pension funds today have invested nearly $5 trillion into capital markets, much of which is directly managed by ESG-promoting asset managers. Leading governors and treasurers in red states began to express consternation in 2022 about their newfound knowledge that their state funds were being used to promote one-sided environmental and social agendas, but the reality is that the decisions of their own pension funds had contributed to the problem.

In 2022, I traveled the country to meet with many of these pension fund boards in a diverse range of states, including red states. When I arrived and asked pension fund staff and board members about the proclamations of their elected officials against ESG and compared them to how their own states' funds had been used to support ESG proposals in corporate America, the most candid answers I received tended to be shared when the elected officials weren't present. "We don't report to them," staff members often said. I often asked whom they *did* report to. They said to their boards. When I then asked who the pension fund boards reported to, I never got a straight answer.

That's a matter for governmental reform of the bureaucratic-managerial class—but it falls outside the scope of this book. The point is that if there are market alternatives available, red states (and for that matter purple and blue states, too) have two options to address the fiduciary gap raised by ESG without having to pass or implement a single new law or regulation.

The first is to redirect funds away from ESG-promoting asset managers and toward asset managers that invest with the sole objective of maximizing investment return. To the extent that a manager is uncertain about the argument I have advanced in this book—that the long-termism justification behind ESG is a farce—and instead genuinely believes that ESG may sometimes maximize financial value, there is an intermediate approach. It's one that is familiar to any fund manager: diversification. If you find the arguments in this book plausible but also find BlackRock's arguments plausible, you can split the difference and at least diversify between the strategies. The perfect need not be the enemy of the good—and restoring true diversity of views to corporate boardrooms is a good thing.

Pension fund managers are notoriously slow at moving money, however. They are generally not rewarded for taking risks, even small ones. The status quo is perceived as "safe"; moving money is not. Moving money away from a fund manager such as BlackRock is a big deal for a pension fund manager. (Note that although plenty of Republican state treasurers were quick to issue press releases in 2022 about their divestment of funds from BlackRock, the amounts divested were a pittance compared to the amounts invested into BlackRock products by pension funds in those very same states.)

But for Republicans who care about staying true to their free market principles and who are reluctant to use regulation or new legislation to address ESG, and even for pension fund managers who are reluctant to move funds (even nonrationally so), there's another step that these states can take. These states could collectively demand that large asset managers restore their proxy voting power, but do so as a large bloc of twenty or more states whose pension fund system assets, *in the aggregate*, would rival those of the larger players such as California and New York. CalPERS and CalSTRS may control in the neighborhood of $800 billion and NYSLRS and NYCPPF about $500 billion, but red states combined control more than $6.6 trillion. This bloc could then hire a third party—an alternative to either the ISS/Glass Lewis duopoly or the Big Three—not only to vote its proxies but also to engage with public companies to offer a competing message to that advanced by BlackRock, State Street, Vanguard, and other ESG-promoting asset managers. This voting bloc could speak with a unified pro-fiduciary voice that would have a more significant impact on the behavior of corporations by putting their boards on notice that there is an alternative perspective—with voting power to back it up—that demands that companies behave in a manner different from that assumed by the ESG orthodoxy in recent years. That would likely be the single most effective means of states' driving pro-fiduciary behavioral change in corporate America—not as regulators but as market participants on behalf of their constituents.

The EleFink in the Room

The foregoing solutions address what can be done to address ESG in the future, but they still fail to address ESG-related wrongdoings over the past decade. In my last book, *Nation of Victims: Identity Politics, the Death of Merit, and the Path Back to Excellence,* I argued that the path from victimhood to excellence runs through forgiveness but that there can be no forgiveness without repentance.

There's no party more suitable to ask for repentance than the world's largest asset manager: BlackRock. At BlackRock, things have gone very, very wrong. To date its board has done nothing to recompense its ultimate clients for its breaches of trust. The company has made only token gestures toward mending its relationships with clients who did not consent to their money being used to promote BlackRock's ESG agenda, but none of those gestures will carry any weight without addressing the elephant in the room: Larry Fink.

Arguably, Fink masterminded the largest financial scam in modern history. BlackRock amassed *trillions* of dollars by promising non-ESG clients that it would invest their money with purely financial interests in mind. The product page for BlackRock's largest index fund, its iShares Core S&P 500 ETF, for example, expressly states, **"This fund does not seek to follow a sustainable, impact or ESG investment strategy."**[10] [Note that the emphasis is BlackRock's.]

Investors took BlackRock at its word. But it's a promise BlackRock never intended to keep. Rather, as one of BlackRock's many "sustainable investing" pages touts, BlackRock integrates ESG "across all our portfolios," including in its ESG-disavowing index funds.[11] As I discussed in Chapter 5, BlackRock votes nearly all of its shares the same way, and it engages with portfolio companies with one ESG-aligned voice. And as discussed in Chapter 3, none of this advocacy is helping investors make money—not in the short term, not in the long term, not ever. Regular investors, and their money, are simply being taken along for BlackRock's ESG ride.

Larry Fink's scam is on a scale at least three orders of magnitude greater than that of Sam Bankman-Fried, impacting tens of millions of people in the United States alone. Sure, this wasn't a case where investors lost all their money as they did with SBF. But they were cheated nonetheless. Yet rather than jail time, Larry Fink's been rewarded with a board seat on the World Economic Forum at Davos and eight-figure compensation packages while US citizens are left holding the bag.

Recently, BlackRock has taken microscopic steps to try to regain clients' trust. Its new Voting Choice program, as you've read, purports to allow clients to take back their ballots and vote their own shares. But the program is available to only a fraction of clients. It applies to voting only and so does nothing to address the soft engagements that BlackRock enters into. And third-party voting options are limited to slates offered by ISS and Glass Lewis, both of which promote ESG. When it comes to choosing a third party to vote your shares, the choices are ESG 1, ESG 2, and ESG 3.

If BlackRock truly wanted to offer a choice, it would need to provide real alternatives to its clients who do not want to be held hostage by its proxy voting or shareholder engagement practices. An apolitical option that would maximize value over politics and focus on products over social agendas would go a long way toward doing that. But in the absence of substantive change at BlackRock, this isn't likely to happen. So long as BlackRock prioritizes the appearance of choice over choice, another firm—say, Strive—could not possibly partner with BlackRock, or else it would just be signing up for the charade and its cover-up.

What will substantive change look like? There's no silver bullet, but whatever it is, it will likely have to involve real sacrifices for the people who have benefited from the game so far. BlackRock cannot claim to offer investors "proxy choice" without also substantially modifying its pro-ESG engagement policy. And astoundingly, the leader of its Voting Choice program is none other than Larry Fink[12]—as preposterous as if FTX, postcollapse, were to offer a new crypto coin that it promises will be different, only to rehire SBF as its CEO.

BlackRock should extricate itself from the industrywide commitments that it has signed, including the Net Zero Asset Managers initiative, the United Nations Principles for Responsible Investment, and the Climate Action 100+ network. If this costs it the support of CalPERS as a client, so be it; that has no bearing on or benefit to any of its other clients that do not benefit from BlackRock's relationship with CalPERS.

The most palpable gesture of good faith of all would be the simplest: BlackRock should force Larry Fink to step down as CEO. Some of BlackRock's clients are already calling for that to happen. In December 2022, North Carolina's treasurer did so[13]—as did BlackRock's former sustainable investment chief, who called his former boss an "emperor with no clothes" who has "lock[ed] himself in the bathroom" rather than "enter the [ESG] debate to clarify what he's saying."[14] So did the BlackRock shareholder and European asset management firm Bluebell Capital Partners, which said that Larry Fink's "hypocrisy" has "unnecessarily politicized the ESG debate."[15]

So far, BlackRock has refused, saying "It is absurd [to] suggest a chief executive step down who has delivered a cumulative total return to shareholders over 23 years of 7,700%—the best performing financial firm in the S&P."[16] Yet BlackRock's response may be the more absurd suggestion—ironically, by touting its own stock price. It's almost as if it admits that shareholders really care only about long-term financial metrics yet imposes different, value-laden objectives on portfolio companies anyway. ESG for thee, but not for me.

That jig may soon be up. In October 2022, UBS downgraded BlackRock, explaining that its "proactive ESG stance has recently drawn pushback from both sides," increasing the risk that its clients will pull out funds.[17] As of the end of 2022, BlackRock's stock price was down by 9.4 percent from its April 2022 high. Its AUM is down, too. The castle is under siege.

BlackRock's board would do well to eat its own cooking with some real "governance"—by creating a special committee of independent directors to investigate what went wrong and why. Once the committee makes its findings, BlackRock needs a plan to move forward. One very real possibility is for it to break itself into two: BlackRock Financial and BlackRock ESG. It's the only way for it to be truly loyal to its ESG and non-ESG clients alike.

There's a legal way to do it. It's called a spin-off: the company breaks itself in two, and existing shareholders get proportionate pieces of each of the new companies. This is not unprecedented; Viacom was spun off of CBS in the 1970s, and AOL was spun off of Time Warner in 2009. The reasons vary, but often board members think that the two companies would be more successful separately than they are combined. In August 2022, for example, the activist investor Daniel Loeb asked Disney to consider spinning off ESPN. He believed that a spin-off would be better for both companies because it would give ESPN "greater flexibility to pursue business initiatives that may be more difficult as part of Disney, such as sports betting."[18] In other words, Disney fans don't like sports betting, ESPN fans do, so ESPN should spin off into its own company to do its own thing.

That sounds a lot like BlackRock. BlackRock's ESG fans don't like coal, so BlackRock should spin BlackRock Financial off so that it is free to invest in new fracking ventures. And vice versa: BlackRock's financial fans don't love net zero goals, so BlackRock should spin BlackRock ESG into its own company to unabashedly follow its net zero dreams.

I'm typically not a fan of asking companies to form special committees and hire expensive outside auditors to generate reports. But you know who is? BlackRock. Time and again, it has asked other companies to do racial equity audits, gender pay gap reports, and climate reports. If those efforts had BlackRock's support, the effort described in this chapter—to get to the bottom of what I see as the largest financial scam in human history—should have its full support as well.

Conclusion

In May 2011, the Nobel Prize–winning economist Joseph Stiglitz published an essay entitled "Of the 1%, by the 1%, for the 1%," condemning the extreme wealth concentration plaguing the United States: "The upper 1 percent of Americans are now taking in nearly a quarter of the nation's income every year. In terms of wealth rather than income, the top 1 percent control 40 percent."[19] He also pointed out that inequality in the United States had grown starkly worse over the previous twenty-five years and that outside the top 1 percent, income was actually falling. Just a few months later, Occupy Wall Street protesters would take their cue from Stiglitz, proclaiming "We are the 99 percent."

Needless to say, inequality didn't improve much in the ensuing decade. According to Senator Bernie Sanders, "In the year 2022 . . . 45% of all new income goes to the top 1%, and CEOs of large corporations make a record-breaking 350 times what their workers earn."[20] Sanders calls this disparity "obscene."[21]

The 1 percent may be getting a bad rap from these statistics. In reality, inequality in the United States is even *more* skewed. With more granular data, the economists Emmanuel Saez and Gabriel Zucman found that the surge in US wealth inequality over the last couple of decades was "concentrated mostly within the *top .1%*."[22] Regardless, the chasm between rich and poor in the United States is real, and it imperils the American dream of a casteless society in which no hereditary wealthy class exists and all people have an equal opportunity to rise.

However, the relentless focus on rich and poor, on the top 1 percent or top .1 percent—on the have-yachts versus the have-nots—can distract from a wealth concentration of far greater magnitude. Individual wealth disparities in the United States may or may not have reached the highest levels in this country's history. But the *corporate* concentration of wealth today is unprecedented in *world* history.

In terms of asset value, history's wealthiest company prior to the current era may have been the juggernaut known as the VOC—the Vereenigde Oost-Indische Compagnie, or Dutch East India Company. Between 1600 and 1800, the VOC sent roughly 1 percent of the population of Europe abroad to work its trade routes in Asia. It was roughly five times as large as its vast counterpart, the British East India Company. It employed fifty thousand to seventy thousand people and had private armies of up to ten thousand soldiers. Although monetary conversions are tricky and asset valuations trickier, the VOC's total value at its peak may have been in the neighborhood of .06 percent of the entire world's gross domestic product at the time.

That's a stunning figure, but it's chicken feed compared to the asset value of the Big Three today. Taken together, with their $20 trillion in assets under management, BlackRock, Vanguard, and State Street control the equivalent of *about 20 percent* of global GDP. Nothing like this level of corporate wealth has been seen before in the history of the world.

Money is power. The control of billions of dollars confers enormous power. With the control of trillions, the amount of power is incalculable. The Big Three may not have armies at their disposal, but they have more power over all of corporate America than any other person or entity, private or governmental, has ever had before. And they are using that power to impose on Americans a social and political ideology of their own choosing—an ideology with which many citizens disagree, an agenda serving their interests, an agenda that was never voted into law by the country's elected representatives.

The phrase *threat to democracy* is wildly overused today. So I won't say that the Big Three's jamming ESG down American throats is a threat to democracy. Rather, as former attorney general William Barr and law professor Jed Rubenfeld put it, it is a *usurpation* of democracy.[23]

This is not—and should not be—a partisan issue. In fact, the dangers of excessive corporate power have historically been a core concern more for the Left than for the Right. It's the Left that most vociferously protests *Citizens United* and the power of corporate money in US elections. The original target of the Occupy protests included not only income inequality but "corporate influence on democracy."[24] But when it comes to ESG, the Left has lost its way.

Today, liberal, progressive, and woke Americans worship, rather than fight against, Wall Street behemoths imposing their preferred social and political ideology of them. The simple explanation is that the Left finds the ideology Wall Street is currently promoting to be congenial. The Left likes ESG and as a result has abandoned its own principles. If instead of ESG, Wall Street were forcing corporate America to deny medical coverage for gender transitions or to make employees acknowledge that biological sex is a fact, progressives would be up in arms. Democratic attorneys general would be making the same fiduciary duty arguments that today only Republican attorneys general advance. Democratic politicians would be apoplectic that the White House had passed new regulations allowing pension fiduciaries to use Americans' money to promote that agenda while concealing it from the very people whose money they're managing.

The United States' social and political policies should be decided by the American people through uncensored First Amendment public discourse and elections. They should not be made by a handful of corporations in control of a staggering, historically unprecedented share of worldwide wealth. Only then will we have a government that is "of the people, by the people, for the people."

ACKNOWLEDGMENTS

I would like to thank Chris Nicholson, Stephanie Solomon, and Jed Rubenfeld, who were instrumental in preparing this book. Without their sheer brilliance and commitment, this book would not have been possible.

I am grateful to the team at HarperCollins for taking such interest in this book; to the entire team at Strive who helped me turn many of the ideas in this book into positive solutions; to all of the people who ever took a bet on me when they didn't have to; and to my wife and family for supporting me at every step in one seemingly crazy endeavor after another.

NOTES

Introduction

1. Steve Eder and Karey Wutkowski, "Goldman's 'Fabulous' Fab's Conflicted Love Letters," Reuters, April 25, 2010, https://www.reuters.com/article/us-goldman-emails/goldmans-fabulous-fabs-conflicted-love-letters-idUSTRE63O26E20100425.
2. Gregory White, "Fabrice Tourre, 'The Fabulous Fab,'" Business Insider, April 26, 2010, https://www.businessinsider.com/fabrice-tourre-fabulous-fab-2010-4.
3. Greg Gordon, "How Hank Paulson's Inaction Helped Goldman Sachs," Truthout.org (Truthout, October 10, 2010), https://truthout.org/articles/how-hank-paulsons-inaction-helped-goldman-sachs/.
4. Dave Michaels, "SEC Is Investigating Goldman Sachs over ESG Funds," *Wall Street Journal*, June 10, 2022, https://www.wsj.com/articles/sec-is-investigating-goldman-sachs-over-esg-funds-sources-say-11654895917.
5. "Summary Prospectus," Goldman Sachs U.S. Equity ESG Fund, Dec. 27, 2019, https://www.sec.gov/Archives/edgar/data/822977/000119312520234885/d96499d497k.htm.
6. Somini Sengupta, "How Greenwashing Fools Us," *New York Times*, August 23, 2022, https://www.nytimes.com/2022/08/23/climate/climate-greenwashing.html.
7. Ryan Young, "If You Play with Antitrust Fire, You Might Get Burned," *The Wall Street Journal* (Dow Jones & Company, March 13, 2022), https://www.wsj.com/articles/esg-investing-environment-activism-antitrust-brnovich-11647138672.
8. Vivek Ramaswamy, "Shareholders Stand up for Profit and Against ESG at Chevron," Strive Asset Management, October 24, 2022, https://strive.com/strive-asset-managementshareholders-stand-up-for-profit-and-against-esg-at-chevron/.
9. Xu Yihe, "PetroChina Aims for Start-up from Chevron-Abandoned Block in China," Upstream Online, August 15, 2022, https://www.upstreamonline.com/field-development/petrochina-aims-for-start-up-from-chevron-abandoned-block-in-china/2-1-1277849?zephr_sso_ott=bGEuKV.
10. Joseph Stiglitz, "What Next for Sri Lanka?," World Economic Forum, February 1, 2016, https://www.weforum.org/agenda/2016/02/what-next-for-sri-lanka/.

11. "Srilanka: MONLAR Backs Government Decision to Ban Import of Chemical Fertil-izers," La Via Campesina, May 11, 2021, https://viacampesina.org/en/srilanka-monlar-backs-government-decision-to-ban-import-of-chemical-fertilizers/.

12. World Bank, "World Bank and European Union Support Sri Lanka's Agriculture Modernization and Job Creation," World Bank, May 25, 2021, https://www.world bank.org/en/news/press-release/2021/05/25/world-bank-and-eu-support-sri-lankas -agriculture-modernization.

13. Indrajit Samarajiva, "Sri Lanka Collapsed First, but It Won't Be the Last," *New York Times*, August 15, 2022, https://www.nytimes.com/2022/08/15/opinion/international -world/sri-lanka-economic-collapse.html.

14. David Blackmon, "Rising Social Unrest over Energy, Food Shortages Threatens Global Stability," *Forbes*, July 11, 2022, https://www.forbes.com/sites/davidblack mon/2022/07/10/rising-social-unrest-over-energy-food-shortages-threatens-global -stability/?sh=3e685c96568b.

Chapter 1: WHAT IS ESG?

1. Ethan Peck, "Who Are the World Economic Forum's 'Young Global Leaders?' The Names May Surprise You," Human Events, November 11, 2022, https://humanevents com/2022/11/10/world-economic-forum-young-global-leaders.

2. E. Merrick Dodd, "For Whom Are Corporate Managers Trustees?," *Harvard Law Review* 45, no. 7 (May 1932): 1145–63, https://www.jstor.org/stable/1331697#metadata _info_tab_contents.

3. Milton Friedman, "A Friedman Doctrine: The Social Responsibility Of Business Is to Increase Its Profits," *New York Times*, September 13, 1970, https://www.nytimes .com/1970/09/13/archives/a-friedman-doctrine-the-social-responsibility-of-business -is-to.html.

4. I explained this in detail in my first book, *Woke, Inc.: Inside Corporate America's Social Justice Scam*, chap. 6.

5. Klaus Schwab, "Davos Manifesto 1973: A Code of Ethics for Business Leaders," World Economic Forum, December 2, 2019, https://www.weforum.org/agenda/2019/12 /davos-manifesto-1973-a-code-of-ethics-for-business-leaders/.

6. Neelam Jhawar and Shasta Gupta, *Understanding CSR: Its History and the Recent De-velopments* (IOSR Journal of Business and Management, 2017), https://www.iosrjour nals.org/iosr-jbm/papers/Vol19-issue5/Version-6/P1905061051o9.pdf.

7. Ramon Mullerat, "Corporate Social Responsibility: A European Perspective," Miami–Florida European Union Center of Excellence, June 2013, https://aei.pitt.edu/43368/1 /Mullerat_CSR_Europa.pdf.

8. Judy Oh, "3 Paradigm Shifts In Corporate Sustainability Marks New Era of ESG," World Economic Forum, September 30, 2021, https://www.weforum.org /agenda/2021/09/3-paradigm-shifts-in-corporate-sustainability-to-esg/.

9. Ibid.

10. "The Evolution of ESG Investing," MSCI, https://www.msci.com/esg-101-what-is -esg/evolution-of-esg-investing.

11. CFI Team, "Socially Responsible Investment (SRI)," CFI, January 12, 2023, https:// corporatefinanceinstitute.com/resources/esg/socially-responsible-investment-sri/.

12. Curtis King, "A Brief History of Sustainable Investing," (JPMorgan Chase & Co., April 18, 2022), https://www.chase.com/personal/investments/learning-and-insights/article/a-brief-history-of-sustainable-investing#:~:text=In%20the%201960s%20and%20%2770s,way%20to%20influence%20corporate%20behavior.

13. Janet Lorin and Sergio Chapa, "Harvard's Status as Wealthiest School Faces Oil-Rich Contender in the University of Texas," Bloomberg, August 26, 2022, https://saylordotorg.github.io/text_the-sustainable-business-case-book/s16-02-pax-world.html.

14. Ibid.

15. Ramaswamy, *Woke, Inc.*, 110.

16. Will Hild, Twitter, December 15, 2022, https://twitter.com/WillHild/status/1603492415410692111.

17. "ESG," State Street Corporation, https://www.statestreet.com/us/en/individual/solutions/ESG#:~:text=ESG%20informs%20our%20long%2Dterm,resilient%20markets%2C%20economies%20and%20societies.

18. International Finance Corporation, World Bank Group, *Who Cares Wins: Connecting Financial Markets to a Changing World*, International Finance Corporation, World Bank Group, June 2004, https://www.unepfi.org/fileadmin/events/2004/stocks/who_cares_wins_global_compact_2004.pdf.

19. "Investment Philosophy," IMPAX Asset Management, https://impaxam.com/investment-philosophy/.

20. Tetsushi Kajimoto and Takaya Yamaguchi, "Japan Unveils Record Budget in Boost to Military Spending," Reuters, December 23, 2022, https://www.reuters.com/markets/asia/japan-unveils-record-budget-boost-military-capacity-2022-12-23/.

21. Vivienne Machi, "EU Scrambles to Channel Hefty Defense-Spending Boost into Joint Buys," DefenseNews, December 8, 2022, https://www.defensenews.com/global/europe/2022/12/08/eu-scrambles-to-channel-hefty-defense-spending-boost-into-joint-buys/.

22. Brent Sadler, "NDAA's Boost in Defense Spending Sends Message to Russia, China," The Heritage Foundation, January 3, 2023, https://www.heritage.org/defense/commentary/ndaas-boost-defense-spending-sends-message-russia-china.

23. Ron Lieber, "Socially Responsible, with Egg on Its Face," *New York Times*, August 22, 2008, https://www.nytimes.com/2008/08/23/business/yourmoney/23money.html.

24. "Impax Large Cap Fund," IMPAX Asset Management, 2022, https://impaxam.com/products/sustainability-lens-equities/us-large-cap-strategy/impax-large-cap-fund/.

25. "Morningstar's U.S. Fund Fee Study," Morningstar, Inc., https://www.morningstar.com/lp/annual-us-fund-fee-study.

26. Andrew Ross Sorkin, "BlackRock's Message: Contribute to Society, or Risk Losing Our Support," *New York Times*, January 15, 2018, https://www.nytimes.com/2018/01/15/business/dealbook/blackrock-laurence-fink-letter.html.

27. "BlackRock's Approach to Companies That Manufacture and Distribute Civilian Firearms," BlackRock, March 2, 2018, https://www.blackrock.com/corporate/newsroom/press-releases/article/corporate-one/press-releases/blackrock-approach-to-companies-manufacturing-distributing-firearms.

28. Sarah Krouse, "BlackRock Plans to Block Walmart, Dick's from Some Funds over Guns," *Wall Street Journal*, April 5, 2018, https://www.wsj.com/articles/blackrockd-plans-to-block-walmart-dicks-from-some-funds-over-guns-1522940521.

29. Akhilesh Ganti, "What Is Investing for Sustainability Impact (IFSI)?," Investopedia,

October 30, 2022, https://www.investopedia.com/investing-for-sustainability-impact-5210477.

30. "About Climate Action 100+," Climate Action 100+, https://www.climateaction100.org/about/.

31. "The Net Zero Asset Managers Commitment," Net Zero Asset Managers initiative, https://www.netzeroassetmanagers.org/commitment/.

32. "About Us," Glasgow Financial Alliance for Net Zero, https://www.gfanzero.com/about/.

33. Nick Schifrin, "COP27 and International Climate Action: A Conversation with John Kerry," Council on Foreign Relations, October 25, 2022, https://www.cfr.org/event/cop27-and-international-climate-action-conversation-john-kerry.

34. "ESG vs. CSR | Differences, Definitions & Implementation," TRC, June 20, 2022, https://www.trccompanies.com/insights/esg-vs-csr-how-environmental-social-governance-differs-from-corporate-social-responsibility/.

35. Persefoni Team, "UN PRI: Everything You Need to Know," Persefoni, August 4, 2022, https://persefoni.com/learn/un-pri.

36. Jackie Ferguson, "How DEI, CSR and ESG Are Already Changing the Way We Work Today," *Forbes*, October 18, 2022, https://www.forbes.com/sites/forbesbusinesscouncil/2022/10/18/how-dei-csr-and-esg-are-already-changing-the-way-we-work-today/?sh=1590bdc22b2c.

37. "Frequently Asked Questions," United Nations Environment Program—Finance Initiative, https://www.unepfi.org/legal-framework-for-impact/faq/.

38. Mister Accountability, Twitter, January 2, 2023, https://twitter.com/accountabletome/status/1609976787756519424.

Chapter 2: THE BIGGEST FIDUCIARY BREACH IN US HISTORY

1. "AG Brnovich Letter to BlackRock, Inc. RE: ESG Concerns," August 4, 2022, Arizona Attorney General Kris Mayes, https://www.azag.gov/media/interest/ag-brnovich-letter-blackrock-inc-re-esg-concerns.

2. "SEC Charges Goldman Sachs Asset Management for Failing to Follow its Policies and Procedures Involving ESG Investments," US Securities and Exchange Commission, November 22, 2022, https://www.sec.gov/news/press-release/2022-209.

3. Frederick Pollock and Frederic William Maitland, *The History of English Law Before the Time of Edward I*, 2nd ed., vol. 2 (Cambridge, UK: Cambridge University Press, 1898), http://files.libertyfund.org/files/2314/Pollock_1541-02_LFeBk.pdf, 231.

4. "Since the tax only applied to land that a man owned in his own name at death, the tax did not apply if the land legally belonged to a trustee, rather than to the deceased." John Morley, *The Common Law Corporation: The Power of the Trust in Anglo-American Business History* 116 Colum. L. Rev. 2145, 2152 (2016).

5. *McNally v. United States*, 483 U.S. 350, 362–63 n. 1 (1987).

6. Morley, *The Common Law Corporation*, 2157–66.

7. Banking Exchange Staff, "Some Sustainable Funds Are 'Expensive S&P 500 Trackers,'" Banking Exchange, May 11, 2021, https://m.bankingexchange.com/recent-articles/item/8695-some-sustainable-funds-are-expensive-s-p-500-trackers.

8. https://investor.vanguard.com/investment-products/etfs/profile/esgv.

9. Lauren Foster, "Sustainable Investing Failed Its First Big Test. A Reckoning Is Coming," *Barron's*, April 17, 2022, https://www.barrons.com/articles/esg-investing-big-test-reckoning-51650041442.

10. Ibid.

11. Ibid.

12. "Total Assets of Pension Funds in the United States from 2010 to 2020," Statista, May 23, 2022, https://www.statista.com/statistics/421729/pension-funds-assets-usa.

13. "Secretary-General Proposes Global Compact on Human Rights, Labour, Environment, in Address to the World Economic Forum in Davos," United Nations, February 1, 1999, https://www.un.org/press/en/1999/19990201.sgsm6881.html; Elizabeth Pollman, "The Origins and Consequences of the ESG Moniker," University of Pennsylvania Carey Law School Research Paper No. 22-23, https://ecgi.global/sites/?default/files/Paper%3A%20Elizabeth%20Pollman.pdf.

14. "What Are the Principles for Responsible Investment?," UNPRI, https://www.unprib.org/about-us/what-are-the-principles-for-responsible-investment.

15. "Private Equity Sustainable Investment Guidelines," CalPERS, https://www.calpers.ca.gov/docs/private-equity-sustainable-investment-guidelines.pdf.

16. 3 Restatement (Third) of Trusts § 78(1); see Uniform Trust Code §?802(a) (2000); Uniform Prudent Investor Act § 5 (1994).

17. *Central States, Southeast & Southwest Areas Pension Fund v. Central Transport, Inc.*, 472 U.S. 559, 570–71 (1985).

18. *Fifth Third Bancorp v. Dudenhoeffer*, 573 U.S. 409, 421 (2014).

19. T. Leigh Anenson, "Public Pensions and Fiduciary Law: A View from Equity," *University of Michigan Journal of Law Reform* 50, no. 2 (2016): 251, 258.

20. South Carolina Constitution, Art. X, sec. 16.

21. Opinion of the Attorney General of Kentucky, OAG 22-05, May 26, 2022 ("mixed-motive" investing violates pension trustees' fiduciary duty), 5; Opinion of the Attorney General of Indiana, No. 2022-3, September 1, 2022 ("A fiduciary breaches this duty merely by having a mixed motive"), 11; *Donovan v. Bierwirth*, 680 F.2d 263, 271 (2nd Cir. 1982) (pension fund fiduciary must "act for the exclusive purpose" of providing financial benefits to plan beneficiaries) (emphasis added); Max M. Schanzenbach and Robert H. Sitkoff, "Reconciling Fiduciary Duty and Social Conscience: The Law and Economics of ESG Investing by a Trustee," *Stanford University Law Review* 72 (2020): 381, 401.

22. Schanzenbach and Sitkoff, "Reconciling Fiduciary Duty," 401.

23. 3 Restatement (Third) of Trusts § 78(1)–(2) cmt. b.

24. Uniform Prudent Investor Act, § 5, cmt. (1994).

25. "BlackRock 2020 Sustainability Disclosure," BlackRock, https://www.blackrock.com/corporate/literature/continuous-disclosure-and-important-information/blackrock-2020-sasb-disclosure.pdf, 6.

26. "Sustainability: The Path to Net Zero," BlackRock, https://www.blackrock.com/ca/institutional/en/insights/blackrock-future-forum/sustainability-path-to-net-zero; "ESG: Trends, Opportunities and Solutions," https://www.blackrock.com/ca/institutional/en/education/esg-endowments-foundations?switchLocale=y&siteEntryPassthrough=true.

27. Douglas M. Grim and Daniel B. Berkowitz, "ESG, SRI, and Impact Investing: A Primer for Decision-Making," August 2018, at 4, https://perma.cc/42T2-K35T, 4.

28. Javier El-Hage, "Fixing ESG: Are Mandatory ESG Disclosures the Solution to Misleading ESG Ratings?," *Journal of Corporate and Finance Law* 26, no. 2 (2021): 366 (2021), https://ir.lawnet.fordham.edu/cgi/viewcontent.cgi?article=1499&context=jcfl.

29. "In index portfolios where the objective is to replicate a predetermined market benchmark, we engage with investee companies on ESG issues." "BlackRock ESG Integration Statement," revised December 13, 2022, https://www.?blackrock.com /corporate/literature/publication/blk-esg-investment-statement-web.pdf, 2.

30. Mark T. Uyeda, "Remarks at the 2022 Cato Summit on Financial Regulation," U.S. Securities & Exchange Commission, November 17, 2022, https://www.sec.gov/news /speech/uyeda-remarks-cato-summit-financial-regulation-111722.

31. Farhad Manjoo, "What BlackRock, Vanguard and State Street Are Doing to the Economy," *New York Times*, May 12, 2022, https://www.nytimes.com/2022/05/12/opinion /vanguard-power-blackrock-state-street.html.

32. BlackRock owns more than 1 trillion shares—or 5.7%—of PetroChina. "BlackRock Inc. ownership in PTR/PetroChina Co., Ltd.," February 3, 2022, https://fintel.io/so /us/ptr/blackrockd.

33. "About Color of Change," Color of Change, https://colorofchange.org/about/.

34. "Official Opinion 2022-3," Office of the Attorney General, State of Indiana, September 1, 2022, https://www.in.gov/attorneygeneral/files/Official-Opinion-2022-3.pdf.

35. *Securities and Exchange Commission v. Capital Gains Research Bureau, Inc.*, 375 U.S. 180, 194 (1963) (advisors are fiduciaries under federal and common law); "Commission Interpretation Regarding Standard of Conduct for Investment Advisers," U.S. Securities and Exchange Commission, June 5, 2019, https://www.sec.gov/rules/interp /2019/ia-5248.pdf ("Under federal law, an investment adviser is a fiduciary").

36. "Commission Interpretation Regarding Standard of Conduct for Investment Advisers," 7-8.

37. 1 Investment Advisers: Law & Compliance § 8.02 (2022), citing *TSC Industries v. Northway, Inc.*, 426 U.S. 438, 449 (1976); *Basic, Inc. v. Levinson*, 485 U.S. 224 (1988); and *SEC v. Capital Gains Research Bureau, Inc.*, 375 U.S. 180 (1963).

38. *Securities and Exchange Commission v. Capital Gains Research Bureau, Inc., et al.*, 375 U.S. 200; see also *Chiarella v. United States*, 445 U.S. 222, 228 (1980); *Securities and Exchange Commission v. Washington Investment Network*, 475 F.3d 392, 404 (D.C. Cir. 2007).

39. Cam Simpson and Saijel Kishan, "How BlackRock Made ESG the Hottest Ticket on Wall Street," Bloomberg, December 31, 2021, https://www.bloomberg.com/news/arti cles/2021-12-31/how-blackrock-s-invisible-hand-helped-make-esg-a-hot-ticket.

40. "Larry Fink's 2022 Letter to CEOs," BlackRock, https://www.blackrock.com/corpo rate/investor-relations/larry-fink-ceo-letter.

41. Dean Emerick, "What Is ESG and Why Is It Important?," ESG The Report, https:// www.esgthereport.com/what-is-esg-and-why-is-it-important.

42. "What Is Environmental, Social, and Governance (ESG) Investing?," Investopedia, September 27, 2022, https://www.investopedia.com/terms/e/environmental-social -and-governance-esg-criteria.asp.

43. Thomas Lee Hazen, "Corporate and Securities Law Impact on Social Responsibility and Corporate Purpose," *Boston College Law Review* 62 (2021): 851, 853-4.

44. "What Is Responsible Investment?," United Nations, https://www.unpri.org/an-in troduction-to-responsible-investment/what-is-responsible-investment/4780.article.

45. "Secretary-General Proposes Global Compact on Human Rights, Labour, Environment, in Address to the World Economic Forum in Davos," United Nations, February 1, 1999, https://www.un.org/press/en/1999/19990201.sgsm6881.html; Elizabeth Pollman, "The Origins and Consequences of the ESG Moniker," University of Pennsylvania Carey Law School Research Paper No. 22-23, https://ecgi.global/sites/default/files/Paper%3A%20Elizabeth%20Pollman.pdf.

46. "What Are the Principles for Responsible Investment?," United Nations, https://www.unpri.org/about-us/what-are-the-principles-for-responsible-investment.

47. BlackRock, "BlackRock Advantage ESG U.S. Equity Fund," BlackRock, as of Sept. 30, 2021, https://tickerfunds.com/uploads/prospectus/1638973859BlackRock%20Advantage%20ESG%20U.S.%20Equity%20FundQ3.pdf.

48. "One Fund, Three Names and Lots of Questions for 'ESG.'" Bloomberg Law, July 25, 2022, https://news.bloomberglaw.com/esg/one-fund-three-names-and-lots-of-questions-for-esg.

49. Schanzenbach and Sitkoff, "Reconciling Fiduciary Duty," 401.

50. *Green v. Fund Asset Management, L.P.*, 245 F.3d 214, 227 n.14 (3d Cir. 2001) (citing *Geddes v. Anaconda Copper Mining Co.*, 254 U.S. 590, 599 (1921)).

51. *Howard v. Shay*, 100 F.3d 1484, 1488–89 (9th Cir. 1996) (quoting *Leigh v. Engle*, 727 F.2d 113, 125–26 (7th Cir. 1984)).

Chapter 3: DOES ESG MAKE MONEY?

1. Vivek Ramaswamy, *Woke, Inc.: Inside Corporate America's Social Justice Scam* (New York: Center Street, 2021), 225.

2. Attorneys General Letter, BlackRock, August 4, 2022, https://www.blackrock.com/us/individual/literature/press-release/blackrock-response-attorneys-general.pdf, 5.

3. "Sustainable Data Insights Research," BlackRock, 2021, https://www.blackrock.com/corporate/literature/investor-education/sustainable-data-in-sights-research.pdf.

4. "Seeking Outperformance Through Sustainable Insights," BlackRock, 2021, https://web.archive.org/web/20211019143531/https://www.blackrock.com/corporate/literature/investor-education/sustainable-data-insights-research.pdf.

5. Ibid., 2.

6. Ibid., 3.

7. Iain Esau, "Net Zero By 2050 'Clearly Not Happening,' Warns Jefferies Executive," Upstream, August 31, 2022, https://www.upstreamonline.com/energy-transition/net-zero-by-2050-clearly-not-happening-warns-jefferies-executive/2-1-1287987.

8. Ramaswamy, *Woke, Inc.*, chap. 5.

9. Taylor Tepper, "It's Not Easy Being Green: Why Is ESG Underperforming in 2022?," *Forbes*, February 17, 2022, https://www.forbes.com/advisor/investing/why-is-esg-underperforming/.

10. Esther Whieldon and Robert Clark, "Most ESG Funds Outperformed S&P 500 in Early 2021 as Studies Debate Why," S&P Global, https://www.spglobal.com/marketintelligence/en/news-insights/latest-news-headlines/most-esg-funds-outperformed-s-p-500-in-early-2021-as-studies-debate-why-64811634.

11. Evie Liu, "Sustainable Funds Are Off to a Rough Start to the Year," *Barron's*, Febru-

ary 14, 2022, https://www.barrons.com/articles/esg-sustainable-funds-performance
-51644844397.

12. Guido Giese et al., "Performance and Risk Analysis of Index-Based ESG Portfolios,"
MSCI, Spring 2019, https://www.msci.com/documents/10199/b07d04e1-2cce-9f35
-5400-0e5cf4a0c76a.

13. Steve Johnson, "ESG Outperformance Narrative 'Is Flawed,' New Research Shows,"
Financial Times, May 2, 2021, https://www.ft.com/content/be140b1b-2249-4dd9-859c
-3f8f12ce6036.

14. "ESG Funds Set for First Annual Outflows in a Decade After Bruising Year," Reuters,
December 19, 2022, https://money.usnews.com/investing/news/articles/2022-12-19
/esg-funds-set-for-first-annual-outflows-in-a-decade-after-bruising-year.

15. Attorneys General Letter, BlackRock, 6.

16. "Taking Stock of the Energy Shock," BlackRock, March 2022, https://www.blackrock
.com/corporate/literature/whitepaper/bii-macro-perspectives-march-2022.pdf, 1.

17. Ibid., 8.

18. Ibid.

19. Ibid.

20. Tommy Wilkes and Patturaja Murugaboopathy, "ESG Funds Set for First Annual
Outflows in a Decade After Bruising Year," Reuters, December 19, 2022, https://www
.reuters.com/business/sustainable-business/esg-funds-set-first-annual-outflows-de
cade-after-bruising-year-2022-12-19/.

21. Elaine Chen, "ESG Fund Closures Pile Up as Do-Good Investing Takes Back Seat,"
Bloomberg, July 21, 2022, https://www.bloomberg.com/news/articles/2022-07-21/esg
fund-closures-pile-up-as-do-good-investing-takes-back-seat.

22. "BlackRock Closes ESG Absolute Return Fund over Lack of Demand," CityWire Se-
lector, March 16, 2022, https://citywire.com/selector/news/blackrock-closes-esg-ab
solute-return-fund-over-lack-of-demand/a2382539.

23. "Seeking Outperformance Through Sustainable Insights," BlackRock, 4.

24. Ibid., 5.

25. Ibid., 6.

26. Ibid., 12.

27. Steven E. Koonin, *Unsettled: What Climate Science Tells Us, What It Doesn't, and Why It
Matters* (Dallas: BenBella Books, 2021).

28. Richard P. Allan et al., "Summary for Policymakers," Intergovernmental Panel on
Climate Change, 2021, https://www.ipcc.ch/report/ar6/wg1/downloads/report/IPCC
_AR6_WGI_SPM.pdf, 5.

29. William Nordhaus, "Climate Change: The Ultimate Challenge for Economics," The
Nobel Prize, December 8, 2018, https://www.nobelprize.org/uploads/2018/10/nord
haus-lecture.pdf, 451.

30. Ibid., 449.

31. David Wallace-Wells, "Beyond Catastrophe: A New Climate Reality Is Coming
Into View," *New York Times*, October 26, 2022, https://www.nytimes.com/interac
tive/2022/10/26/magazine/climate-change-warming-world.html.

32. Ibid.

33. "The CAT Thermometer," Climate Action Tracker, November 2022, https://climate
actiontracker.org/global/cat-thermometer/.

34. Intergovernmental Panel on Climate Change, *Climate Change 2014: Impacts, Adaptation, and Vulnerability. Part A: Global and Sectoral Aspects* (New York: Cambridge University Press, 2014), https://www.ipcc.ch/site/assets/uploads/2018/02/WGIIAR5 -PartA_FINAL.pdf, p. 690.
35. Koonin, *Unsettled*, 178.
36. David R. Henderson, "Good Reasoning on Global Warming," *Financial and Economic Review* 21, no. 2 (June 2021), https://en-hitelintezetiszemle.mnb.hu/letoltes/fer-21-2 -br2-henderson.pdf, 207.
37. Richard S. J. Tol, "The Distributional Impact of Climate Change," *Annals of the New York Academy of Sciences* 1504, no. 1 (November 2020): 63–75, https://nyaspubs.on linelibrary.wiley.com/doi/10.1111/nyas.14497.
38. Nordhaus, "Climate Change," 452.
39. Ibid., 460.

Chapter 4: TERRIBLE AT PICKING STOCKS, GREAT AT PICKING LAWS

1. Barry Ritholtz, "Eric Balchunas on the Vanguard Effect," *Masters in Business* (podcast), Bloomberg Radio, 2023, https://podcasts.apple.com/us/podcast/eric-balchunas -on-the-vanguard-effect/id730188152?i=1000577386118.
2. Paul A. Samuelson, "Challenge to Judgment," *Journal of Portfolio Management* 1, no. 1 (1974): 17–19, https://jpm.pm-research.com/content/1/1/17.
3. John C. Bogle, "Bogle Sounds a Warning on Index Funds," *Wall Street Journal*, November 29, 2018, https://www.wsj.com/articles/bogle-sounds-a-warning-on-index -funds-1543504551.
4. Tim Harford, "Why the World's Biggest Investor Backs the Simplest Investment," BBC, July 17, 2017, https://www.bbc.com/news/business-40189970.
5. "ETF Versus Mutual Fund Taxes," Fidelity, https://www.fidelity.com/learning-center /investment-products/etf/etfs-tax-efficiency.
6. *The ETF Story* (podcast)), Bloomberg Radio, 2018, https://www.audible.com/pd /The-ETF-Story-Podcast/episodes/B08JJNJQ6S?clientContext=135-6411885 -0172547&ref=a pd_The-ET_c3_episodes_view_all&showAuthLoginBanner=true.
7. "Vanguard 500 Index Investor (VFINX)," YCharts, https://ycharts.com/mutual _funds/M:VFINX/total_assets_under_management.
8. "Trends in the Expenses and Fees of Funds," Investment Company Institute, March 2021, https://www.ici.org/doc-server/pdf%3Aper27-03.pdf.
9. Leo E. Strine, Jr., "One Fundamental Corporate Governance Question We Face: Can Corporations Be Managed for the Long Term Unless Their Powerful Electorates Also Act and Think Long Term?," *Business Lawyer* 66, no. 1 (November 2010)): 1–26, https://www.jstor.org/stable/25758524#metadata_info_tab_contents.
10. John C. Coates, IV, "The Future of Corporate Governance Part I: The Problem of Twelve," Harvard Public Law Working Paper No. 19-07, March 14, 2019, https://pa pers.ssrn.com/sol3/papers.cfm?abstract_id=3247337, 2.
11. Ibid., 13.
12. Ibid., 14.
13. Ibid., 19.

14. Lucian Bebchuck and Scott Hirst, "Index Funds and the Future of Corporate Governance: Theory, Evidence, and Policy," *Columbia Law Review* 119, no. 8 (December 2019), https://www.jstor.org/stable/26844587#metadata_info_tab_contents, 2053.

15. Jeff Sommer, "A Mutual Fund Master, Too Worried to Rest," *New York Times*, August 11, 2012, https://www.nytimes.com/2012/08/12/business/john-bogle-vanguards -founder-is-too-worried-to-rest.html.

16. Bogle, "Bogle Sounds a Warning on Index Funds."

Chapter 5: NO MANAGER CAN SERVE TWO MASTERS

1. Liz Hoffman, "An Activist Investor Has a Garbage Plan for Coca-Cola," Semafor, October 18, 2022, https://www.semafor.com/article/10/18/2022/coca-cola-activist-inves tor-engine-no-1-garbage.

2. Emily Stewart, "The Firm Behind Wall Street's Fearless Girl Statue Isn't as Pro-Woman as It Could Be," Vox, April 3, 2019, https://www.vox.com/business-and-fi nance/2019/4/3/18293611/fearless-girl-state-street-etf-she-nyse.

3. Paul Sullivan, "In Fledgling Exchange-Traded Fund, Striking a Blow for Women," *New York Times*, March 4, 2016, https://www.nytimes.com/2016/03/05/your-money /in-fledgling-exchange-traded-fund-striking-a-blow-for-women.html.

4. Larry Fink, "To Our Shareholders," BlackRock, April 9, 2018, https://s24.q4cdn .com/856567660/files/oar/2017/letter-to-shareholders.html.

5. "China's Expanding Middle Class is Starting to Look a Lot like the US', but It's Not a Good Thing," Business Insider, December 8, 2021, https://www.scmp.com/economy /china-economy/article/3158753/chinas-expanding-middle-class-starting-look-lot-us -its-not.

6. "China's Fund Industry Predicted to Grow Fivefold by 2025," *Financial Times*, April 18, 2018, https://www.ft.com/content/ca76b3a8-398a-11e8-8b98-2f31af407cc8.

7. Lingling Wei, Bob Davis, and Dawn Lim, "China Has One Powerful Friend Left in the U.S.: Wall Street," *Wall Street Journal*, December 2, 2020, https://www.wsj.com /articles/china-has-one-powerful-friend-left-in-the-u-s-wall-street-11606924454.

8. U.S. Securities and Exchange Commission, "The SEC, China & Offshore Shell Companies," YouTube, August 16, 2021, https://www.youtube.com/watch?v=6dKrRoU4O_k; Gary Gensler, "Statement on Investor Protection Related to Recent Developments in China," U.S. Securities and Exchange Commission, July 30, 2021, https://www .sec.gov/news/public-statement/gensler-2021-07-30; "Investor Bulletin: U.S.-Listed Companies Operating Chinese Businesses Through a VIE Structure," U.S. Securities and Exchange Commission, September 20, 2021, https://www.investor.gov/introduc tion-investing/general-resources/news-alerts/alerts-bulletins/investor-bulletins-95.

9. "The Role of Chinese Assets," BlackRock, May 2021, https://www.blackrock.com /us/individual/insights/blackrock-investment-institute/investing-in-chinese-assets; "Which Chinese Asset Do You Favor?," BlackRock, April 1, 2021, https://www.black rock.com/corporate/insights/blackrock-investment-institute/publications/question -of-the-week/april-1-2021; "Investing in China," BlackRock, https://www.blackrock .com/us/individual/insights/investing-in-china.

10. "iShares by BlackRock, 2022 Prospectus," BlackRock, December 1, 2022, https://

www.blackrock.com/us/financial-professionals/literature/prospectus/p-ishares-msci
-china-a-etf-7-31.pdf, 18.

11. Vivek Ramaswamy and Mike Pompeo, "China's Threat to Taiwan Semiconductors," *Wall Street Journal*, October 10, 2022, https://www.wsj.com/articles/investing-silicon
-semiconductors-chips-taiwan-invasion-tsmc-china-intel-blackrock-asset-manager
-11665408814.

12. Tom Donilon et al., "Geopolitical Risk Dashboard," BlackRock, September 22, 2022, https://www.blackrock.com/corporate/literature/whitepaper/geopolitical-risk-dash
board-september-2022.pdf.

13. BlackRock, Twitter, October 11, 2022, https://twitter.com/BlackRock/status/1579839
711862226945.

14. "BlackRock Investment Stewardship: Proxy Voting Guidelines for Chinese Securities," BlackRock, January 2023, https://www.blackrock.com/corporate/literature
/publication/blk-corporate-governance-and-proxy-voting-guidelines-for-chinese-se
curities.pdf.

15. "BlackRock Investment Stewardship: Proxy Voting Guidelines for U.S. Securities," BlackRock, January 2022, https://web.archive.org/web/20220119003458/https:/www
.blackrock.com/corporate/literature/fact-sheet/blk-responsible-investment-guide
lines-us.pdf.

16. Ibid.

17. Philippe Benoit and Kevin Tu, "Is China Still a Developing Country? And Why It Matters for Energy and Climate," Center on Global Energy Policy at Columbia University, School of International and Public Affairs, July 23, 2020, https://www.energypolicy
.columbia.edu/research/report/china-still-developing-country-and-why-it-matters
-energy-and-climate; Maxine Joselow, Michael Birnbaum, and Lily Kuo, "How China, the World's Top Polluter, Avoids Paying for Climate Change," *Washington Post*, November 23, 2022, https://www.washingtonpost.com/climate-environment/2022/11/23
/china-climate-finance-cop27/.

18. "Xi's ESG Boom Funnels Billions Into Coal, Liquor, Defense Stocks," Bloomberg News, September 26, 2022, https://www.bloomberg.com/news/articles/2022-09-06
/china-s-esg-fund-investing-boom-follows-xi-s-political-agenda#xj4y7vzkg.

19. Eduardo Corrochio, "BlackRock CEO Larry Fink: 'Markets Like Totalitarian Governments' (2011)" YouTube, September 6, 2022), https://www.youtube.com/watch?v-MF
VecfbffUE.

20. "BGF China Impact Fund," BlackRock, https://www.blackrock.com/ch/individual/en
/products/310252/blackrock-china-impact-fund.

21. Natalie Sauer, "Russia Formally Joins Paris Climate Agreement," Climate Home News, September 23, 2019, https://www.climatechangenews.com/2019/09/23/russia
-formally-joins-paris-climate-agreement/.

22. "Russia says sanctions will stop it cutting carbon emissions, but does it have a climate plan?," Euronews, March 18, 2022, https://www.euronews.com/green/2022/03/18
/russia-says-sanctions-will-stop-it-cutting-carbon-emissions-but-does-it-have-a-cli
mate-pla.

23. Angelina Davydova, "Will Russia Ever Leave Fossil Fuels Behind?," BBC, November 23, 2021, https://www.bbc.com/future/article/20211115-climate-change-can-russia
-leave-fossil-fuels-behind.

24. Valerie Richardson, "Leaked Emails Show Hillary Clinton Blaming Russians for

Funding 'Phony' Anti-Fracking Groups," *Washington Times*, October 10, 2016, https://www.washingtontimes.com/news/2016/oct/10/clinton-blames-russians-anti-fracking-groups/.

25. https://web.archive.org/web/20220310230148/https://republicans-energycommerce.house.gov/wp-content/uploads/2022/03/3.10.22-Letter-to-Sierra-Club.pdf; Letter to Natural Resources Defense Council, U.S. House of Representatives, March 10, 2022, https://web.archive.org/web/20220310205124/https://republicans-energycommerce.house.gov/wp-content/uploads/2022/03/3.10.22-Letter-to-NRDC.pdf.

26. Glenn Kessler, "The Bogus 'Allegation' That Putin Is Funding a California Environmental Charity," *Washington Post*, March 17, 2022, https://www.washingtonpost.com/politics/2022/03/17/bogus-allegation-that-putin-is-funding-california-environmental-charity/.

27. "BlackRock's Exxon and Chevron Votes are Good Steps but Not Enough, Say Climate Advocates," Sierra Club, May 27, 2020, https://www.sierraclub.org/press-releases/2020/05/blackrock-s-exxon-and-chevron-votes-are-good-steps-not-enough-say-climate.

28. Adele Shraiman, "This Shareholder Season, Big Banks Are Feeling the Heat on Climate," Sierra Club, April 19, 2022, https://www.sierraclub.org/articles/2022/04/shareholder-season-big-banks-are-feeling-heat-climate.

29. Oisin Breen, "Suddenly Vanguard, BlackRock, State Street Not Only Have the Assets but the Power of ESG Mandates, Which Make Them a Growing Threat to Shareholder Democracy, Critics Say," RIABiz, July28, 2021, https://riabiz.com/a/2021/7/28/suddenly-vanguard-blackrock-state-street-not-only-have-the-assets-but-the-power-of-esg-mandates-which-make-them-a-growing-threat-to-shareholder-democracy-critics-say.

30. Simon Jessop and Ross Kerber, "Sierra Club Warns BlackRock It May Pull $12 Million Over Climate Stance—Letter," Reuters, May 24, 2022, https://money.usnews.com/investing/news/articles/2022-05-24/sierra-club-warns-blackrock-it-may-pull-12-million-over-climate-stance-letter.

31. NRDC et al., Brief to Shareholders of Procter & Gamble re: Proposal to Improve the Sustainability of its Forest Supply Chains, Natural Resources Defense Council, October 6, 2020, https://www.nrdc.org/sites/default/files/pg-investor-brief-20201006.pdf.

32. DT Analysis, "Gazprom: Even If the War Ends Tomorrow, the Good Days Are Gone Forever," Seeking Alpha, March 10, 2022, https://seekingalpha.com/article/4494327-gazprom-sanctions-good-days-gone-forever.

33. Carl Surran, "Gazprom Posts Record Half-Year Profit, Will Pay Dividends," Seeking Alpha, August 30, 2022, https://seekingalpha.com/news/3878084-gazprom-posts-record-half-year-profit-will-pay-dividends.

34. Ibid.

35. Peter Millard, "Petrobras CEO Calls Net Zero a Fad, Echoing Exxon's Focus on Oil," *Houston Chronicle*, December 2, 2020, https://www.houstonchronicle.com/business/energy/article/Petrobras-CEO-Calls-Net-Zero-a-Fad-Echoing-15769038.php.

36. "Vote Bulletin: Petróleo Brasileiro S.A.," BlackRock, April 2022, https://www.blackrock.com/corporate/literature/press-release/vote-bulletin-petrobras-april-2022.pdf.

37. Christine Murray, "BlackRock-Owned Mexican Prison Opens in Coahuila," Reuters, October 25, 2018, https://www.reuters.com/article/us-mexico-blackrock-prison/blackrock-owned-mexican-prison-opens-in-coahuila-idUSKCN1MZ1K5.

38. 2022 Summary Prospectus iShares ESG Advanced MSCI USA ETF, BlackRock, December 29, 2022, https://www.blackrock.com/us/financial-professionals/literature/summary-prospectus/sp-ishares-esg-advanced-msci-usa-etf-8-31.pdf; 2022 Prospectus iShares ESG Advanced Total USD Bond Market ETF, BlackRock, June 29, 2022, https://www.blackrock.com/us/financial-professionals/literature/prospectus/p-ishares-esg-advanced-total-usd-bond-market-etf-2-28.pdf.

39. "Our Approach to Engagement with the Palm Oil Industry," BlackRock, 2022, https://www.blackrock.com/corporate/literature/publication/blk-commentary-engaging-on-palm-oil.pdf.

40. Primrose Riordan and Stefania Palma, "BlackRock Accused of ESG Inconsistency over Indonesia Palm Oil," *Financial Times*, May 4, 2021, https://www.ft.com/content/479b9dd2-c738-4310-8b1e-afdfbd3921b0.

41. Andrew Ross Sorkin, "A Free Market Manifesto that Changed the World, Reconsidered," *New York Times*, September 11, 2020, https://www.nytimes.com/2020/09/11/business/dealbook/milton-friedman-doctrine-social-responsibility-of-business.html; BlackRock, "From Ambition to Action – the Path to Net Zero," https://www.blackrock.com/dk/individuel/about-us/road-to-net-zero.

42. CalPERS 2015-16 Comprehensive Annual Financial Report, June 30, 2016, https://www.calpers.ca.gov/docs/forms-publications/cafr-2016.pdf.

43. "BlackRock Joins Climate Action 100+ to Ensure Largest Corporate Emitters Act on Climate Crisis," Ceres, January 9, 2020, https://www.ceres.org/news-center/press-releases/blackrock-joins-climate-action-100-ensure-largest-corporate-emitters-act.

44. Senate Bill 262, West Virginia Legislature, 2022 Regular Session, https://www.wvlegislature.gov/Bill_Text_HTML/2022_SESSIONS/RS/bills/SB262%20INTR.pdf.

45. Steven Allen Adams, "West Virginia Treasurer Riley Moore Joins Other Financial Officers Opposing ESG," The Intelligencer, 2022, https://www.theintelligencer.net/news/top-headlines/2022/06/west-virginia-treasurer-riley-moore-joins-other-financial-officers-opposing-esg/.

46. "Governor Ron DeSantis Takes Action Against Communist China and Woke Corporations," Ron DeSantis, December 20, 2021, https://www.flgov.com/2021/12/20/governor-ron-desantis-takes-action-against-communist-china-and-woke-corporations/.

47. Rob Davies and Josephine Moulds, "Green Credentials of World's Largest Investor Questioned over Oil Industry Emails," *Guardian*, March 9, 2022, https://www.theguardian.com/environment/2022/mar/09/blackrock-privately-soothes-oil-industry-fears-over-its-new-green-credentials.

48. "Texas Comptroller Glenn Hegar Seeks Information from 19 Companies That May Be Boycotting Fossil Fuel Industry," Texas Comptroller of Public Accounts, March 16, 2022, https://comptroller.texas.gov/about/media-center/news/20220316-texas-comptroller-glenn-hegar-seeks-information-from-19-companies-that-may-be-boycotting-fossil-fuel-industry-1647296122533.

49. Mark Brnovich, "Arizona Defends Retirees Against ESG," *Wall Street Journal*, August 15, 2022, https://www.wsj.com/articles/arizona-defends-retirees-against-esg-blackrock-asset-management-retirement-net-zero-greenhouse-gas-fiduciary-duty-pension-gender-quota-california-11660571998.

50. Letter from Nineteen State Attorneys General to BlackRock, August 4, 2022, https://www.azag.gov/sites/default/files/2022-08/BlackRock%20Letter.pdf.

51. Ibid.

52. Open Letter from Fourteen State Treasurers, September 14, 2022, https://www.forthe longterm.org/current.

53. Letter from Brad Lander to Laurence D. Fink, Re: BlackRock Inc.'s Commitment to Net Zero Emissions, City of New York, Office of the Comptroller, September 21, 2022, https://comptroller.nyc.gov/wp-content/uploads/2022/09/Letter-to-BlackRock -CEO-Larry-Fink.pdf.

54. Brad Johnson, "'Fossil Fuel Divestor' BlackRock CEO Touts Decarbonization, ESG at Clinton Global Initiative Meeting," The Texan, September 22, 2022, https://the texan.news/fossil-fuel-divestor-blackrock-ceo-touts-decarbonization-esg-at-clinton -global-initiative-meeting/.

55. Andy Puzder, "ESG: BlackRock's Hard Place," NR Capital Matters, November 15, 2022, https://www.nationalreview.com/2022/11/esg-blackrocks-hard-place/.

56. "BlackRock Expands Voting Choice to Additional Clients," BlackRock, June 13, 2022, https://www.blackrock.com/corporate/newsroom/press-releases/article/corporate -one/press-releases/2022-blackrock-voting-choice.

57. "Vote Bulletin: Chevron Corporation," BlackRock, May 26, 2021, https://www.black rock.com/corporate/literature/press-release/blk-vote-bulletin-chevron-may-2021.pdf.

58. "Vote Bulletin: China Shenhua Energy," BlackRock, June 25, 2021, https://www.black rock.com/corporate/literature/press-release/blk-vote-bulletin-china-shenhua-en ergy-aug-2021.pdf.

59. "Keeping the Promise: Getting Politics Out of Pensions," American Legislative Exchange Council, 2016, https://alec.org/wp-content/uploads/2016/12/Getting-Politics -Out-Of-Pensions-Final-WEB-2.pdf.

60. Jason Perez, "Candidate Statement," August 2018, https://www.nakedcapitalism .com/wp-content/uploads/2018/08/Jason-Perez-final-ballot-statements.pdf.

61. Randy Diamond, "CalPERS Rejects Reinvesting in Tobacco Again," Chief Investment Officer, March 16, 2021, https://www.ai-cio.com/news/calpers-rejects-reinvesting-to bacco/; Chris Butera, "New CalPERS Board Member Has Concerns About Private Equity Plan," Chief Investment Officer, January 14, 2019, https://www.ai-cio.com/news /fitch-rebuts-kentucky-governors-ratings-allegation/.

62. "2022 Paris-Aligned Climate Lobbying Shareholder Proposals," Interfaith Center on Corporate Responsibility, https://www.iccr.org/2022-paris-aligned-climate-lobbying -shareholder-proposals.

63. Aaron Omer Ammons et al., letter to Laurence Fink, January 25, 2021, SEIU, https://static1.squarespace.com/static/5d4df99c531b6d0001b48264/t/600f52645de 93024ba6f361f/1611616887756/Capitol+Invasion+Asset+Manager+Letter.

64. Daphne Zhang, "ESG Ratings Are Business Insurance's New, Contested Frontier," Bloomberg Law, September 15, 2022, https://news.bloomberglaw.com/esg/esg-rat ings-are-business-insurances-new-contested-frontier.

65. Brad Cornell and Aswath Damodaran, "Valuing ESG: Doing Good or Sounding Good?," The Journal of Impact and ESG Investing, Fall 2020, Vol. 1, 76-93, https://jesg.pm-re search.com/content/1/1/76.

66. Vicky Xiuzhong Xu and James Leibold, "Your Favorite Nikes May Be Made from Forced Labor. Here's Why," Washington Post, March 17, 2020, https://www.washing tonpost.com/opinions/2020/03/17/your-favorite-nikes-might-be-made-forced-labor -heres-why/; Nury Turkel, "I Grew Up Witnessing Forced Labor. U.S. Companies Must

Step Up," *New York Times*, January 20, 2021, https://www.nytimes.com/2021/01/20/opinion/uighur-forced-labor.html; Jacey Fortin, "Facing Droughts, California Challenges Nestlé Over Water Use," *New York Times*, April 29, 2021, https://www.nytimes.com/2021/04/29/us/nestle-water-california.html.

67. Theo Wayt, "Elon Musk Rips 'Phony Social Justice Warriors' as Tesla Booted from S&P 500 ESG Index," *New York Post*, May 18, 2022, https://nypost.com/2022/05/18/elon-musk-rips-phony-social-justice-warriors/.

68. David Katz and Laura McIntosh, "ESG in 2023: Politics and Polemics," Harvard Law Forum for Corporate Governance, February 6, 2023, https://corpgov.law.harvard.edu/2023/02/06/esg-in-2023-politics-and-polemics/.

69. Ross Kerber and Hyunjoo Jin, "Tesla Cut from S&P 500 ESG Index, and Elon Musk Tweets his Fury," Reuters, May 19, 2022, https://www.reuters.com/business/susbtainable-business/tesla-removed-sp-500-esg-index-autopilot-discrimination-concerns-2022-05-18/.

70. Keith Williams, "Tesla, Exxon Mobil And S&P 500's ESG: How Does This Work?," Seeking Alpha, June 3, 2022, https://seekingalpha.com/article/4516270-tesla-exxon-mobil-sp-500-esg-how-does-this-work.

71. "MSCI: This Might Be the Most Attractive Business in the World," Seeking Alpha, June 16, 2022, https://seekingalpha.com/article/4518681-msci-attractive-business-strong-business-model.

72. Cam Simpson, Akshat Rathi, and Saijel Kishan, "The ESG Mirage," Bloomberg, December 9, 2021, https://www.bloomberg.com/graphics/2021-what-is-esg-investing-msci-ratings-focus-on-corporate-bottom-line/.

73. D E Shaw & Co, "Keep the Change: Analyzing the Increase in ESG Ratings for U.S. Equities," D E Shaw & Co, April 2022, https://www.deshaw.com/assets/articles/DESCO_Market_Insights_ESG_Ratings_20220408.pdf.

74. "ESG Industry Materiality Map," MSCI, https://www.msci.com/our-solutions/esg-investing/esg-industry-materiality-map.

75. "MSCI: This Might Be the Most Attractive Business in the World," Seeking Alpha, June 16, 2022, https://seekingalpha.com/article/4518681-msci-attractive-business-strong-business-model.

76. Dragon Yongjun Tang, Jiali Yan and Chelsea Yaqiong Yao, "The Determinants of ESG Ratings: Rater Ownership Matters," Proceedings of Paris December 2021 Finance Meeting EUROFIDAI – ESSEC, July 22, 2021, https://papers.ssrn.com/sol3/papers.cfm?abstract_id=3889395.

77. "Measuring sustainability. Creating value," Accenture, January 20, 2022, https://www.accenture.com/us-en/insights/strategy/measuring-sustainability-creating-value?c=acn_glb_brandexpressionbing_12819208&n=psbs_0122&&msclkid=cb94833ba29e18a1553ae0ddfa4388d1&utm_source=bing&utm_medium=cpc&utm_campaign=US_INS_CORP_SUSBLTY_BREXSUST_BRAND_PHRS_STND_EN_BAS1651SUST_CMAC-BRND-GLOADSM-NA_SUSSVC_NA&utm_term=accenture%20sustainability%20firms&utm_content=CONS_ENT_SUSBLTY_BREXSUST_BAS1651SUST_CMAC-BRND-GLOADSM-NA_SUSSVC_Sustainability%20Chain%20Value&gclid=cb94833ba29e18a1553ae0ddfa4388d1&gclsrc=3p.ds.

78. "Examining the Market Power and Impact of Proxy Adivsory Firms," Hearing Before the Subcommittee on Capital Markets and Government Sponsored Enter-

prises of the Committee on Financial Services, U.S. House of Representatives, June 5, 2013, https://www.govinfo.gov/content/pkg/CHRG-113hhrg81762/html/CHRG-113hhrg81762.htm.

79. Chong Shu, "The Proxy Advisory Industry: Influencing and Being Influenced," May 20, 2022, https://chong-shu.com/papers/shu2020proxy.pdf.

80. Tao Li, "Outsourcing Corporate Governance: Conflicts of Interest and Competition in the Proxy Advisory Industry," ECGI Finance Working Paper no. 389/201, November 12, 2013, https://papers.ssrn.com/sol3/papers.cfm?abstract_id=2287196.

81. California Public Employees' Retirement System, *2020–2021 Annual Comprehensive Financial Report, Fiscal Year Ended June 30, 2021*, California Public Employees' Retirement System, 2021, https://www.calpers.ca.gov/docs/forms-publications/acfr-2021.pdf.

82. California Public Employees' Retirement System, "2022 Proxy Season," https://news.calpers.ca.gov/2022-proxy-season/.

83. John G. Matsusaka and Chong Shu, "A Theory of Proxy Advice When Investors Have Social Goals," USC Marshall School of Business Research Paper, April 6, 2021, https://deliverypdf.ssrn.com/delivery.php?ID=01110600906711912310100512612611002403803900006500303410308711108709509085120070078010118005034010099113066096022000083125114039035093009046117073120092030089099025086069046115070065083115107002028125093001084028031091127091067018126072111074028096066&EXT=pdf&INDEX=TRUE.

84. Ibid.

85. Harvey Pitt," Statement of the U.S. Chamber of Commerce, ON: 'Examining the Market Power and Impact of Proxy of Advisory Firms,'" U.S. Chamber of Commerce, June 5, 2013, https://www.centerforcapitalmarkets.com/wp-content/uploads/2010/04/2013-6.3-Pitt-Testimony-FINAL.pdf.

86. David F. Larcker, Allan L. McCall, and Gaizka Ormazabal, "Outsourcing Shareholder Voting to Proxy Advisory Firms," Stanford University Graduate School of Business Research Paper no. 14-27, October 30, 2014, https://papers.ssrn.com/sol3/papers.cfm?abstract_id=2101453.

87. *Hearing Before the Subcommittee on Capital Markets and Government Sponsored Enterprises of the Committee on Financial Services, U.S. House of Representatives*, 113th Congress, 1st sess., June 5, 2013, https://www.govinfo.gov/content/pkg/CHRG-113hhrg81762/html/CHRG-113hhrg81762.htm.

88. Darla Stuckey, "Society for Corporate Governance Comment Letter to SEC on Proposed Proxy Rules for Proxy Voting Advice," Harvard Law School Forum on Corporate Governance, February 28, 2020, https://corpgov.law.harvard.edu/2020/02/28/society-for-corporate-governance-comment-letter-to-sec-on-proposed-proxy-rules-for-proxy-voting-advice/.

89. Timothy M. Doyle, "The Conflicted Role of Proxy Advisors," American Council for Capital Formation, May 2018, https://accfcorpgov.org/wp-content/uploads/2018/05/ACCF_The-Conflicted-Role-of-Proxy-Advisors.pdf; "Glass Lewis Launches ESG Scores and Data to Give Investors Insights Needed for Informed Voting and Engagement Decisions," Glass Lewis, February 7, 2022, https://www.glasslewis.com/press-release-esg-profile/.

90. Jonathan Stempel, "Starbucks Executives, Directors Are Sued Over Diversity Policies," Reuters, August 31, 2022, https://www.reuters.com/business/retail-consumer/starbucks-executives-directors-are-sued-over-diversity-policies-2022-08-31/.

91. "6 Ways ESG Policies Benefit Dental Practices," Aprio, November 2, 2021, https://www.aprio.com/6-ways-esg-policies-benefit-dental-practices/.

Chapter 6: TOO BIG TO COMPETE

1. IFRS Foundation, SASB Standards, https://www.sasb.org/investor-use/supporters/.
2. Alastair Marsh, "Vanguard Exit Has Lawyers Mapping Out Wall Street's Top ESG Risk," December 19, 2022, https://www.fa-mag.com/news/vanguard-exit-has-lawyers-mapping-out-wall-street-s-top-esg-risk-71183.html.
3. IFRS Foundation, SASB Standards.
4. "Vanguard Exit Has Lawyers Mapping Out Wall Street's Top ESG Risk."
5. "ExxonMobil Corp: Ownership," Morningstar, https://www.morningstar.com/stocks/xnys/xom/ownership.
6. "Chevron Corp: Ownership," Morningstar, https://www.morningstar.com/stocks/xnys/cvx/ownership.
7. "ConocoPhillips [COP]: Ownership," Morningstar, https://www.morningstar.com/stocks/xnys/cop/ownership; "ConocoPhillips [YCP]: Ownership," Morningstar, https://www.morningstar.com/stocks/xdus/ycp/ownership; "Marathon Oil Corp: Ownership," Morningstar, https://www.morningstar.com/stocks/xnys/mro/ownership.
8. See, e.g., *AMP Inc. v. AlliedSignal Corp.*, 168 F.3d 649 (3d Cir. 1999); Carolina Bona-Sánchez, Jerónimo Pérez Alemán, and Domingo Javier Santana–Martín, "Ultimate Ownership and Earnings Conservatism," *European Accounting Review* 20, no. 1 (2011): 57–80; Dušan Isakov and Jean-Philippe Weisskopf, "Are Founding Families Special Blockholders? An Investigation of Controlling Shareholder Influence on Firm Performance," *Journal of Banking & Finance* 41 (April 2014): 1–16.
9. For a discussion of Nasdaq Rule 5635(c), see Morrison & Foerster LLP Capital Markets, "Frequently Asked Questions About the 20% Rule and Non-Registered Securities Offerings," https://assets.contentstack.io/v3/assets/blt5775cc69c999c255/bltddb24b34603a5afc/faqsthe20percentrulenonregisteredsecurities.pdf.
10. "From Ambition to Action—The Path to Net Zero," BlackRock, https://www.blackrock.com/corporate/sustainability/committed-to-sustainability; see also "Our Approach to Sustainability," BlackRock, July 2020, https://www.blackrock.com/corporate/literature/publication/our-commitment-to-sustainability-full-report.pdf, 4.
11. "Our Target: Net Zero," State Street Global Advisors, https://www.ssga.com/us/en/intermediary/ic/capabilities/esg/our-target-net-zero.
12. "Vanguard's Approach to Climate Change," https://perma.cc/G9ZT-2ERS (captured as of December 22, 2023). Vanguard has now altered this language. "Vanguard's Approach to Climate Risk," https://corporate.vanguard.com/content/corporatesite/us/en/corp/climate-change.html.
13. David G. Victor, "Energy Transformations: Technology, Policy, Capital and the Murky Future of Oil and Gas," Engine No. 1, March 3, 2021, https://reenergizexom.com/documents/Energy-Transformations-Technology-Policy-Capital-and-the-Murky-Future-of-Oil-and-Gas-March-3-2021.pdf, 4.
14. Matt Phillips, "Exxon's Board Defeat Signals the Rise of Social-Good Activists," *New York Times*, June 9, 2021, https://www.nytimes.com/2021/06/09/business/exxon-mobil-engine-no1-activist.html.

15. Jessica Camille Aguirre, "The Little Hedge Fund Taking Down Big Oil," *New York Times Magazine*, June 23, 2021, https://www.nytimes.com/2021/06/23/magazine/exxon -mobil-engine-no-1-board.html.

16. Debbie Carlson, "Engine No. 1 Says Its New Representation on ExxonMobil's Board Has Already Scored a Win," MarketWatch, September 24, 2021, https://www.market watch.com/story/engine-no-1-says-its-new-representation-on-exxonmobils-board -has-already-scored-a-win-11632508131.

17. "Dallas Fed Energy Survey: First Quarter 2022: Special Questions," Federal Reserve Bank of Dallas, March 23, 2022, https://www.dallasfed.org/research/surveys/des /2022/2201.aspx#tab-questions.

18. Collin Eaton, "After Defeating Exxon, Engine No. 1 Works with Oil Giants on Emissions," *Wall Street Journal*, July 14, 2022, https://www.wsj.com/articles/after-defeating -exxon-engine-no-1-works-with-oil-giants-on-emissions-11657803660.

19. Matt Egan, "Gas Prices Are High. Oil CEOs Reveal Why They're Not Drilling More," CNN, March 24, 2022, https://www.cnn.com/2022/03/24/energy/gas-prices-oil-pro duction-wall-street/index.html.

20. Jan Fichtner, Eelke M. Heemskerk, and Javier Garcia-Bernardo, "Hidden Power of the Big Three? Passive Index Funds, Re-concentration of Corporate Ownership, and New Financial Risk," *Business and Politics* 19, special issue 2 (June 2017): 298–326, https://www.cambridge.org/core/journals/business-and-politics/article/hidden -power-of-the-big-three-passive-index-funds-reconcentration-of-corporate-owner ship-and-new-financial-risk/30AD689509AAD62F5B677E916C28C4B6.

21. Net Zero Asset Managers initiative, https://www.netzeroassetmanagers.org/.

22. Ibid.

23. "Network Partners' Expectation of Signatories with Regard to Fossil Fuel Investment Policy," Net Zero Asset Managers initiative, https://www.netzeroassetmanag ers.org/media/2021/12/NZAM-Network-Partners-Fossil-Fuel-Position.pdf.

24. "Commitment," Net Zero Asset Managers initiative, https://www.netzeroassetman agers.org/commitment/.

25. "About Climate Action 100+," Climate Action 100+, https://www.climateaction100 .org/about/.

26. "How We Work," Climate Action 100+, https://www.climateaction100.org/approach /how-we-work.

27. "Climate Action 100+ Net Zero Company Benchmark," Climate Action 100+, https://www.climateaction100.org/wp-content/uploads/2021/03/Climate-Action -100-Benchmark-Indicators-FINAL-3.12.pdf.

28. "About Climate Action 100+," Climate Action 100+, https://www.climateaction100 .org/about/.

29. "The Three Asks," Climate Action 100+, https://www.climateaction100.org/approach /the-three-asks/.

30. "Investor Signatories," Climate Action 100+, https://www.climateaction100.org /whos-involved/investors/.

31. "Engagement Process," Climate Action 100+, https://www.climateaction100.org/ap proach/engagement-process/.

32. "How We Work."

33. See, e.g., "Disclaimer," Climate Action 100+, https://www.climateaction100.org/dis claimer.

34. Dalia Blass, letter to Attorneys General of the States Listed as Signatories of the August 4, 2022 Letter, August 4, 2022, https://www.blackrock.com/us/individual/lit erature/press-release/blackrock-response-attorneys-general.pdf.

35. "Engagement Process," Climate Action 100+, https://www.climateaction100.org/ap proach/engagement-process.

36. "An Update on Vanguard's Engagement with the Net Zero Asset Managers Initiative (NZAM)," Vanguard, December 7, 2022, https://corporate.vanguard.com/content /corporatesite/us/en/corp/articles/update-on-nzam-engagement.html.

37. Tim Quinson, "Cost of Capital Spikes for Fossil-Fuel Producers," Bloomberg, November 9, 2021, https://www.bloomberg.com/news/articles/2021-11-09/cost-of-capi tal-widens-for-fossil-fuel-producers-green-insight#xj4y7vzkg; "Why Oil Prices Are Surging but Investment Is Drying Up," Goldman Sachs, January 20, 2022, https:// www.goldmansachs.com/insights/pages/from-briefings-20-january-2022.html.

38. Brad Plumer and Henry Fountain, "Trump Administration Finalizes Plan to Open Arctic Refuge to Drilling," *New York Times*, August 17, 2020, https://www.nytimes .com/2020/08/17/climate/alaska-oil-drilling-anwr.html.

39. Henry Fountain and Lisa Friedman, "Drilling in Arctic Refuge Gets a Green Light. What's Next?," *New York Times*, December 20, 2017, https://www.nytimes.com/2017 /12/20/climate/drilling-arctic-anwr.html.

40. Rachel Koning Beals, "Bank of America Joins Big U.S. Banks That Won't Finance Oil in the Arctic Refuge Trump Opened to Drilling," MarketWatch, December 5, 2020, https://www.marketwatch.com/story/bank-of-america-joins-big-u-s-banks -that-wont-finance-oil-in-the-arctic-refuge-trump-opened-to-drilling-11606843342; Christopher M. Matthews and Orla McCaffrey, "Banks' Arctic Financing Retreat Rattles Oil Industry," *Wall Street Journal*, October 8, 2020, https://www.wsj.com/articles /banks-arctic-financing-retreat-rattles-oil-industry-11602157853; Lananh Nguyen, "Bank of America Says It Won't Finance Oil and Gas Exploration in the Arctic," Bloomberg, November 30, 2020, https://www.bloomberg.com/news/articles/2020-11 -30/bofa-says-it-won-t-finance-oil-and-gas-exploration-in-the-arctic.

41. Ibid.

42. Steven Mufson and Joshua Partlow, "Once Eager to Drill, Oil Companies Exit Leases in Arctic Refuge," *Washington Post*, June 2, 2022, https://www.washingtonpost.com /climate-environment/2022/06/02/arctic-national-wildlife-refuge-drilling.

43. Dan Mornoff, "Break Up the ESG Investing Giants," *Wall Street Journal*, August 31, 2022, https://www.wsj.com/articles/break-up-the-esg-investing-giants-state-street -blackrock-vanguard-voting-ownership-big-three-competitor-antitrust-11661961693.

44. "Members: Net-Zero Banking Alliance," United Nations Environment Programme Finance Initiative, https://www.unepfi.org/net-zero-banking/members.

45. "Texas Comptroller Glenn Hegar Announces List of Financial Companies That Boycott Energy Companies," Texas Comptroller of Public Accounts, August 24, 2022, https://comptroller.texas.gov/about/media-center/news/20220824-texas-comptrol ler-glenn-hegar-announces-list-of-financial-companies-that-boycott-energy-compa nies-1661267815099; David Gelles, "West Virginia Punishes Banks That It Says Don't Support Coal," *New York Times*, July 28, 2022, https://www.nytimes.com/2022/07/28 /business/west-virginia-fossil-fuel-banks.html.

46. See, e.g., Mark Brnovich, "ESG May Be an Antitrust Violation," *Wall Street Journal*, March 6, 2022, https://www.wsj.com/articles/esg-may-be-an-antitrust-violation-cli

mate-activism-energy-prices-401k-retirement-investment-political-agenda-coordi
nated-influence-11646594807.

47. Paul Clarke, "Bank of America CEO Brian Moynihan: ESG Transition Is a 'Big Business Opportunity,'" *Financial News*, May 24, 2022, https://www.fnlondon.com
/articles/bank-of-america-ceo-brian-moynihan-esg-transition-is-a-big-business-op
portunity-20220524.

48. OECD, World Bank, and UN Environment, "Financing Climate Futures: Rethinking
Infrastructure: Policy Highlights," https://www.oecd.org/environment/cc/climate-fu
tures/policy-highlights-financing-climate-futures.pdf.

49. William Wilkes, Hayley Warren, and Brian Parkin, "Germany's Failed Climate Goals:
A Wake-Up Call for Governments Everywhere," Bloomberg, August 15, 2018), https://
www.bloomberg.com/graphics/2018-germany-emissions.

50. Michael Shellenberger, "If Solar and Wind Are So Cheap, Why Are They Making
Electricity So Expensive?," *Forbes*, April 23, 2018, https://www.forbes.com/sites/mi
chaelshellenberger/2018/04/23/if-solar-and-wind-are-so-cheap-why-are-they-mak
ing-electricity-more-expensive; Michael Shellenberger, "The Real Reason They Hate
Nuclear Is Because It Means We Don't Need Renewables," *Forbes*, February 14, 2019,
https://www.forbes.com/sites/michaelshellenberger/2019/02/14/the-real-reason
-they-hate-nuclear-is-because-it-means-we-dont-need-renewables.

51. Frank Jordans, "Explainer: Why Germany Is Delaying Its Nuclear Shutdown," AP
News, October 18, 2022, https://apnews.com/article/russia-ukraine-technology-ger
many-nuclear-power-olaf-scholz-7b22d8d55cea98b76925376a94ffdcff; Joanna Par-
tridge, "Germany at a Crossroads: What a Nuclear Power Station Tells Us about its
Energy Dilemma," *The Guardian*, December 9, 2022, https://www.theguardian.com
/world/2022/dec/09/neckarwestheim-delay-phasing-out-nuclear-power-dividing
-german-village.

52. Daniel Moore, "Nuclear Power's Climate Credentials, Footprint Spark Climate Debate," Bloomberg Law, May 9, 2022, https://news.bloomberglaw.com/environment
-and-energy/nuclear-powers-climate-credentials-footprint-spark-esg-debate; Soňa
Stadtelmeyer-Petrů and Scarlet O'Shea, "The Role of Nuclear Power in the Energy
Transition," J.P.Morgan Asset Management, November 2022, https://am.jpmorgan
.com/fr/en/asset-management/institutional/investment-strategies/sustainable-in
vesting/nuclear-power-transition.

53. 15 U.S.C. § 18.

54. See Einer Elhauge, "Horizontal Shareholding," *Harvard Law Review* 129,
no. 5 (March 2016): 1267–1317, https://harvardlawreview.org/wp-content/uploads
/2016/03/1267-1317-Online.pdf; Einer Elhauge, "How Horizontal Shareholding Harms
Our Economy—and Why Antitrust Law Can Fix It," *Harvard Business Law Review* 10
(2020): 207–86, https://www.hblr.org/wp-content/uploads/sites/18/2020/08/HLB203
_crop.pdf; Eric A. Posner, Fiona M. Scott Morton, and E. Glen Weyl, "A Proposal
to Limit the Anti-competitive Power of Institutional Investors," *Antitrust Law Journal* 81, no. 3 (2017): 669–728, https://papers.ssrn.com/sol3/papers.cfm?abstract_id
=2872754.

55. Elhauge, "Horizontal Shareholding," 1267.

56. *United States v. ITT Continental Baking Co.*, 420 U.S. 223, 240-42 (1975).

57. *Denver & Rio Grande Western Railroad Co. et al. v. United States*, 387 U.S. 485, 501 (1967).

58. Ibid. See also Elhauge, "Horizontal Shareholding," 1268-69.

59. José Azar, Martin C. Schmalz, and Isabel Tecu, "Anticompetitive Effects of Common Ownership," *Journal of Finance* 73, no. 4 (2018): 1513–65.

60. José Azar, Sahil Raina, and Martin Schmalz, "Ultimate Ownership and Bank Competition," *Financial Management* 51, no. 1 (Spring 2022): 227–69.

61. Melissa Newham, Jo Seldeslachts, and Albert Banal-Estañol, "Common Ownership and Market Entry: Evidence from the Pharmaceutical Industry," DIW Discussion Papers, no. 1738, 2022, https://www.econstor.eu/bitstream/10419/261499/1/dp1738rev2.pdf, 4.

62. See Elhauge, "Horizontal Shareholding," 1291–301; Eric Posner and E. Glen Weyl, "Mututal Funds' Dark Side," Slate, April 16, 2015, https://slate.com/news-and-politics/2015/04/mutual-funds-make-air-travel-more-expensive-institutional-investors-reduce-competition.html.

63. Morenoff, "Break Up the ESG Investing Giants."

64. Ibid.

65. 17 C.F.R. § 240.13d-1.

66. 17 C.F.R. § 240.12b-2.

67. Mark T. Uyeda, "Remarks at the 2022 Cato Summit on Financial Regulation," November 17, 2022, U.S. Securities and Exchange Commission, https://www.sec.gov/news/speech/uyeda-remarks-cato-summit-financial-regulation-111722.

68. Elhauge, "How Horizontal Shareholding Harms Our Economy," 269–70.

Chapter 7: GOVERNMENT CONSCRIPTS EMPLOYEES INTO ESG WARFARE

1. *Nathaniel Hiers v. The Board of Regents of the University of North Texas System, et al.*, U.S. District Court Eastern District of Texas, Case 4:20-cv-00321-SDJ, 2022, https://www.thefire.org/research-learn/nathaniel-hiers-v-university-north-texas.

2. Denise L. Nappier, letter to Gayle Slossberg, State of Connecticut Treasurer's Office, March 1, 2018, https://si-interactive.s3.amazonaws.com/prod/plansponsor-com/wp-content/uploads/2018/03/02135009/CTESGLetter.pdf.

3. "Proposal Number 16: Stockholder Proposal Regarding a Report on Content Governance," U.S. Securities and Exchange Commission, 2019, https://www.sec.gov/Archives/edgar/data/1652044/000130817919000205/lgoog2019_def14a.htm#lgooga075.

4. "Schedule 14A Information: Berkshire Hathaway, Inc.," U.S. Securities and Exchange Commission, 2021, https://www.sec.gov/Archives/edgar/data/1067983/000119312521080418/d938053ddef14a.htm.

5. Andrew Napolitano, "PRIM Board Approves Plan to Vote Against Directors at High Polluting Portfolio Companies," Massachusetts Office of the Treasurer and Receiver General, February 18, 2022, https://www.masstreasury.org/single-post/prim-board-approves-plan-to-vote-against-directors-at-high-polluting-portfolio-companies.

6. Brad Lander, "New York City and State Pension Funds Launch 'VOTE NO' Campaign Against Against [*sic*] the Re-election of Two Amazon Board Directors Responsible for Oversight of Human Capital Management," New York City Comptroller, April 21, 2022, https://comptroller.nyc.gov/newsroom/new-york-city-and-state-pension-funds-launch-vote-no-campaign-against-against-the-re-election-of-two-amazon-board-directors-responsible-for-oversight-of-human-capital-management/.

7. *TRS Board of Trustees Meeting*, Teacher Retirement System of Texas, February 2021, https://www.trs.texas.gov/TRS%20Documents/board_book_february_2021.pdf, 5.

8. "Corporate Governance Principles Proxy Voting Guidelines, 2022," SBA Florida, 2022, https://www.sbafla.com/fsb/Portals/FSB/Content/CorporateGovernance/ProxyVoting/2022%20SBA%20Corporate%20Governance%20Voting%20Guidelines.pdf?ver=2022-07-11-153613-893.

9. Allie Morris, "Texas Lt. Gov. Dan Patrick 'Outraged' by State Pension Fund's Climate Change Vote," *Dallas Morning News*, May 2, 2022, https://www.dallasnews.com/news/politics/2022/05/02/texas-lt-gov-dan-patrick-outraged-by-state-pension-funds-climate-change-vote/.

10. Katherine Greifeld, "'God Bless America ETF' May Be Coming Soon with the Ticker YALL," Bloomberg, July 12, 2022, https://www.bloomberg.com/news/articles/2022-07-12/-god-bless-america-etf-may-be-coming-soon-with-the-ticker-yall?leadSource=uverify%20wall; "Fund Details," God Bless America ETF, https://www.godblessamericaetf.com/fund-details/.

11. "Corporate Governance," Office of the New York State Comptroller, https://www.osc.state.ny.us/common-retirement-fund/corporate-governance.

12. Joe Guszkowski, "Shareholders Push Denny's and Dine to Look at Ending Tip Credit," Restaurant Business, May 5, 2022, https://www.restaurantbusinessonline.com/workforce/shareholders-push-dennys-dine-look-ending-tip-credit; "2022 Notice of Annual Meeting and Proxy Statement," Denny's, April 7, 2022, https://d18rn0p25nwr6d.cloudfront.net/CIK-0000852772/af0116ac-c369-4070-8e71-843a7d518fa7.pdf.

13. "Corporate Governance"; Richard Vanderford, "Texas Blacklists BlackRock, UBS and Other Financial Firms over Alleged Energy Boycotts," *Wall Street Journal*, August 24, 2022, https://www.wsj.com/articles/texas-blacklists-blackrock-ubs-and-other-financial-firms-over-alleged-energy-boycotts-11661381425; Texas Senate Bill No. 13, 2021, https://capitol.texas.gov/tlodocs/87R/billtext/pdf/SB00013F.pdf.

14. Lander, "New York City and State Pension Funds Launch 'VOTE NO' Campaign."

15. Anne Sheehan, "Letter from JANA Partners & CalSTRS to Apple, Inc.," Harvard Law School Forum on Corporate Governance, January 19, 2018, https://corpgov.law.harvard.edu/2018/01/19/joint-shareholder-letter-to-apple-inc/.

16. Brad Lander, Twitter, April 21, 2022, https://twitter.com/NYCComptroller/status/1517187459599192065.

17. Shawn T. Wooden, Memorandum, State of Connecticut, Office of the Treasurer, April 9, 2021, https://portal.ct.gov/-/media/OTT/Pension-Funds/Investment-Advisory-Council/041421IAC_InfoPacket.pdf.

18. Brad Lander, "Comptroller Stringer, Neva Goodwin, Miranda Kaiser Op-Ed Demanding a Cleaner Energy Future Now: Why JPMorgan Chase Should Boot Lee Raymond off Its Board," Office of the New York City Comptroller, May 19, 2020, https://comptroller.nyc.gov/newsroom/comptroller-stringer-neva-goodwin-miranda-kaiser-op-ed-demanding-a-cleaner-energy-future-now-why-jpmorgan-chase-should-boot-lee-raymond-off-its-board/.

19. Eugene Volokh and William Baude, "Compelled Subsidies and the First Amendment," *Harvard Law Review* 132, no. 1 (November 2018): 171–204, https://harvardlawreview.org/wp-content/uploads/2018/11/171-204_Online.pdf.

20. *Summit Medical Center of Alabama, Inc. v. Riley*, 274 F. Supp. 2d 1262 (M.D. Ala. 2003), U.S. District Court for the Middle District of Alabama, July 5, 2003, https://law.justia.com/cases/federal/district-courts/FSupp2/274/1262/2493503/.

21. Volokh and Baude, "Compelled Subsidies and the First Amendment"; *Board of Regents of the University of Wisconsin System v. Southworth et al.*, Certiorari to the United States Court of Appeals for the Seventh Circuit, No. 98-1189, March 22, 2000, https://supreme.justia.com/cases/federal/us/529/217/case.pdf.

22. Micah L. Berman, "Clarifying Standards for Compelled Commercial Speech," *Washington University Journal of Law & Policy* 50 (2016): 53–87, https://openscholarship wustl.edu/cgi/viewcontent.cgi?article=1910&context=law_journal_law_policy.

23. *McIntyre v. Ohio Elections Commission*, U.S. Supreme Court, April 19, 1995, https://supreme.justia.com/cases/federal/us/514/334/.

24. *Citizens United v. Federal Election Commission*, U.S. Supreme Court, January 21, 2010, https://supreme.justia.com/cases/federal/us/558/310/#tab-opinion-1963051.

25. UFCW, "Private Sector Workers Notice," (UFCW Local 1459, 2023), https://ufcw1459.com/private-sector-workers-notice/.

26. *Crowe et al. v. Oregon State Bar et al.*, United States Court of Appeals for the Ninth Circuit, February 25, 2021, https://cdn.ca9.uscourts.gov/datastore/opinions/2021/02/26/19-35463.pdf.

27. Rafael Shimunov, Twitter, May 4, 2022, https://twitter.com/rafaelshimunov/status/1521950088272171008.

28. Da Lin, "*Janus* and Public Pension Funds," Harvard Law Review Blog, September 17, 2018, https://blog.harvardlawreview.org/janus-and-public-pension-funds/.

29. "California Constitution: Article XVI—Public Finance: Section 17," Justia US Law, https://law.justia.com/constitution/california/article-xvi/section-17/.

30. "California Code, Government Code—GOV § 7513.6," FindLaw, January 1, 2019, https://codes.findlaw.com/ca/government-code/gov-sect-7513-6.html.

31. "California Code, Government Code—GOV § 7513.7," FindLaw, January 1, 2019, https://codes.findlaw.com/ca/government-code/gov-sect-7513-7.html.

32. *McDonald v. Longley*, No. 20-50448 (5th Cir. 2021), Justia Law, https://law.justia.com/cases/federal/appellate-courts/ca5/20-50448/20-50448-2021-07-02.html.

33. "Active Members' Handbook," New York State Teachers' Retirement System, https://www.nystrs.org/NYSTRS/media/PDF/Library/Publications/Active%20Members/handbook.pdf.

34. "Mandatory vs. Optional Membership," Office of the New York State Comptroller, https://www.osc.state.ny.us/retirement/members/mandatory-vs-optional-membership.

35. "New York City Pension Funds," Office of the New York City Comptroller, https://comptroller.nyc.gov/wp-content/uploads/documents/2021-NYCRS_Shareowner_Initiatives_Postseason_Report.pdf.

36. "Transferring or Terminating Your Membership," Office of the New York State Comptroller, https://www.osc.state.ny.us/retirement/members/transferring-or-terminating-your-membership.

Chapter 8: THE POWER OF THE PRESIDENTIAL PEN

1. Joseph R. Biden, Jr., "Executive Order on Advancing Racial Equity and Support for Underserved Communities Through the Federal Government," The White House, January 20, 2021, https://www.whitehouse.gov/briefing-room/presidential-actions/2021

/01/20/executive-order-advancing-racial-equity-and-support-for-underserved-com munities-through-the-federal-government/.

2. Antony J. Blinken, "The United States Officially Rejoins the Paris Agreement," U.S. Department of State, February 19, 2021, https://www.state.gov/the-united-states-offi cially-rejoins-the-paris-agreement/.

3. Joseph R. Biden, Jr., "Executive Order on Tackling the Climate Crisis at Home and Abroad," The White House, January 27, 2021, https://www.whitehouse.gov/briefing -room/presidential-actions/2021/01/27/executive-order-on-tackling-the-climate-cri sis-at-home-and-abroad/.

4. Ibid.

5. Joseph R. Biden, Jr., "Executive Order on Climate-Related Financial Risk," The White House, May 20, 2021, https://www.whitehouse.gov/briefing-room/presidential -actions/2021/05/20/executive-order-on-climate-related-financial-risk/.

6. "Financial Factors in Selecting Plan Investments," Federal Register 85, no. 220 (No-vember 12, 2020): 72846–85, https://www.govinfo.gov/content/pkg/FR-2020-11-13/pdf /2020-24515.pdf.

7. "US Department of Labor Releases Statement on Enforcement of Its Final Rules on ESG Investments, Proxy Voting by Employee Benefit Plans," U.S. Department of Labor, March 10, 2021, https://www.dol.gov/newsroom/releases/ebsa/ebsa20210310.

8. "Prudence and Loyalty in Selecting Plan Investments and Exercising Shareholder Rights," Employee Benefits Security Administration, U.S. Department of Labor, Oc-tober 14, 2021, https://www.federalregister.gov/documents/2021/10/14/2021-22263 /prudence-and-loyalty-in-selecting-plan-investments-and-exercising-shareholder -rights.

9. Vivek Ramaswamy and Alex Acosta, "Biden's ESG Tax on Your Retirement Fund," *Wall Street Journal*, July 19, 2022, https://www.wsj.com/articles/bidens-esg-tax-on -your-retirement-fund-pension-planning-regulation-climate-change-investment-re turns-portfolios-11658245467.

10. "Final Rule on Prudence and Loyalty in Selecting Plan Investments and Exercising Shareholder Rights," U.S. Department of Labor, 2022, https://www.dol.gov/agencies /ebsa/about-ebsa/our-activities/resource-center/fact-sheets/final-rule-on-prudence -and-loyalty-in-selecting-plan-investments-and-exercising-shareholder-rights; see also Max M. Schanzenbach and Robert H. Sitkoff, "No, Biden Isn't Forcing Your Re-tirement Money into ESG Funds," *Wall Street Journal*, December 22, 2022, https:// www.wsj.com/articles/no-biden-isnt-forcing-your-retirement-money-into-esg-funds -pension-labor-department-investing-11671742012.

11. Roger Lowenstein, "The End of Pensions," *New York Times Magazine*, October 30, 2005, https://www.nytimes.com/2005/10/30/magazine/the-end-of-pensions.html.

12. "Fiduciary Duties," Employee Retirement Income Security Act, 29 U.S.C. § 1104, https://www.govinfo.gov/content/pkg/USCODE-2011-title29/pdf/USCODE-2011-title 29-chap18-subchapI-subtitleB-part4-sec1104.pdf.

13. Complaint, *Utah v. Walsh*, N.D. Tex., January 26, 2023, https://attorneygeneral.utah .gov/wp-content/uploads/2023/01/2023.01.26_1-Complaint.pdf.

14. "The Enhancement and Standardization of Climate-Related Disclosures for Inves-tors," U.S. Securities and Exchange Commission, March 21, 2022, https://www.sec .gov/rules/proposed/2022/33-11042.pdf.

15. Paul Kiernan, "SEC Floats Mandatory Disclosure of Climate-Change Risks, Emissions," *Wall Street Journal*, March 21, 2022, https://www.wsj.com/articles/sec-to-float-mandatory-disclosure-of-climate-change-risks-emissions-11647874814.

16. Hester M. Peirce, "We Are Not the Securities and Environment Commission—At Least Not Yet," U.S. Securities and Exchange Commission, March 21, 2022, https://www.sec.gov/news/statement/peirce-climate-disclosure-20220321#_ftnref66.

17. "The Enhancement and Standardization of Climate-Related Disclosures for Investors," U.S. Securities and Exchange Commission, March 21, 2022, https://www.sec.gov/rules/proposed/2022/33-11042.pdf.

18. "Enhanced Reporting of Proxy Votes by Registered Management Investment Companies; Reporting of Compensation Votes by Institutional Investment Managers," U.S. Securities and Exchange Commission, Oct. 15, 2021, https://www.federalregister.gov/documents/2021/10/15/2021-21549/enhanced-reporting-of-proxy-votes-by-registered-management-investment-companies-reporting-of.

19. Peirce, "Statement on Enhanced Reporting of Proxy Votes by Registered Management Investment Companies; Reporting of Executive Compensation Votes by Institutional Investment Managers," September 29, 2021, https://www.sec.gov/news/public-statement/peirce-open-meeting-2021-09-29.

20. John J. Brennan and Edward C. Johnson 3d, "No Disclosure: The Feeling Is Mutual," *Wall Street Journal*, January 14, 2003, https://www.wsj.com/articles/SB1042509880551133904.

21. Hester M. Peirce, "Statement on Enhanced Reporting of Proxy Votes by Registered Management Investment Companies; Reporting of Executive Compensation Votes by Institutional Investment Managers," U.S. Securities and Exchange Commission, September 29, 2021, https://www.sec.gov/news/public-statement/peirce-open-meeting-2021-09-29#_ftnref2.

22. "Enhanced Reporting of Proxy Votes by Registered Management Investment Companies; Reporting of Executive Compensation Votes by Institutional Investment Managers," U.S. Securities and Exchange Commission, November 2, 2022, https://www.sec.gov/rules/final/2022/33-11131.pdf.

23. Paul Kiernan, "SEC Proposes More Disclosure Requirements for ESG Funds," *Wall Street Journal*, May 25, 2022, https://www.wsj.com/articles/sec-to-propose-more-disclosure-requirements-for-esg-funds-11653498000.

24. Hester M. Peirce, "Statement on Environmental, Social, and Governance Disclosures for Investment Advisers and Investment Companies," U.S. Securities and Exchange Commission, May 25, 2022, https://www.sec.gov/news/statement/peirce-statement-esg-052522; see also "Enhanced Disclosures by Certain Investment Advisers and Investment Companies About Environmental, Social, and Governance Investment Practices," U.S. Securities and Exchange Commission, May 25, 2022, https://www.sec.gov/rules/proposed/2022/33-11068.pdf.

25. Jaime Lizárraga, "Meeting Investor Demand for High Quality ESG Data," U.S. Securities and Exchange Commission, October 17, 2022, https://www.sec.gov/news/speech/lizarraga-speech-meeting-investor-demand-high-quality-esg-data.

26. Hester M. Peirce, "It's Not Just Scope 3: Remarks at the American Enterprise Institute," U.S. Securities and Exchange Commission, December 7, 2022, https://www.sec.gov/news/speech/peirce-remarks-american-enterprise-institute-120722.

27. Peirce, "Statement on Environmental, Social, and Governance Disclosures for Investment Advisers and Investment Companies."

28. "SEC Announces Enforcement Task Force Focused on Climate and ESG Issues," U.S. Securities and Exchange Commission, March 4, 2021, https://www.sec.gov/news/press-release/2021-42.

29. "Environmental, Social and Governance (ESG) Funds—Investor Bulletin," U.S. Securities and Exchange Commission, February 26, 2021, https://www.sec.gov/oiea/investor-alerts-and-bulletins/environmental-social-and-governance-esg-funds-investor-bulletin.

30. "Shareholder Proposals: Staff Legal Bulletin No. 14L (CF)," U.S. Securities and Exchange Commission, November 3, 2021, https://www.sec.gov/corpfin/staff-legal-bulletin-14l-shareholder-proposals.

31. Brian Croce, "SEC Staff Having Trouble Keeping Up with Rule-Making Pace—Report," Pensions & Investments, October 19, 2022, https://www.pionline.com/regulation/sec-staff-having-trouble-keeping-rule-making-pace-report.

32. Nicholas Padilla, Jr., memorandum to Gary Gensler, U.S. Securities and Exchange Commission, October 13, 2022, https://www.sec.gov/files/inspector-generals-statement-sec-mgmt-and-perf-challenges-october-2022.pdf.

33. Ibid., 3.

34. Allysia Finley, "Where Was Biden's SEC Sheriff on Sam Bankman-Fried?," *Wall Street Journal*, December 18, 2022, https://www.wsj.com/articles/where-was-bidens-sec-sheriff-on-sam-bankman-fried-gary-gensler-ftx-crypto-fraud-alameda-11671384862.

35. "I CARE," U.S. Department of Veterans Affairs, https://www.va.gov/icare/#:~:text=Our%20mission%2C%20as%20the%20Department,actions%20toward%20service%20to%20others; "VA Supports Women Veteran Entrepreneurs in How to Obtain Government Contracts," U.S. Department of Veterans Affairs, March 3, 2022, https://www.va.gov/opa/pressrel/pressrelease.cfm?id=5769.

36. "2018-2022 Strategic Plan," U.S. Patent and Trademark Office, https://www.uspto.gov/sites/default/files/documents/USPTO_2018-2022_Strategic_Plan.pdf; "The Importance of Equity in Innovation," U.S. Patent and Trademark Office, https://www.uspto.gov/initiatives/equity/importance-equity-innovation; "USPTO Announces Launch of Climate Change Mitigation Pilot Program," U.S. Patent and Trademark Office, June 3, 2022, https://www.uspto.gov/about-us/news-updates/uspto-announces-launch-climate-change-mitigation-pilot-program.

37. Peirce, "We Are Not the Securities and Environment Commission."

38. "About Us," Office of the Comptroller of the Currency, https://www2.occ.gov/about/index-about.html.

39. "Fair Access to Financial Services," Office of the Comptroller of the Currency, 2021, https://www.occ.gov/news-issuances/news-releases/2021/nr-occ-2021-8a.pdf.

40. "OCC Finalizes Rule Requiring Large Banks to Provide Fair Access to Bank Services, Capital, and Credit," Office of the Comptroller of the Currency, 2021, https://www.occ.gov/news-issuances/news-releases/2021/nr-occ-2021-8.html.

41. "Fair Access to Financial Services."

42. Marta Belcher, "New OCC Rule Is a Win in the Fight Against Financial Censorship," Electronic Frontier Foundation, January 19, 2021, https://www.eff.org/deeplinks/2021/01/new-occ-rule-win-fight-against-financial-censorship.

43. Meaghan Winter, "Why It's So Hard to Run an Abortion Clinic—and Why So Many

Are Closing," Bloomberg, February 24, 2016, https://www.bloomberg.com/fea tures/2016-abortion-business/; MacKenzie Sigalos, "Bitcoin Has Become a Lifeline for Sex Workers, like This Former Nurse Who Made $1.3 Million Last Year," CNBC, February 5, 2022, https://www.cnbc.com/2022/02/05/bitcoin-a-lifeline-for-sex-work ers-like-ex-nurse-making-1point3-million.html; Alana Evans, "Wells Fargo Closed My Account for Being a Porn Star—and It's Time to Fight Back," Daily Beast, Sep tember 10, 2022, https://www.thedailybeast.com/wells-fargo-closed-my-account-for -being-a-porn-star-and-its-time-to-fight-back; "JPMorgan, Condoms and the Prob lem of Reputational Risk," American Banker, March 26, 2014, https://www.american banker.com/opinion/jpmorgan-condoms-and-the-problem-of-reputational-risk.

44. "Fair Access to Financial Services," U.S. Office of the Comptroller of Currency, Nov. 25, 2020, https://www.regulations.gov/document/OCC-2020-0042-0001.

45. William Isaac, "Don't Like an Industry? Send a Message to Its Bankers," *Wall Street Journal*, November 21, 2014, https://www.wsj.com/articles/william-isaac-dont-like -an-industry-send-a-message-to-its-bankers-1416613023.

46. Walter Olson, "Republicans Kill Obama's Awful 'Operation Choke Point,'" CATO In stitute, August 21, 2017, https://www.cato.org/commentary/republicans-kill-obamas -awful-operation-choke-point.

47. "OCC Puts Hold on Fair Access Rule," Office of the Comptroller of the Cur rency, 2021, https://www.occ.gov/news-issuances/news-releases/2021/nr-occ-2021-14 .html.

48. Anna Hrushka, "OCC Halts Controversial Fair Access Rule," Banking Dive, Janu ary 28, 2021, https://www.bankingdive.com/news/office-comptroller-currency-fair-ac cess-rule-2021/594145/.

49. "Principles for Climate-Related Financial Risk Management for Large Banks," Office of the Comptroller of the Currency, 2022, https://www.occ.treas.gov/news-issuances /news-releases/2021/nr-occ-2021-138a.pdf.

50. Jacob Bernstein, "OnlyFans Reverses Its Decision to Ban Explicit Content," *New York Times*, August 25, 2021, https://www.nytimes.com/2021/08/25/style/onlyfans-ban-re versed.html.

51. Tasos Vossos, "Porn Is Worse than Pollution in Ethical Investing Portfolios," Bloomberg, June 12, 2019, https://www.bloomberg.com/news/articles/2019-06-12 in-ethical-investments porn-is-a-bigger-taboo-than-firearms?leadSource=uverify %20wall#xj4y7vzkg.

52. Miles Weiss and Silla Brush, "Pimco ESG Fund's Fine Print: No Abortion-Related Holdings," Bloomberg, August 26, 2022, https://www.bloomberg.com/news/articles /2022-08-26/pimco-esg-fund-has-unusual-screen-no-abortion-related-holdings#x j4y7vzkg.

53. Megan Keller, "A Socially Conscious but Politically Incorrect Company," *Wall Street Journal*, September 15, 2022, https://www.wsj.com/articles/a-socially-conscious -but-politically-incorrect-company-black-rifle-coffee-initial-public-offering-finance -law-firms-reputational-risk-military-veterans-evan-hafer-11663258552.

54. "PayPal Says Policy to Fine Customers for 'Misinformation' was an 'Error,'" Reuters, October 10, 2022, https://www.reuters.com/business/finance/paypal-says-it-never -intended-fine-users-misinformation-bloomberg-news-2022-10-10/.

55. Christopher Hutton, "PayPal Polices 'Intolerance,' Even After Free Speech Backlash," The Washington Examiner, October 14, 2022, https://www.washingtonexaminer

.com/restoring-america/equality-not-elitism/paypal-misinformation-penalties-free
-speech-legal-concerns.

56. "Federal Insurance Office Request for Information on the Insurance Sector and Climate-Related Financial Risks," Federal Insurance Office, August 31, 2021, https://www.federalregister.gov/documents/2021/08/31/2021-18713/federal-insurance-office-request-for-information-on-the-insurance-sector-and-climate-related.

57. "Comments Due to the Federal Insurance Office on its Wide-Ranging Work Relating to the Insurance Sector and Climate-Related Financial Risks," Hinshaw & Culbertson LLP, October 12, 2021, https://www.hinshawlaw.com/newsroom-updates-insights-for-insurers-federal-insurance-office-climate-change-rfi-comments.html.

58. "Net-Zero Insurance Alliance," United Nations Environment Programme Finance Initiative, https://www.unepfi.org/net-zero-insurance/.

59. Steven Mufson, "What Could Finally Stop New Coal Plants? Pulling the Plug on Their Insurance," *Washington Post*, October 26, 2021, https://www.washingtonpost.com/climate-environment/2021/10/26/climate-change-insurance-coal/.

60. Jen Frost, "The Investors Taking on Fossil Fuel Insurers," Insurance Business Magazine, May 20, 2022, https://www.asyousow.org/press-releases/2022/6/1/investors-greenhouse-gas-reduction-message-insurance-companies.

61. "Shareholder Proposal to The Hartford Financial Services Group, Inc. from The Green Century Funds," U.S. Securities and Exchange Commission, March 28, 2022, https://www.sec.gov/divisions/corpfin/cf-noaction/14a-8/2022/greencentury hartford032822-14a8.pdf; "The Travelers Companies, Inc.—Omission of Shareholder Proposal from Proxy Materials Pursuant to Rule 14a-8," U.S. Securities and Exchange Commission, March 30, 2022, https://www.sec.gov/divisions/corpfin/cf-noaction/14a-8/2022/greencenturytravelers033022-14a8.pdf; "Chubb Limited—Shareholder Proposal Submitted by Green Century Equity Fund—Rule 14a-8," U.S. Securities and Exchange Commission, March 26, 2022, https://www.sec.gov/divisions/corpfin/cf-noaction/14a-8/2022/greencenturychubb032522-14a8.pdf.

62. "Investors Send Greenhouse Gas Reduction Message to National Insurance Companies."

63. "Treasury's Federal Insurance Office Continues Efforts on Climate-Related Financial Risks in the Insurance Sector, Joins the NGFS," U.S. Department of the Treasury, February 17, 2022, https://home.treasury.gov/news/press-releases/jy0598; "About us," Network for Greening the Financial System, https://www.ngfs.net/ngfs-scenarios-portal/about.

64. Mufson, "What Could Finally Stop New Coal Plants?"

65. "Coal Projects Face 40% Premium Increases as Insurer Retrenchment Continues," The Insurer, 2020, https://www.theinsurer.com/news/coal-projects-face-40-premium-increases-as-insurer-retrenchment-continues/.

66. Isabella Kaminski, "Coal Projects Outside China Becoming 'Uninsurable,' Says Climate Group," *Guardian*, October 18, 2022, https://www.theguardian.com/environment/2022/oct/19/coal-projects-outside-china-becoming-uninsurable-says-climate-group.

67. Corbin Hiar, "Coal, Oil Sands Companies Feel Growing Insurance Squeeze," ClimateWire, September 20, 2021, https://www.eenews.net/articles/coal-oil-sands-companies-feel-growing-insurance-squeeze/; Jonathan Saul and Simon Jessop, "Ship-

ping Companies Feel the Heat as Investors Shun Coal," Reuters, November 12, 2021, https://www.reuters.com/business/energy/shooting-messenger-shipping-carries -can-investors-shun-coal-2021-11-12/utm_source=reddit.com.

68. Kashmir Hill and Corey Kilgannon, "Madison Square Garden Uses Facial Recognition to Ban Its Owner's Enemies," *New York Times*, December 22, 2022, https://www .nytimes.com/2022/12/22/nyregion/madison-square-garden-facial-recognition.html.

69. *West Virginia et al. v. Environmental Protection Agency et al.*, Supreme Court of the United States, 597 U.S. __, June 30, 2022, https://www.supremecourt.gov/opinions /21pdf/20-1530_n758.pdf.

70. Joby Warrick, "White House Set to Adopt Sweeping Curbs on Carbon Polluting," *Washington Post*, August 1, 2015, https://www.washingtonpost.com/national /health-science/white-house-set-to-adopt-sweeping-curbs-on-carbon-pollution /2015/08/01/ba6627fa-385c-11e5-b673-1df005a0fb28_story.html.

71. 31 U.S.C. § 313, Federal Insurance Office, https://uscode.house.gov/view.xhtml ?req=(title:31%20section:313%20edition:prelim).

72. Securities Act of 1933, 15 U.S.C. § 77a, https://www.govinfo.gov/content/pkg /COMPS-1884/pdf/COMPS-1884.pdf; Bernard S. Sharfman and James R. Copland, "The SEC Can't Transform Itself into a Climate-Change Enforcer," *Wall Street Journal*, September 14, 2022, https://www.wsj.com/articles/securities-exchange-sec -climate-change-esg-major-questions-doctrine-west-virginia-v-epa-supreme-court -disclosure-rule-11663178488.

73. Biden, "Executive Order on Tackling the Climate Crisis at Home and Abroad"; Biden, "Executive Order on Advancing Racial Equity and Support for Underserved Communities Through the Federal Government."

Chapter 9: HOW ESG'S EFFORTS TO SAVE THE WORLD ARE HURTING IT

1. Kelsey Piper, "Sam Bankman-Fried Tries to Explain Himself," Vox, November 16, 2022, https://www.vox.com/future-perfect/23462333/sam-bankman-fried-ftx-crypto currency-effective-altruism-crypto-bahamas-philanthropy.

2. Brian Tayan, "ESG Ratings: A Compass Without Direction," Harvard Law School Forum on Corporate Governance, August 24, 2022, https://corpgov.law.harvard .edu/2022/08/24/esg-ratings-a-compass-without-direction/.

3. George Calhoun, "FTX and ESG: A Panorama af Failed Governance (Pt 1—The Internal Failures)," *Forbes*, November 21, 2022, https://www.forbes.com/sites /georgecalhoun/2022/11/21/ftx-and-esg-a-panorama-of-failed-governance-pt-1— the-internal-failures/sh=20871ffb2d9d.

4. Allison Morrow, "'Complete failure:' Filing reveals staggering mismanagement inside FTX," Cable News Network, November 18, 2022, https://www.cnn.com/2022/11/17 /business/ftx-ceo-complete-failure/index.html#:~:text=%E2%80%9CNever%20 in%20my%20career%20have,2000s%2C%20among%20other%20bankruptcy%20 cases.

5. Sigal Samuel, "Effective Altruism Gave Rise to Sam Bankman-Fried. Now It's Facing a Moral Reckoning," Vox, November 16, 2022, https://www.vox.com/future-per fect/23458282/effective-altruism-sam-bankman-fried-ftx-crypto-ethics.

6. muzzlightyear, "Larry David FTX Commercial Super Bowl Ad," YouTube, November 20, 2022, https://www.youtube.com/watch?v=pWV9ZdMwL98.

7. Colormatics, "Stephen Curry's Crypto Commercial," YouTube, March 29, 2022, https://www.youtube.com/watch?v=kJTwwfS4vBs.

8. Calhoun, "FTX and ESG: A Panorama of Failed Governance (Pt 1—The Internal Failures)."

9. Amy Shoenthal, "Gisele Bündchen Partners with FTX CEO Sam Bankman-Fried to Address Crypto's Sustainability Challenges," *Forbes*, April 28, 2022, https://www.forbes.com/sites/amyshoenthal/2022/04/28/gisele-bndchen-partners-with-ftx-ceo-sam-bankman-fried-to-address-cryptos-sustainability-challenges/sh=73c099822d78.

10. Manny Ramos, "Cryptocurrency Exchange Opens Headquarters in Fulton Market," *Chicago Sun-Times*, May 10, 2022, https://chicago.suntimes.com/news/2022/5/10/23065531/cryptocurrency-exchange-opens-headquarters-fulton-market-launches-guaranteed-basic-income-pilot.

11. muzzlightyear, "All 3 Tom Brady FTX Commercial," YouTube, November 20, 2022, https://www.youtube.com/watch?v=_aCGMyrFn-8.

12. Web3, "FTX Shaq Full Advert Comemrcial," YouTube, June 1, 2022, https://www.youtube.com/watch?v=XSu76VUIkEg.

13. Ian Allison, "Divisions in Sam Bankman-Fried's Crypto Empire Blur on His Trading Titan Alameda's Balance Sheet," CoinDesk, November 2, 2022, https://www.coindesk.com/business/2022/11/02/divisions-in-sam-bankman-frieds-crypto-empire-blur-on-his-trading-titan-alamedas-balance-sheet/.

14. Kathleen Marshall, "Binance to Liquidate Its Entire FTT Tokens Following FTX's Insolvency Rumors," Investopedia, November 7, 2022, https://www.investopedia.com/binance-to-sell-ftt-6826211.

15. David Z. Morris, "FTX's Collapse Was a Crime, Not an Accident," CoinDesk, November 30, 2022, https://www.coindesk.com/layer2/2022/11/30/ftxs-collapse-was-a-crime-not-an-accident/.

16. Oliver Knight, "FTX CEO Sam Bankman-Fried Denies Insolvency Rumors as Binance Liquidates FTT Token," CoinDesk, November 7, 2022, https://www.coindesk.com/business/2022/11/07/ftx-ceo-sam-bankman-fried-denies-insolvency-rumors-as-binance-liquidates-ftt-token/.

17. Morris, "FTX's Collapse Was a Crime."

18. Piper, "Sam Bankman-Fried Tries to Explain Himself."

19. Koh Gui Qing, "Bankman-Fried's FTX, Senior Staff, Parents Bought Bahamas Property Worth $300 Mln," Reuters, November 22, 2022, https://www.reuters.com/technology/exclusive-bankman-frieds-ftx-parents-bought-bahamas-property-worth-121-mln-2022-11-22/.

20. Paul Kiernan and Stgephanic Stamm, "Sam Bankman-Fried, FTX Team Among Top Political Donors Before Bankruptcy," *Wall Street Journal*, November 21, 2022, https://www.wsj.com/articles/sam-bankman-fried-ftx-team-among-top-political-donors-before-bankruptcy-11668949205.

21. Marco Quiroz-Gutierrez, "Sam Bankman-Fried Says He Donated Just as Many Millions to Republicans as Democrats, but Didn't Publicize It Because Reporters Would 'Freak the F—k Out,'" *Fortune*, November 29, 2022, https://fortune.com

/crypto/2022/11/29/sam-bankman-fried-political-donations-democrats-republicans
-dark-money/.

22. "Transcript of Sam Bankman-Fried's Interview at the DealBook Summit," *New York Times*, December 1, 2022, https://www.nytimes.com/2022/12/01/business/dealbook/sam-bankman-fried-dealbook-interview-transcript.html.

23. Calhoun, "FTX and ESG: A Panorama of Failed Governance (Pt 1—The Internal Failures)."

24. Vivek Ramaswamy and Mark Lurie, "Centralization Caused the FTX Fiasco," *Wall Street Journal*, November 27, 2022, https://www.wsj.com/articles/centralization-caused-the-ftx-fiasco-sam-bankman-fried-regulation-lobbying-assets-funds-cryptocurrency-exchange-11669566906?st=4g828ugbj3vigbp&reflink=share_mobilewebshare.

25. "FactSet Enters into Agreement to Acquire Truvalue Labs," (FactSet Research Systems, October 20, 2020), https://www.globenewswire.com/news-release/2020/10/20/2110924/7768/en/FactSet-Enters-into-Agreement-to-Acquire-Truvalue-Labs.html.

26. Vivek Ramaswamy, *Woke, Inc.: Inside Corporate America's Social Justice Scam* (New York: Center Street, 2021), chap. 1.

27. Kay Smythe, "'I Am Legend' Set a Prediction for Gas Prices in the Apocalypse. Prices in Beverly Hills Just Surpassed It," Daily Caller, March 7, 2022, https://dailycaller.com/2022/03/07/i-am-legend-gas-prices-apocalypse-will-smith-beverly-hills/.

28. "Our Letter to Chevron," Strive Asset Management, September 6, 2022, https://strive.com/strive-asset-management-letter-to-chevron/.

29. "US Crude Oil in the Strategic Petroleum Reserve Stocks," YCharts, https://ycharts.com/indicators/us_ending_stocks_of_crude_oil_in_the_strategic_petroleum_reserve.

30. Kayla Tausche, "White House Weighs Future Release of Emergency Heating, Crude Oil Reserves as Winter Nears," CNBC, November 30, 2022, https://www.cnbc.com/2022/11/30/white-house-weighs-future-release-of-emergency-heating-crude-oil-reserves-as-winter-nears.html.

31. Ellie Potter, "Senate Drops $3B Oil Reserve Funding from Final Coronavirus Bill, Senator Says," S&P Global Market Intelligence, March 25, 2020, https://www.spglobal.com/marketintelligence/en/news-insights/latest-news-headlines/senate-drops-3b-oil-reserve-funding-from-final-coronavirus-bill-senator-says-57756971.

32. "Russian Oil Industry," Statista, November 28, 2022, https://www.statista.com/topics/5399/russian-oil-industry/.

33. Al Jazeera Staff, "How Much of Your Country's Gas Comes from Russia?," Al Jazeera, March 17, 2022, https://www.aljazeera.com/news/2022/3/17/infographic-how-much-of-your-countrys-gas-comes-from-russia-interactive.

34. Katie Stallard-Blanchette, "Putin Comes Clean on Crimea's Little Green Men," Sky News, March 10, 2015, https://news.sky.com/story/putin-comes-clean-on-crimeas-little-green-men-10368423.

35. Gabriel Rinaldi, "Berlin's Push for Nord Stream 2 Contributed to Ukraine War, German Minister Says," Politico, November 29, 2022, https://www.politico.eu/article/nord-stream-2-germany-bears-responsibility-for-ukraine-war-minister/.

36. Brian Parkin, "Germany Paid Record $38 Billion for Green Power Growth in 2020," Bloomberg, January 12, 2021, https://www.bloomberg.com/news/articles/2021-01-12/germany-paid-record-38-billion-for-green-power-growth-in-2020.

37. Lea Booth, "Germany's Energy Catastrophe," Quillette, July 14, 2022, https://quil lette.com/2022/07/14/germanys-energy-catastrophe/.

38. "Germany Natural Gas," Worldometer, 2015, https://www.worldometers.info/gas /germany-natural-gas/.

39. Katrin Bennhold and Erika Solomon, "Shadowy Arm of a German State Helped Russia Finish Nord Stream 2," *New York Times*, December 2, 2022, https://www.nytimes .com/2022/12/02/world/europe/germany-russia-nord-stream-pipeline.html.

40. "Germany Approves Welfare Reform, Extends Nuclear Power," Deutsche Welle, November 25, 2022, https://www.dw.com/en/germany-approves-welfare-reform-ex tends-nuclear-power/a-63892209.

41. Jen Kirby, "Why Firewood Is Suddenly in High Demand in Germany," Vox, October 17, 2022, https://www.vox.com/world/2022/10/17/23390663/europe-energy-crisis -explained-firewood-germany.

42. Rob Schmitz, "Amid an Energy Crisis, Germany Turns to the World's Dirtiest Fossil Fuel," NPR, September 27, 2022, https://www.npr.org/2022/09/27/1124448463/ger many-coal-energy-crisis.

43. "Energy Crisis: Germany Sees Rising Trend in Wood Burning Stoves to Save on Gas," Euronews.green, November 14, 2022, https://www.euronews.com/green/2022/11/11 /energy-crisis-in-germany-rising-trend-in-wood-burning-stoves-to-save-on-gas.

44. Hans-Werner Sinn, "Will Germany's Energy Policy Lead to Economic Failure?," *Guardian*, November 25, 2022, https://www.theguardian.com/business/2022/nov/25 /germany-energy-policy-economic-failure-green-russian-gas.

45. Richard Heinberg, "Can We Abandon Pollutive Fossil Fuels and Avoid an Energy Crisis?," Resilience, May 4, 2022, https://www.resilience.org/stories/2022-05-04/can-we -abandon-pollutive-fossil-fuels-and-avoid-an-energy-crisis/.

46. "What the Inflation Reduction Act Means for Your Solar Installation," Energy Solution Providers, September 21, 2022, https://energysolutionsolar.com/blog/what-infla tion-reduction-act-means-your-solar-installation.

47. Niccolo Conte, "Visualizing China's Dominance in the Solar Panel Supply Chain," Visual Capitalist, August 30, 2022, https://www.visualcapitalist.com/visualizing-chinas -dominance-in-the-solar-panel-supply-chain/.

48. Nichola Groom, "Exclusive: U.S. Blocks More than 1,000 Solar Shipments over Chinese Slave Labor Concerns," Reuters, November 11, 2022, https://www.reuters.com /world/china/exclusive-us-blocks-more-than-1000-solar-shipments-over-chinese -slave-labor-2022-11-11/.

49. "Solar Energy Boom Could Worsen Forced Labor in China, Group Says," Bloomberg, March 28, 2022, https://www.bloomberg.com/news/articles/2022-03-28/solar-energy -boom-could-worsen-forced-labor-in-china-group-says.

50. Dave Merrill, "The U.S. Will Need a Lot of Land for a Zero-Carbon Economy," Bloomberg, June 3, 2022, https://www.bloomberg.com/graphics/2021-energy-land-use -economy/.

51. Jake Lahut and John Haltiwanger, "Biden Fist Bumps Saudi Crown Prince Mohammed Bin Salman at Start of Their First Face-to-Face Meeting, Less than 3 Years After Vowing to Make Saudi Arabia a 'Pariah' State," Business Insider, July 15, 2022, https:// www.businessinsider.com/biden-fist-bump-mbs-mohammed-bin-salman-saudi-arabia -video-2022-7.

52. Mark Mazzetti, Edward Wong, and Adam Entous, "U.S. Officials Had a Secret Oil

Deal with the Saudis. Or So They Thought," *New York Times*, October 25, 2022, https://www.nytimes.com/2022/10/25/us/politics/us-saudi-oil-deal.html.

53. Alex Marquardt, "US Determines Saudi Crown Prince Is Immune in Case Brought by Jamal Khashoggi's Fiancée," CNN, November 18, 2022, https://www.cnn.com/2022/11/17/politics/saudi-crown-prince-immunity-state-department-jamal-khashoggi/index.html.

54. Stephanie Kirchgaessner, "US Judge Dismisses Case Against Saudi Crown Prince over Khashoggi Killing," *Guardian*, December 6, 2022, https://www.theguardian.com/world/2022/dec/06/us-judge-saudi-crown-prince-mohammed-bin-salman-khashoggi.

55. Sam Meredith, "OPEC+ to Consider Deeper Oil Output Cuts Ahead of Russia Sanctions and Proposed Price Cap," CNBC, December 2, 2022, https://www.cnbc.com/2022/12/02/opec-meeting-oil-output-cuts-on-the-table-ahead-of-russia-sanctions.html.

56. Wolf-Georg Ringe and Alperen A. Gözlügöl, "Private Companies, Brown-Spinning, and Climate-Related Disclosures in the U.S.," Harvard Law School Forum on Corporate Governance, April 14, 2022, https://corpgov.law.harvard.edu/2022/04/14/private-companies-brown-spinning-and-climate-related-disclosures-in-the-u-s/.

57. Fiona Harvey, "Methane Leak at Russian Mine Could Be Largest Ever Discovered," *Guardian*, June 14, 2022, https://www.theguardian.com/world/2022/jun/15/methane-leak-at-russian-mine-could-be-largest-ever-discovered.

58. "I Will Not Eat the Bugs," Know Your Meme, July 22, 2022, https://knowyourmeme.com/memes/i-will-not-eat-the-bugs.

59. Klaus Schwab, "Now Is the Time for a Great Reset," World Economic Forum, June 3, 2020, https://www.weforum.org/agenda/2020/06/now-is-the-time-for-a-great-reset/.

60. World Economic Forum, "8 Predictions for the World in 2030," Facebook, November 18, 2016, https://www.facebook.com/watch/?v=10153920524981479.

61. Noam Blum, Twitter, November 15, 2019, https://twitter.com/neontaster/status/1196071987543728129.

62. Michael Shellenberger, Twitter, August 14, 2022, https://twitter.com/shellenbergermd/status/1558807160351608832.

Chapter 10: SOLUTIONS

1. Marty Flanagan, "Greater Possibilities Together," Invesco, 2020, https://www.corporatereport.com/invesco/2020/crr/strategy/ceo-message.php; Marty Flanagan, "Seeing Opportunity in a Post-Pandemic World," Invesco, November 10, 2021, https://www.invesco.com/corporate/en/news-and-insights/ceo-insights/seeing-opportunity-in-post-pandemic-world.html.

2. Marty Flanagan, "Greater Possibilities Together," Invesco, 2020, https://www.corporatereport.com/invesco/2020/crr/strategy/ceo-message.php.

3. Silla Brush, "One Fund, Three Names and Lots of Questions for 'ESG,'" Bloomberg, July 25, 2022, https://www.bloomberg.com/news/articles/2022-07-25/how-blackrock-rebranded-one-sustainable-mutual-fund.

4. Alan Murray and David Meyer, "Coca-Cola and Novartis's CEOs Don't Care If 'ESG' Has Become A Toxic Phrase Among Some," *Fortune*, January 23, 2023, https://fortune.com/2023/01/23/coca-cola-novartis-ceos-esg-quincey-narasimhan/.

5. *ERI Consulting Engineers, Inc. v. Swinnea*, 318 S.W.3d 867, 874 (Tex. 2010).

6. "Disgorging an agent of all compensation received during a period of employment in which the agent was also breaching a fiduciary duty to the principal, without a requirement for the principal to demonstrate financial loss, is an equitable, not legal remedy"; ordering disgorgement of three months' salary for fiduciary breach. *Wenzel v. Hopper & Galliher, P.C.*, 830 N.E.2d. 996, 1001 (Ind. Ct. App. 2005).

7. Coco Khan, "Can I Make an Ethical Killing on the Stock Market? We Ask an Expert," *Guardian*, April 22, 2022, https://www.theguardian.com/lifeandstyle/2022/apr/22/ethical-killing-on-stock-market-we-ask-an-expert.

8. "Free Enterprise Project," National Center for Public Policy Research, https://nationalcenter.org/programs/free-enterprise-project/.

9. "Overview," Ave Maria Mutual Funds, https://avemariafunds.com/fund-family/.

10. "iShares Core S&P 500 ETF," BlackRock, https://www.ishares.com/us/products/239726/ishares-core-sp-500-etf.

11. "ESG Integration," BlackRock, https://www.blackrock.com/institutions/en-us/solutions/sustainable-investing/esg-integration.

12. Larry Fink, "The Transformative Power of Choice in Proxy Voting," BlackRock, https://www.blackrock.com/corporate/about-us/investment-stewardship/blackrock-voting-choice/proxy-voting-power-of-choice.

13. Ross Kerber, "North Carolina Treasurer Calls for BlackRock CEO Fink to Resign," Reuters, December 9, 2022, https://www.nasdaq.com/articles/north-carolina-treasurer-calls-for-blackrock-ceo-fink-to-resign-0.

14. Theo Andrew, "BlackRock's Fink Should Resign over ESG Says Former Sustainability Chief," E T F Stream, December 19, 2022, https://www.etfstream.com/news/blackrock-s-fink-should-resign-over-esg-says-former-sustainability-chief-reports/.

15. Will Schmitt, "Activist Investor Calls for Fink to Resign as BlackRock CEO over ESG 'Hypocrisy,'" Citywire, December 7, 2022, https://citywire.com/pro-buyerznews/activist-investor-calls-for-fink-to-resign-as-blackrock-ceo-over-esg-hypocrisy/a2404388.

16. Andrew, "BlackRock's Fink Should Resign over ESG Says Former Sustainability Chief."

17. Will Schmitt, "BlackRock Downgraded by UBS over ESG Risks, Market Headwinds," Citywire, October 12, 2022, https://citywire.com/pro-buyer/news/blackrock-downgraded-by-ubs-over-esg-risks-market-headwinds/a2399720.

18. Alexandra Canal, "Dan Loeb Buys New Stake in Disney, Lays Out Key Initiatives to 'Unlock Further Value,'" Yahoo Finance, August 15, 2022, https://finance.yahoo.com/news/dan-loeb-buys-new-stake-in-disney-lays-out-key-initiatives-to-unlock-further-value-151539090.html.

19. Joseph E. Stiglitz, "Of the 1%, by the 1%, for the 1%," *Vanity Fair*, March 31, 2011, https://www.vanityfair.com/news/2011/05/top-one-percent-201105.

20. Bernie Sanders, "The US Has a Ruling Class—and Americans Must Stand Up to It," *Guardian*, September 2, 2022, https://www.theguardian.com/commentisfree/2022/sep/02/the-us-has-a-ruling-class-and-americans-must-stand-up-to-it.

21. Brett Wilkins, "'Obscene,' Says Sanders After CBO Reports Richest 1% Now Owns over 1/3 of US Wealth," Bernie Sanders, U.S. Senator for Vermont, September 28, 2022, https://www.sanders.senate.gov/in-the-news/obscene-says-sanders-after-cbo-reports-richest-1-now-owns-over-1-3-of-us-wealth/.

22. Emmanuel Saez and Gabriel Zucman, "Wealth Inequality in the United States Since 1913," October 2014, https://eml.berkeley.edu/~saez/SaezZucman14slides.pdf; Emmanuel Saez and Gabriel Zucman, "The Rise of Income and Wealth Inequality in America: Evidence from Distributional Macroeconomic Accounts," *Journal of Economic Perspectives* 34, no. 4 (Fall 2020): 3–26, https://eml.berkeley.edu/~saez/SaezZucman2020JEP.pdf.

23. David Gothard, "ESG Can't Square with Fiduciary Duty," *Wall Street Journal*, September 6, 2022, https://www.wsj.com/articles/esg-cant-square-with-fiduciary-duty-blackrock-vanguard-state-stree-the-big-three-violations-china-conflict-of-interest-investors-11662496552.

24. Andrew Fleming, "Adbusters Sparks Wall Street Protest," *Vancouver Courier*, September 27, 2011, https://web.archive.org/web/20121011160015/http://www.vancourier.com/Adbusters+sparks+Wall+Street+protest/5466332/story.html.